The Philosophy of Education: An Introduction

Also available from Continuum

An Introduction to Education Studies, Sue Warren
Philosophy of Education, Richard Pring
The Study of Education: An Introduction, Jane Bates and Sue Lewis

From the Continuum Library of Educational Thought

Aristotle, Alexander Moseley
Jean-Jacques Rousseau, Jürgen Oelkers
John Dewey, Richard Pring
Michel Foucault, Lynn Fendler
Plato, Robin Barrow

The Philosophy
of Education:
An Introduction

Edited by
Richard Bailey

continuum

Continuum International Publishing Group

The Tower Building   80 Maiden Lane
11 York Road   Suite 704
London SE1 7NX   New York, NY 10038

www.continuumbooks.com

British Library Cataloguing-in-Publication Data
A catalogue record for this book is available from the British Library.

ISBN: 9781847060198 (paperback)
9781441126856 (hardcover)

Library of Congress Cataloging-in-Publication Data
The philosophy of education: an introduction / edited by Richard Bailey.
    p. cm.
Includes bibliographical references.
ISBN 978-1-84706-019-8 (pbk.)
ISBN 978-1-4411-2685-6 (hardcover)
1. Education–Philosophy. I. Bailey, Richard. II. Title.

LB14.7.P543 2010
370.1–dc22

                          2009015983

Typeset by Newgen Imaging Systems Pvt Ltd, Chennai, India
Printed and bound in Great Britain by the MPG Books Group

Contents

8 Should the State Control Education?   99
Judith Suissa

9 Educational Opportunities – Who Shall We Leave Out?   113
Carrie Winstanley

List of Contributors

Richard Bailey is a writer and academic who has worked at a number of institutions, and was most recently appointed founding Chair of Sport and Education at the University of Birmingham. He is the author of *Education in the Open Society: Karl Popper and Schooling* (Ashgate), and is author/editor of 14 other books on theoretical and practical aspects of schooling and sport. He also edits the 25-volume *International Encyclopaedia of Educational Thought* (Continuum).

Harry Brighouse is Professor of Philosophy and Affiliate Professor of Educational Policy Studies at University of Wisconsin, Madison. He is author of *On Education* (Routledge, 2006) and is currently working with Adam Swift on a book entitled *Family Values* to be published by Princeton University Press.

James C. Conroy is Professor of Religious and Philosophical Education and Dean of the Faculty of Education at the University of Glasgow. He is currently Principal Investigator on an ESRC/AHRC funded project asking the question 'Does RE Work?' and his publications include *Betwixt and Between: The Liminal Imagination, Education and Democracy* (2004).

Dianne Gereluk is senior research fellow at Roehampton University and a visiting scholar at University of Calgary. She is the author of *Education and Community* (Continuum, 2006) and *Symbolic Clothing in Schools* (Continuum, 2008) and is currently working on a book entitled, *Education, Extremism and Terrorism: What Should Be Taught in Citizenship Education and Why* to be published by Continuum.

John Gingell is Reader and Course Leader in Philosophy at the University of Northampton. His interests are in value theories in Ethics, Aesthetics, Politics and Education and his most recent book is *Philosophy and Educational Policy* [with Chris Winch].

Michael Hand is Reader of Philosophy of Education at the Institute of Education, University of London. His research interests are in the areas of moral, religious, political and philosophical education and his books include *Is Religious Education Possible?* (Continuum, 2006) and *Philosophy in Schools* (Continuum, 2008).

Roger Marples is Principal Lecturer in Education at Roehampton University, London. He is the editor of *Aims of Education* (Routledge, 1999).

Paula McAvoy is a doctoral candidate in the department of Educational Policy Studies at the University of Wisconsin-Madison. Her area of study is the philosophy of education with specific interests in political theory and the aims of public schooling, and the ethics of teaching. Her dissertation is an argument for how public schools should respond to requests for cultural and religious accommodation.

Tristan McCowan is Lecturer in Education and International Development at the Institute of Education, University of London. His current research focuses on the right to education, citizenship and curriculum theory, and his recent publications include *Rethinking Citizenship Education: A Curriculum for Participatory Democracy* (Continuum, 2009).

Richard Pring is lead director of the Nuffield Review of 14–19 Education and Training for England and Wales. He was for 14 years Director of the Department of Educational Studies, University of Oxford.

Richard Smith is Professor of Education at the University of Durham. His principal research interests are in the philosophy of social science and the philosophy of education; his most recent book is (with Paul Smeyers and Paul Standish) *The Therapy of Education: Philosophy, Happiness and Personal Growth* (Palgrave Macmillan, 2006).

Paul Standish is Professor of Philosophy of Education at the Institute of Education, University of London. His interests span such topics as teaching and learning, democracy and education, and higher education; recent books include *The Therapy of Education* (Palgrave Macmillan, 2006), co-authored with Paul Smeyers and Richard Smith, and *The Philosophy of Nursing Education* (Palgrave Macmillan, 2007), co-edited with John Drummond.

Judith Suissa is Senior Lecturer in Philosophy of Education at the Institute of Education, University of London. Her research interests include radical and libertarian education, utopian theory, liberal theory, and philosophical aspects of the parent-child relationship. She is the author of *Anarchism and Education: A Philosophical Perspective* (Routledge, 2006).

Carrie Winstanley is Principal Lecturer and Subject leader for Education at Roehampton University, London. Her main research interest concerns highly able children with special educational needs, social justice concerns and pedagogy in and beyond the classroom.

Acknowledgements

I'd like to thank Ada Mau for her help and support in the preparation of this book. It is literally the case that the book would not have been completed without her. Thanks are due to Alison Clark, Joanne Allcock and Ania Leslie-Wujastyk at Continuum for their sterling support. Undergraduate students on the Education Studies programme at Roehampton University offered extremely valuable feedback on each of the chapters in this book. Their contribution is greatly appreciated.

I'd like to use editor's privilege to take this opportunity to dedicate this book to Morgan and Maddie Bailey. They are just starting their schooling. I hope that theirs will be a long and exhilarating experience.

Introduction

Richard Bailey

Here is a very old story: A famous philosopher had to move house from one part of the city to another. His wife, knowing that her husband was extremely absent-minded, decided to train the philosopher in preparation for the move. So for weeks in advance, she reminded him that they would shortly be moving house, and that he would need to take a different bus home from the University, and get off at a different stop. She even wrote down the new address on a piece of paper and put it in his pocket. On the day of the move the philosopher forgot his training, and took his usual bus home. The house was empty, of course, as his family had moved. Then he remembered the piece of paper and found his new address. After a very indirect series of bus journeys, the philosopher finally found himself on his correct bus, and he got off at the right stop. Then he realized that he had absolutely no idea where his street was, or even what his new house looked like. He wandered around for an hour, until he saw a little girl playing in the street. 'Excuse me, young lady, would you happen to know where this house is?' he asked, showing her the piece of paper. The child took his hand, and said, 'Don't worry Daddy, I'll take you home.'

This story represents the stereotypical image of philosophers. Some people, especially in my experience those with a background in the sciences, criticize philosophy for being a never-ending series of discussions and arguments. They are, as Bertrand Russell put it, 'inclined to doubt whether philosophy is anything better than innocent but useless trifling, hair-splitting distinctions, and controversies on matters concerning which knowledge is impossible' (Russell, 1959, p. 153).

The real world for many readers of this book is likely to be the world of the classroom, and it is reasonable to ask 'what can philosophy offer here?' The central goal of this book is to demonstrate the relevance of philosophy (or, more accurately, that sub-discipline called the Philosophy of Education) to the world of schools. It aims to show that the popular idea of philosophy is plain wrong.

Philosophy (from the Greek for the love of knowledge or wisdom) requires thinkers to think for themselves. This is why the great philosopher Kant asserted that it is not possible to learn philosophy; it is only possible to learn how to philosophize. This does not mean that the philosopher ought to live a life of solitary contemplation (although some have done just that), but it does mean that the philosopher is compelled to think for himself. This is perhaps why philosophical conversations often seem characterized by ambiguity and perplexity. Important questions are rarely resolved with simple answers unless, of course, we choose to borrow uncritically the dogmas and doctrines of others. For Russell, the person who does decide to live so uncritically 'goes through life imprisoned in the prejudices derived from common sense, from the habitual beliefs of his age or his nation, and from convictions which have grown up in his mind without the co-operation or consent of his deliberate reason'.

We might pause for a moment to consider Russell's use of masculine pronouns as generic terms referring to all humans. This was common usage when he wrote, but has increasingly become replaced by gender-neutral language (his/her, abandoning pronouns, pluralizing, etc.) following claims that gendered language is misleading, inappropriate or simply sexist. Is this a reasonable evolution of language use or 'political correctness run mad'? As soon as we start to reflect on these questions we are engaging in philosophy.

It is possible to think and act without philosophizing. It is certainly possible to teach without giving a moment's thought to philosophy. But it is not possible to think for ourselves, especially to think about matters of value, without philosophizing in some way. Education is a subject rich in philosophical issues:

- What should we teach?
- What experiences are most valuable/relevant/necessary for students?
- Who should pay for schooling?
- Are some ways of organizing or presenting the curriculum inappropriate?
- Should schooling be compulsory?
- Should all students be taught together, or grouped according to their ability?
- Should schools prepare their students for the world of work?
- Is the ideal outcome of schooling a happy/rational/spiritual/good person?
- What type of person should teachers aim to develop?
- What should the values and ethos of the school be?

We might turn to sociology or psychology to help us gather evidence for our enquiries. For example, psychology might help us understand how children's minds develop. But psychology can never tell the psychologist which forms of development are worth supporting. Questions of value are questions of philosophy.

There is a lot to learn from reading the works of the great thinkers. In this book you will encounter some of the most influential philosophers to have written about education: 'classical' thinkers like Plato and Aristotle; and more recent philosophers, such as Dewey and Peters. There is little doubt that reading their work will help you think more deeply about education. It would be a mistake, however, to presume that memorizing their words amounts to philosophizing. Kant warned us that these philosophers 'should not be a model of judgement, but simply an opportunity to make a judgement of them, even against them' (in Comte-Sponville, 2000). The same can be said for the contributors to this book. Each of the authors has thought a great deal about their specialist topic and their personal positions. Yet their chapters are certainly not the final words on their subjects; on the contrary, they should be understood as starting points for your own philosophizing. In fact, each has sought to be clear and explicit in their arguments, so that you, the reader, can follow their thinking and can challenge their conclusions. In each case, the goal is to inspire and provoke you to think for yourself.

This introduction has an unusual structure. With the exceptions of the introductory and closing chapters, each author has addressed a key question for educationalists. Throughout the book you will find opportunities to reflect on questions and debates for yourself. You will also find numerous suggestions of further reading that encourage a deeper and more comprehensive understanding of the field. You are strongly encouraged to take the time to do the suggested tasks and follow the readings.

If you read these contributions carefully, you will note that there are substantial disagreements. This is the life-blood of philosophy. By choosing to engage with these discussions, you are choosing to philosophize.

What Is the Philosophy of Education?

Paul Standish

Consider three cases: Gary is a student in a B.Ed. course, currently preparing the dissertation that he has decided to do as one of his option modules. This involves him first choosing a topic and then setting about writing a 'dissertation plan', which will explain how he expects to go about the research and the methodology he has chosen to adopt. All this seems quite daunting. He has done the compulsory course in Educational Research Methods, so he has some idea of the various methodologies and of the interpretive paradigms that are available, and he realizes that at an early stage he will need to identify a research question and, following from this, a set of sub-questions. Gary has already spent several blocks of time in the classroom on teaching practice, as well as participating in a variety of other day-visits to schools. He has found himself particularly interested in the question of children's moral education. It's not that he is particularly religious, but he has some sense of the importance of being moral and realizes that this is somehow bound up with how children behave in school and how well they do in their education. This he thinks is the topic he will choose. He wants his work to have some real connection to his practice as a teacher, so on the day that he goes for the first meeting with the tutor who has been assigned to him, the research question he is ready to propose is: *Which kind of moral education works best with elementary school children?* He has in mind an empirical study, based on questionnaires given to teachers and parents.

Rajinder has just become head of a large high school. The school is a competitive one, with a good reputation, and it is highly regarded by the local community. Rajinder has been concerned, however, by the obvious signs of stress that are apparent amongst its staff, and the recent spate of cases of self-harm and anorexia, not to mention incidents of aggression and bullying, that have made her realize that stress is a problem for the students too. She remembers reading in *The Guardian* that between 600 and 800 15- to 24-year-olds in the UK kill themselves each year, equivalent to the population of a small secondary school. Of course, there are calls for a coordinated approach to these problems; but what steps, she wonders, can her school take to make matters better? How can she improve the well-being of students and teachers alike? She finds that in the press and on the radio people are increasingly talking about the need for happiness to counterbalance the pressures of the time we live in, and so she has a brainwave: why not teach happiness in schools, and succeeds in enthusing the staff with the idea. She explains that happiness teaching is based on 'positive psychology', a relatively new branch of science focusing on helping people to live lives that are flourishing. It is agreed that classes will be given to all pupils aged 14 to 16, providing them with skills on how to manage relationships, physical and mental health and negative emotions, and how to achieve their ambitions, alongside a strong emphasis on the promotion of self-esteem and practice in meditation.

Sam is a senior advisor in the Department for Education, with a particular responsibility for the curriculum for secondary schools. Plans are underway to revise the curriculum for pupils aged 11–14, and Sam has been asked to scrutinize policy regarding History, a subject whose value today has been seriously called into question. There is a common perception in the Department that curricula need to be updated in order to equip pupils with skills relevant to a knowledge economy. Sam sees her role as one of persuading policy-makers and curriculum planners that this can be done in History. What is needed is for the emphasis to move away from content – say, learning about a particular period – and towards the development of historical skills.

These three cases provide examples of people engaged in educational practice, at different levels and in different circumstances, and all need to think about what they are doing. How are they best to think about these matters? Hold this question in your mind, because we shall return to it later. But for now let's address more directly the topic at hand and see how we can best think about answering the question 'What is the philosophy of education?'

What is philosophy? What is education?

How do you answer a 'what is' question? One way is to consult the dictionary. So we find that the *Cambridge Advanced Learner's Dictionary* gives four definitions for 'philosophy':

1 [U] the use of reason in understanding such things as the nature of reality and existence, the use and limits of knowledge and the principles that govern and influence moral judgment: *René Descartes is regarded as the founder of modern philosophy.* See also PhD.

2 the philosophy of sth a group of theories and ideas related to the understanding of a particular subject: *the philosophy of education/religion/science*

3 [C] a particular system of beliefs, values and principles: *the Ancient Greek philosophy of Stoicism*

4 [C usually singular] INFORMAL someone's approach to life and their way of dealing with it: *Live now, pay later – that's my philosophy of life!*

(*Cambridge Advanced Learner's Dictionary*, http://dictionary.cambridge.org/define.asp?key=59385& dict=CALD. Accessed 6 March 2009.)

The third and fourth definitions are less relevant to our purposes here, and the second helpfully uses the very phrase that we are trying to explain. But this clearly depends on the first, which is the one that we need to consider most. Philosophy, it says, involves the use of reason in relation to the understanding of three things: knowledge, moral judgement and the nature of reality. So far so good, you might think. But this is heady stuff, isn't it? So far so good, but abstract and vague. The dictionary will take us only so far. And this impression is confirmed when we look up 'education', which is said to be:

the process of teaching or learning in a school or college, or the knowledge that you get from this:

As a child he received most of his education at home.
It's a country which places great importance on education.
She lectures in education (= *the study of education*) at the teacher training college.
It's important for children to get a good education.

(http://dictionary.cambridge.org/define.asp?key=24811&dict=CALD. Accessed 6 March 2009.)

The examples of usage almost seem to acknowledge that the definition, as it stands, does not tell us very much. Furthermore, it is not clear that it is adequate as it is. For a start, we can use the word 'education' in a range of cases not covered by this definition. We can speak of our experience in travelling abroad as an education, just as we can deny that what happened to us in school educated us. The sense here is not metaphorical. To say that someone received most of her education at home may mean that she had a private tutor, but it may also say something broader about the quality of life in her home – that living there was an education in itself, more important than any systematic tuition she may have had. An interesting point emerges from this. If one is asked the question 'what are the purposes of education?' it is possible to give two kinds of response:

First type of answer: *to control the working classes in order to advance the interests of those in power.*

Second type of answer (three possibilities): *to serve the needs of society / to advance knowledge and understanding / the self-realization of the individual.*

It is important that each of these kinds of answers can be appropriate, though what is understood by 'education' may be rather different in each case. The first response seems to take it that the question is asking about the actual effects of current educational systems. Its purpose is to describe and (probably) to imply a judgement about what is in fact going on, in schools and other educational institutions. The second type of answer treats the question in a rather different way. Its intention is to say what the purposes of education should be, regardless of what is in fact going on now. These responses can be thought of respectively as *descriptive/ sociological* and *normative/philosophical*. But two points should be made about this. In the first place, it is, of course, the case that sometimes sociologists make judgements of the latter kind, and philosophers should be concerned also to describe what is actually happening (to be realistic). But we need to be clear about which way the question is being taken. In the second place, it is important to realize also that it is difficult to criticize the way things *are* without some sense of how they *ought to be*. This makes the normative/philosophical at some point unavoidable.

We have seen then that the definition of 'education' takes us only so far, while what the dictionary offers for 'philosophy' is helpful but remains rather abstract. It is unlikely that anyone coming across this definition would understand well what the subject was like unless they already had some sense of this before. This can be a problem with definitions more generally – that sometimes they involve the use of terms that in themselves stand in need of fuller explanation. So let us take a slightly different approach and ask how can we characterize better what philosophers do.

Philosophers are interested in basic ideas or concepts (including knowledge, understanding, truth, goodness), and how they relate to each other. But their approach to these matters is distinctive. Philosophy *does not* involve doing experiments or collecting data empirically; it *does* involve exploring how we think and the assumptions lying behind our thinking, and becoming clear about the concepts we use; it *is* concerned with the nature of knowledge (and the grounds for knowledge claims); it is concerned especially with reasons or justifications for thoughts and opinions; and it *is* concerned with questions of value. The purpose of philosophy has often been thought of as concerned with bringing clarity to thought, so that concepts are carefully analysed and arguments are robust. Hence, it is sometimes thought to be what John Locke called an 'underlabourer' to other ways of thinking (i.e. an assistant): the philosopher (of education) takes concepts that are in use in other aspects of educational research, such as intelligence and IQ, self-esteem, skill, objectivity; she clarifies them and tidies them up, and then hands them back to the empirical researchers. Some have thought that conceptual analysis can actually show you the heart of what education is about – that it has its own logic, which a close examination of its central concepts (such as teaching, learning and knowledge) will reveal. (See, for example, John Wilson, as well as the work of Israel Scheffler, R. S. Peters, Paul Hirst, Harvey Siegel and Christopher Winch in certain respects.)

But does philosophy just clarify our thinking about such questions of value (a second order activity)? Or does it enter into the business of making direct judgements about what is good or right (a first order activity)? Some of the most influential philosophies that have a bearing on education have certainly done the latter. But philosophical approaches can also reject this assumption that the nature of education can be discovered by analysis of the concepts in favour of the view that there is no avoiding the direct consideration of questions of value. This makes philosophy less like a matter of technical expertise; instead it becomes something like an intensified version of the kind of enquiry that people generally engage in with regard to such questions. It is precisely this kind of intense enquiry that characterizes so much of the work of the great philosophers. (Not that they are *not* concerned with clarity, logic, etc!)

If you pursue practical questions in education far enough, as the thinking teacher is likely to find, they usually lead to 'big' questions about the nature of knowledge and the nature of the good life. These are addressed in some way or other in various aspects of educational research. But they are the kind of thing that cannot be resolved by empirical study. They need reflection and judgement and argument. This is central to philosophy.

These then are big claims, and we can imagine a number of questions being raised about them as well as some continuing confusion over what it is that philosophy is about. 'I get the picture,' someone might say. 'Philosophy is a kind of qualitative research particularly concerned with values. So it's subjective and touchy-feely, not objective and rigorous like quantitative research.' Well, no, and no for a number of reasons. First, the distinction between qualitative and quantitative research is one that applies *within* empirical research, and it is clear that philosophy is not an empirical form of enquiry. Second, the relation between quantitative and qualitative research has often been a source of confusion. Not so long ago there were the so-called paradigm wars in educational research, where each side, the qualoids and the quantoids, claimed that theirs was the only game in town, the only appropriate method for studying education. But surely the truth of the matter is that sometimes we need quantitative data and sometimes qualitative data. For example, if you want to consider the relationship between educational achievement and poverty, then you will need to have quantitative measures of poverty – perhaps based on the number of children in a school who have free school meals. If you want to find out about students' impressions of their induction into university, it may be better to interview them. But, third, it is essential to realize, that some questions cannot be answered by empirical methods of any kind. If you want to know whether or not schools should compensate for poverty, you will need to think this through. If you want to know what kind of induction is best, you will need to make judgements about what the priorities should be. This is not because we do not have the technical means to answer these questions but because they cannot be approached in that way. Such questions are what philosophy characteristically addresses. Of course, you can leave someone else to decide these things, but someone somewhere will need to face up to these questions of what ought to be done. Certainly judgements of this kind are likely to be better where they are the result of reasoned argument, where they have been tested against the views of others, and where they are based on a research literature in which such matters are examined. Fourth, it is wrong to think of philosophy, or for that matter of qualitative research, as subjective. The implication here is that these approaches are concerned with values, and values are in the end purely personal things, not part of the real world 'out there', not matters of fact. But even the most uncontroversial fact is already steeped in value, if only because there must have been some human concern that caused us to identify this feature of the world in the first place. In any case, it is a fallacy to suppose that values are not 'out there'. If your preference is for apples as opposed to pears, this really does look like a subjective matter, and it would be crazy for anyone to say that you were wrong. But if the question has to do with the justifiability of capital punishment, say, or for that matter with whether schools should compensate for poverty, there is a very clear sense that we are talking about something that is a public matter, where it is appropriate for us to develop and test our arguments against those of others; it is significant that we feel there is a truth-of-the-matter to these things. Judgements in these matters are not whims; they are to be defended on the basis of reasons.

So, we are likely to find that good philosophy helps us to pursue these questions, and to pursue them where they lead. Sometimes this will involve the presentation of water-tight logical arguments, and sometimes things will be less clear-cut. Some of the greatest philosophers, including Plato and Wittgenstein, test thoughts in various forms of dialogue, grappling with the voice of an interlocutor who takes issue with what seems their preferred point of view. Philosophy can sometimes sound abstract, but this is relieved enormously where examples are given, where possible cases are imagined, sometimes where 'thought experiments' are constructed to expose an idea to its limits. And those possible cases can be drawn from real life, from literature, from film.

We are filling out the picture here, but it may still seem that what has been said so far falls short of providing a definitive account of the philosophy of education. Even the term 'education' remains somewhat fuzzy as it is. But it is important to realize that very often in life, and certainly in connection with what matters most in education, we are dealing with terms that are not susceptible to water-tight definition, in the way that, say, such terms in biology as 'liver', 'pancreas' and 'gall-bladder' are. One reason for this is that the concepts in question are themselves matters of dispute: people disagree about what education consists in such that we lack the stable ground on which to anchor the term. One way of putting this is to say that these most important concepts are essentially contestable: we are in disagreement about what their essence is, and this disagreement is not like a controversy in science, where we await further evidence; it is more like an inevitable part of the human condition. In a sense such questions of value are matters that we cannot just hand over to experts; we must all take them up for ourselves, in our personal and in our professional lives.

In the light of these remarks it is a good thing to think about what *reading* philosophy might entail. Sometimes people come to the subject imagining it to be a kind of technical discipline, and this goes with the assumption that it will somehow provide ready-made answers to difficult questions. But really it is a characteristic of philosophy at its best that it provokes the reader, throwing her back on her own resources, forcing her to think. Hence, there is a particular kind of reading, maybe slow reading, that often serves philosophy best, and this helps most with those difficult matters of judgement discussed above. Often in philosophy it is best not to cover too much but rather to stay with certain texts, to dwell on them, you might say, and then you may find that their words help you to think more fully and more deeply about the problems you are addressing.

> Think of some of the texts you are reading on your course or in your earlier studies. Which of these encourage slow reading? In what ways have these helped you to think more deeply?

These remarks about reading imply something about *writing* too, and in what follows we are going to take a practical turn and ask how one might go about preparing a piece of extended writing, such as a dissertation, based upon a philosophical approach.

Writing philosophy of education

Against the standard pattern?

Let us take first an example of empirical research in order to contrast this with philosophical approaches. Imagine a study into the problem of boys' underachievement at the age of 15. The following outlines the stages through which such a study might proceed.

The standard pattern (perhaps)

Outline of area of research.	*Male underachievement.*
Identification of research question.	*Why do boys do worse in exams at 15+?*
Literature survey (probably exhaustive)	*What others have said about male underachievement – the standard theories.*
Explanation of methodology adopted.	*Attitudinal survey of 14–15 yr old boys and girls.*
[Carrying out empirical research]	*[Carry it out.]*
Presentation of results.	*Summary of attitudes expressed correlated with performance in exams and with gender.*
Analysis/discussion of results.	*Evaluation of evidence gathered in relation to the standard theories discussed above.*
	Suggestions of alternative explanations.
	Reflection on adequacy of methodology and any problems encountered.

How is a philosophical thesis different?

In contrast to the above, we can say that a philosophical thesis is:

- not empirically researchable – hence, it will not have the same pattern of procedure (there is no 'writing-up' of results because there are no results);
- centrally concerned with questions of meaning and value, with conceptual matters and with the coherence of ideas (whether they make sense, whether they are justified); quite often with some kind of struggle with ideas;
- sometimes based on a precise question one sets out to answer or provide a solution to, but often concerned with an area in which one searches with less clear a destination;
- sometimes crystal clear argument organized with precision – for example, a systematic refutation of an established point of view relying on the sheer force of logic; but sometimes more loose and less systematic in style, where the force of ideas (and the language used to express them) is allowed to evolve – sometimes you don't know what you think until you have written it!
- sometimes structured in such a way that one sets out clearly at the start the way one is going to proceed, but sometimes organized in such a way as to avoid showing one's hand at the beginning in order to build up the argument more convincingly.

How does one proceed with these kinds of study?

The significance of sources

Because of its central concern with the nature of ideas a philosophical thesis is likely to draw significantly on a limited number of sources – perhaps on a particular philosopher. There is unlikely to be an exhaustive literature search because very often the topic at issue is one that touches on such broad (and sometimes big) issues that one could never come to the end of it. Imagine one for moral education! There is no end to the books that have been written on the nature of morality and on the ways in which we develop as moral beings. But you do need to identify significant voices in the field and to be prepared to address some, at least, of their arguments. Because of the diversity and the strangeness (?) of philosophy it will not normally work if there are numerous brief references to diverse thinkers. It will be necessary to work within some kind of tradition or frame (and to use language in keeping with this tradition). It may nevertheless be very desirable to isolate an aspect of the work of an influential philosopher or educationalist, or some strand of policy or practice, with which you do *not* agree and to provide a critique of the work (perhaps with the help of a philosopher or other thinker you find more sympathetic).

A thesis usually develops best if at an early stage it considers points of view that are later rejected. It follows from this that much of the thesis will involve a faithful *description* of those points of view in order to lay the way for critique. It's a mistake to think that you must plunge into the presentation of your ideas straight away. (This is the topic. Just what has been said about it? Why do I disagree? That is the better method of approach.) Generally, then, you should hold back the exposition of your own ideas until you have carefully and fairly outlined the points of view that you need to contend with.

Different types of philosophical thesis

Consider now a loose, overlapping and non-complete categorization of possible topics for philosophical study. Many of these are on the broad side. As a rough guide, research tends to develop better if a narrower and more focused topic is selected. Paradoxically there can be more to say about something quite specific and limited than about the meaning of life!

Questions of conceptual clarification

Studies of this kind will typically be concerned with ideas that are current in educational policy and practice. They will try to clarify what is understood by these terms and how cogent the ideas are. The following might be examples:

- The idea of lifelong learning.
- What is quality and how can it be assessed?
- The nature of religious belief and the nature of religious education.

The point, as we saw, is not just to find a kind of dictionary definition so much as to see what is implied by these terms in their current usage. The third of these titles clearly directs us to ideas that are matters of controversy, but the central terms in the other two titles also need exploration in this way. Are these words technical expressions or rhetorical slogans? How useful are they? What values do they enshrine? The purpose of the study here will be to make clear these meanings and to address the questions of value that they raise. And it should be noted that it is likely that most philosophical research will somehow or other involve some clarification of the ideas in question.

Questions of justification and value (What is the point of an activity? Why do we value this activity more than that? Which values are important?)

- A justification for happiness classes in the high school curriculum;
- Personal autonomy as an aim of education;
- The case for mass higher education;
- The value of self-esteem;
- Learning to be tolerant – a critical discussion.

Questions of value (i.e. ethics) are at the heart of education, as of other human practices. There are certain formal principles we can apply to considering these – such as consistency and coherence – but at some point questions of substantive value need to be addressed: what matters most and why? Ultimately these matters open onto the biggest questions about what is important in life.

Questions concerning the nature of knowledge

- Professional expertise and its acquisition in physiotherapy;
- The idea of transferable skills and their place in higher education;
- What is a literary education?

Questions about the nature of knowledge (epistemological questions) are obviously at the heart of education, but – strangely – they are easily forgotten or not addressed clearly. We can distinguish between three kinds of knowledge: *knowing that* (or propositional knowledge – 'I know that H_2O is the chemical formula for water'), *knowing how* (skills and competences – 'I know how to dance'), and *knowing with a direct object* (knowing by acquaintance – 'I know Paris / Beethoven's 5th / *The Wizard of Oz*'). Most subjects involve blends of these kinds of knowledge. Which kind of knowledge is most prominent in different curriculum subjects? Is the blend that currently occurs in a subject justified? Note here how epistemological questions regarding the curriculum also lead us back to ethical questions (questions of value and justification).

Questions concerning social justice

- Children's rights and the nature of compulsory schooling;
- The implications of multiculturalism for the secondary school curriculum;
- Social justice and the funding of higher education;
- The idea of inclusion.

Much of the difficulty here concerns what is meant by terms such as 'rights' and 'inclusion' and 'multiculturalism'. Remember also that everyone is in favour of justice, but there are big differences over what counts as justice; this is true across cultures and within them. 'Justice' is an essentially contestable term.

The significance of particular philosophers/thinkers for education

- Nietzsche's Overman and the aims of education;
- A critical discussion of David Cooper's *Illusions of Equality*;
- The legacy of Vygotsky – a critical discussion;
- The idea of well-being in the work of John White – a critical discussion;
- A. N. Whitehead's conception of education – a discussion;
- Richard Layard's *Happiness: Lessons from a New Science*;
- R. S. Peters' concept of the educated man – a critique.

Obviously the scope here is enormous. The big thing to avoid is writing a kind of eulogy to the person you are interested in. You may, of course, come to be fascinated by a particular thinker, but you need to give space to criticisms of this person's work, and not to be so hooked that you come to believe the person can do no wrong! Similarly, you will probably want to quote extensively from this author, but beware of getting carried away with the words, or of being sycophantic in your repetition of their key phrases. Furthermore, ensure that you relate the ideas of the author in question to the practicalities of education. Show why they matter! . . . And you could, of course, write about someone whose ideas you do *not* like.

Critical discussion of policy documents, influential publications, or current developments in practice

- Religious education and its place in secondary schools;
- ICT in recent further education policy documents;
- Howard Gardner's multiple intelligences;
- The idea of learning styles;
- Social and Emotional Aspects of Learning (SEAL – UK Department for Children, Schools and Families);
- The place of Brain Gym in education.

This gives you the chance, if you wish, to analyse a document in your own area of practice. But it is also a chance to stand back from that practice and to scrutinize the details of the document – its language, its policy context and background, and especially its assumptions and reasoning. Some awareness of suitable comparisons can help to cast light on sense and nonsense in these matters, and seeing how people do things differently elsewhere provides a valuable aid to the imagination when it comes to suggesting improvements.

Broader questions combining various elements of the above

- Education for citizenship;
- Psychology and psychoanalysis and their relevance to education;
- The social construction of childhood;
- European identity and the school curriculum in Malta/Northern Ireland/Lithuania/. . .;
- Education and the free market.

Here the scope is broader, and you can put your own stamp on the approach you take. For example, you could address the question of the free market either in terms of the specific changes that this is currently bringing about in educational policy and practice in your sector, or you could explore the deeper philosophical issues that lie behind these developments – covering such matters as questions of economics and social justice, questions to do with public ownership with reference to arguments from Marx, and metaphysical questions relating to differences between individualism and communitarianism.

Some worked examples

Let us now take three of these topics to see in a little more detail how a philosophical approach to them might be structured. Let us imagine that we are preparing a short dissertation, which will be divided into chapters.

What is a literary education?

Introduction

This explains that the purpose of thesis is to ask what a literary education should amount to. This will be done through the provision of a number of different characterizations of a literary education – in terms of the types of texts that are studied and the different ways in which they are taught.

Chapter 1 – The point of literature

This chapter considers a variety of theories in literary criticism concerning the point of literature and of literary appreciation. With regard to education these are related to ideas concerning (a) aesthetic pleasure, (b) moral and character education, (c) expression and self-expression.

Chapter 2 – What is taught?

Questions are raised concerning the canon *v.* a cafeteria curriculum. How to decide what is to be included in the canon? Standard criticisms of the canon are considered ('books by dead white males'), as well as the problems of multiculturalism in relation to the canon. Particular attention is paid to the work of Allan Bloom and Harold Bloom in relation to the idea of *tradition*, and to Wayne Booth in relation to *multiculturalism*.

Chapter 3 – Subjectivity and objectivity in literary judgement

What kind of knowledge is literary knowledge – knowledge about texts? skills to decode texts? direct acquaintance with texts? What is the nature of value judgements in literary appreciation? Are there objective truths here? (Is Jane Austen better than Jackie Collins?) What role is to be allotted to subjective preference? What is the role of personal response in the appreciation of a text? Is that response something learned or is it a purely personal, natural thing? How is assessment to take place in this subject? This depends crucially on the kind of knowledge (if any) that it is thought is being imparted.

Chapter 4 – How is literature to be taught?

In the light of Chapters 2 and 3, suggestions of principles to guide the choice of texts and the manner of teaching are now provided. What is the role of classroom interaction? What is the point of students' writing? What is the role of knowledge of the 'apparatus' of literary criticism? What is the role of personal response and creativity and how is this to be justified?

The value of self-esteem

Introduction

- This sets the scene with evidence of prominence of talk of self-esteem in both educational research literature and the popular media.
- It identifies recent relevant publications including psychological measures of self-esteem.
- It acknowledges the existence of a critical literature about self-esteem – especially regarding what is meant by it and how far the emphasis on it is desirable.
- It explains structure of the thesis that is to follow.

Chapter 1 – The development of self-esteem as an aim of education

We begin with a discussion (largely descriptive) and with plenty of evidence of the ways in which self-esteem has been adopted as a key value in the curriculum (and beyond?). A brief sketch of the history of this is offered. (When did this come into the educational literature?) Connections are drawn with the culture of therapy and ideas of well-being.

Chapter 2 – Self-esteem and educational psychology

This chapter considers specific ways in which self-esteem is understood within educational psychology, perhaps identifying contrasting approaches (say, in behavioural management, in counselling psychology, and in psychotherapy). It also examines attempts to develop measures for self-esteem.

Chapter 3 – Clarifying the concept of self-esteem and its value

An examination of recent discussions by, for example, Ruth Cigman and Richard Smith that seek to clarify how the idea of self-esteem is understood, how coherent it is, and in what ways it should be valued. (e.g. Can you have too much self-esteem? Is it something that only matters when it is absent? Does self-esteem involve an accurate assessment of one's strengths and weaknesses, or is it to do with something beyond particular characteristics – an absolute matter of what it is to be a human being? What is the nature of low self-esteem?)

Chapter 4 – Subjecting current practice regarding self-esteem to criticism

In view of the above discussion, how far is the current emphasis on self-esteem justified? How are problems of self-esteem to be identified and addressed? Does the emphasis on self-esteem involve looking in the wrong direction – too much at the self? This might lead to recommendations for the practice of educational psychologists.

Education for citizenship

Introduction

- This sets the scene in terms of recent policy developments in citizenship education in the context you are working in – for example, in England and Wales, in relation to the Crick Report and the National Curriculum.
- It makes some brief reference to the value of comparisons with one or two other countries, where practices and the issues are significantly different. Hence, it points to the broader issues beyond the local ones.
- It provides an indication of how the dissertation will proceed.

Chapter 1 – Citizenship in England and Wales: the National Curriculum and the Crick Report

This chapter provides a brief account of the social and political circumstances that led to the preparation of the 1998 *Crick Report, Education for Citizenship and the Teaching of Democracy in Schools*. It goes on to explain the way that its recommendations became part of the National Curriculum. Attention needs to be drawn to the aims of citizenship education as understood by the Report, as well as to its recommendations for the curriculum, in terms of the knowledge, abilities and dispositions to be developed. Criticisms of contemporary policy are considered.

Chapter 2 – Citizenship education in other contexts: some points of comparison

Consideration is given to the different priorities that are evident in citizenship education curricula in different countries. Why, for example, is national identity emphasized in Scotland? Why is tolerance and understanding to the fore in Northern Ireland? And why in some other countries is nation-building made a central theme? Furthermore, how is citizenship in the national (UK) context to be related to European citizenship? And how is it to the idea of world citizenship? Perhaps here there can be consideration also of how citizenship relates to patriotism? And there is also the question of the 'citizenship tests' that have been developed for those who want to become British.

Chapter 3 – The relationship between being educated and becoming a citizen

This chapter takes us into deeper considerations about the aims of education. What is it to be an educated person? Can one become educated alone, or must this be connected to one's involvement in society in some way or other? Certainly some philosophers who have written about these matters have seen an essential connection between being educated and becoming a citizen. Plato's *The Republic* and Rousseau's *Emile* are two classic, utopian texts about education, and both depend on visions of the good society and the good citizen. This chapter explains the aspects of those texts that relate most directly to citizenship.

Chapter 4 – Conclusion: all education is citizenship education

In the light of the discussion of Plato and Rousseau in Chapter 3 the argument is developed that Crick's approach is too narrow. Crick runs the risk of limiting the idea of citizenship to a compartment of our lives, when in fact we need to understand our lives as related to the wider involvement in society in which we find ourselves. This points towards the need to rethink the curriculum as a whole in the light of this larger purpose. To do this it is important to make clear what this does *not* mean: it does not require that everyone be trained to do what the state commands, as in some non-democratic regimes. Rather it involves educating people so that they understand that their own good is not to be separated from the larger good of society; this at the same time is the best source of their fulfilment.

Conclusion: the practical importance of philosophy

We recall that Gary was hoping to do an empirical study on the topic: *Which kind of moral education works best with elementary school children?* This is in fact a mine-field. In the first place, the question repeats that contemporary cliché of education 'What works best?', without beginning to think that what works best depends first upon what you are trying to achieve. So far this remains unanswered – or, if the answer offered is that what we are trying to achieve is moral education, then we can now remember that this notion is essentially contestable, and we have a problem to address. To put this more simply: what does moral education consist of? Does it mean children being quiet and obedient, perhaps through fear, perhaps through habit? Or does it mean that children must come to be responsible for themselves in some way, exercising autonomy, making up their own minds about things and acquiring the strength of character to act on what they believe is right? There are no easy answers here. And – the second point – none of this will be solved by an empirical study. What Gary needs above all is to do some serious reading and thinking, and it is philosophical literature, where others have considered precisely these questions, that is likely to help him best here. And when he does this, let us hope also that he realizes that his topic is really still far too broad. Less, as we saw, is often more.

Like Gary, Rajinder, our headteacher, is surely well-intentioned, but she looks as though she may be rushing in too quickly. She is certainly right to be concerned about rising levels of stress amongst her colleagues and students. But are happiness classes more than a feel-good, cosmetic response to this – too quick, too neat, too easy a solution? She will do better to look carefully at the literature that has brought happiness to the fore in policy agendas. If she reads the many critical responses to this that have emerged in the literature, she may come to look on the idea of happiness classes with more sceptical eyes. The result need not be that she abandons the idea of addressing the problem of stress in the school. It may rather be that she is better placed to see what the real causes are of stress and what there is in education that might better respond to this. She will learn in the process, no doubt, how part of the problem is contemporary educational practice itself, and this may help her to see the need to dismantle some of those structures of anxiety in such a way as to release aspects of teaching and learning that they hold at bay. She too then can make practical progress here by becoming more philosophical in her approach to these matters, and this will involve her in some careful reading and thinking.

It is an irony of Sam's case that she studied some history as part of her undergraduate course, so she has felt some misgivings about the current directive to reframe the curriculum in terms of skills. But somehow the tide of policy change has seemed unstoppable, and she has realized that what is expected of her is to see things through to a result. In these circumstances she finds herself adopting the catch-phrases that she hears in policy circles, which are there every day in the masses of policy literature she is compelled to read, and she feels less and less capable of phrasing arguments in any other way. But what justification can there be for screening out arguments that are relevant to the matter at hand. We saw above the value of attending to the blend of different kinds of knowledge in different subjects. Shifts in that blend amount to a reorientation of the subject, sometimes a change in its very nature. Sam is convinced that History should not be a matter of just learning strings of dates, the way her parents told her they had to do, but on the other hand she remembers well how, when she enjoyed the subject most, there was a sense of becoming familiar with a particular period, of having a vivid sense of what it was that animated people then, what they cared about and how different these things were from life today. Now certainly to gain this sense you needed some knowledge of the facts – concerning, for example, changes in the law, fluctuations in trade or major social movements. But in addition to this, if this was truly History, there was also that sense of familiarity with the time in question, a knowing by acquaintance, and it is this, she now finds, that is most under threat. If Sam reads some philosophy about these matters, this will not by itself enable her to swing the government around to her point of view, but it at least will help her in presenting the case. It will help her to see things more clearly. Ultimately, if one day she has more influence, it may even feed into a more coherent approach to the subject. That may be a lot to hope for, but in all conscience it is surely what Sam should do.

Further reading

Key Questions in Education, edited by William Hare and John Portelli (2007), provides a clear and concise account of some key concepts and issues in education, and it does this in a very accessible way. For a more searching philosophical approach, see *The Blackwell Guide to*

Philosophy of Education (2003), edited by Nigel Blake, Paul Smeyers, Richard Smith and Paul Standish. This book provides a substantial introduction, followed by 20 chapters in which pairs of philosophers address prominent topics. Each chapter provides an initial survey of prevailing lines of thought but then takes some aspect of the topic forward into new terrain. Detailed discussions of developments in teaching and learning can be found in Ruth Cigman and Andrew Davis's *New Philosophies of Learning* (2009). Diverse and conflicting points of view on both topical and enduring educational issues are presented in a thought-provoking way, while the editors' helpful commentary sections offer an invaluable guide to the reader. Paul Standish's 'Rival Versions of the Philosophy of Education' (2007) offers an account of some contemporary trends in the discipline, as well as a rationale for its place in the study of education, with illustrations of its purchase on educational practice.

Does Education Need Philosophy?

2

Richard Pring

Introduction

It might be assumed from observation of what actually happens in practice that the answer to the title's question is 'no'. Thirty or more years ago, philosophy was an essential and much needed component in the education of teachers. Now it is no longer regarded as such. Future teachers, more often than not, are prepared for their professional life without any reference to the philosophical thinking about education – its aims and purposes, its content or its links with the wider preoccupations of society – which has been conducted and argued about over the centuries. But why this has happened is itself worthy of philosophical reflection.

In the more distant past, those trained as teachers through the Diploma of Education or the Post-Graduate Certificate of Education would have been exposed to the 'Great Thinkers' – to Plato's education of a 'guardian' class, to Rousseau's account of Emile, to Dewey's advocacy of experiential learning or the 'experiential continuum', to Froebel's emphasis on 'natural growth', to Whitehead's 'age of romance' followed by the 'age of precision', and (possibly with disapproval) to Locke's description of the child's mind as a *tabula rasa* on which good ideas were to be impressed.

Here are two questions from the examination paper taken 50 years ago by those completing their post-graduate initial training at Oxford University Department of Educational Studies:

> How far are the educational views of Plato and Aristotle relevant only to the training of a meritocracy?
>
> 'Let him not be taught science; let him discover it.' Explain this principle of Rousseau's, and comment on its soundness and on its practicability.

Many would have questioned the philosophical merits of such an exposure to 'the great thinkers', but at least it alerted the future teacher to the world of ideas, inevitably controversial, which enter into our understanding of young people and of what should be taught and of how those learners might be properly treated. Failure to enter into that world of ideas and to be critical of the taken-for-granted assumptions behind educational practice leads to a sense of certainty where there should instead be a measure of doubt, and to dogmatism where there should be critical questioning.

Today, with a few admirable exceptions, there is little room for the critical discussion of ideas, whether philosophical or sociological, which, often unconsciously, underpin educational practice. Teachers are trained to 'deliver' the curriculum. They are assessed on their 'effectiveness'. Their 'training' teaches them to reach the 'targets' set by others. There is no time, and little systematic encouragement, to question what they are instructed to deliver or the mode by which it might be delivered most effectively.

Similarly, courses in educational research methodology (a condition for 'recognition' of university departments by the Economic and Social Research Council) are increasingly training new researchers how to observe, how to conduct surveys, how to interview – techniques equally relevant, for instance, to research into effective management of the retail business – but not to question the relevance of such techniques to the exploration of distinctively educational questions. What counts as *educational* research is not thought to need questioning.

To understand all this, a little history might help.

Recent history of philosophy in educational studies

The early 1960s saw the creation in Britain of a specifically education degree – the B.Ed., which could be taken at Honours Level. To be an Honours degree, it had to be academically respectable. That respectability could be achieved only if the prevailing theory of education (more often than not an introduction to 'the great thinkers', referred to above) was replaced by systematic studies in the so-called 'foundation disciplines'. Posts were created in the philosophy of education in most, if not all, of the many colleges of education, then under the academic wings of university institutes of education.

At the same time, the dominant mode of philosophizing within universities was that of 'conceptual analysis' – the close and disciplined attention to the meaning of key and often contestable concepts as these were revealed in the different usages of particular words. Through a closer and systematic examination of language, one might contribute to the solution of problems which often arise from 'the bewitchment of intelligence' by the unreflective use of language.

Putting the two together – namely, the attempt to make educational studies academically respectable and the contemporary dominance of analytic philosophy in universities – teacher educators developed a particular style of thinking about education, led by a group of philosophers at the Institute of Education, University of London. Professor Richard Peters, who succeeded to the Chair of Philosophy of Education in 1962, spoke at a major conference in 1964 of the need to get rid of the 'undifferentiated mush', which too often passes for educational theory, and to base educational thinking upon sound academic disciplines, not least of which was that of analytic philosophy (see Peters, 1977a, p. 140). The analytic tradition within the philosophy of education took seriously the advice of Wittgenstein: 'My aim is: to teach you to pass from a piece of disguised nonsense to something that is patent nonsense' (Wittgenstein, 1958, 1.464).

Henceforth, the philosophy of education examined such logically interrelated concepts as

- 'education' ('What does it mean to say that someone is educated?'),
- 'indoctrination' ('Can one teach a person to have religious faith without indoctrinating them?'),
- 'teaching' ('Does it make sense to say you are teaching when you don't know the learners' level of understanding?'),
- 'learning' ('Is behaviourism a theory of learning?'),
- 'curriculum subjects' ('Are there logical characteristics of different forms of knowledge which should be reflected in the curriculum?'),
- 'moral development' ('Is "being moral" a relative matter – and therefore beyond the role of the school?').

An excellent, and at the time, very influential example of such analytic thinking was the work of John Wilson in moral education. Wilson's philosophical analysis of what is meant by being and thus becoming moral (namely, having knowledge of key moral principles, the capacity to think in a certain way, the dispositions or virtues to act on that knowledge and thinking, and the strength of will to persevere) was intended to provide the conceptual framework within which the sociologist and the psychologist in the team could then proceed to seek the empirical evidence. First, Wilson argued, you need to clarify what you mean, and only then can you know what evidence is relevant to finding out the truth.

Of course, neither the sociologist nor the psychologist willingly accepted this subservient division of labour. None the less, it resulted in a pioneering book (divided appropriately into three parts – the philosophical analysis, the sociological dimension and the psychological facts about development), entitled *An Introduction to Moral Education* (Wilson et al., 1967).

Similarly, through such systematic analysis, key concepts (and thereby the practices) of 'child-centred education', such as 'growth', 'needs', 'learning through play', were criticized and transferred from the list of 'disguised nonsense' to that of 'patent nonsense'. A philosophical attack on the 1967 Plowden Report *Children and their Schools* had a profound influence on subsequent attitudes towards that Report and towards the conception of primary education which it embodied.

However, the place of philosophy so conceived is no longer assured. A recent paper in *Educational Theory* is entitled 'Why aren't philosophers and educators speaking to each other?' (Arcilla, 2002). Arcilla's diagnosis of the problem is that, in failing to give the guidance to educators, which the social sciences both promise and seem to deliver, philosophers have been excluded from the conversation with educationists and have sought comfort in a purely theoretical world tagged on either to social science or to the post-modern embrace. Teachers do not read the *Journal of the Philosophy of Education*, and, if they did, they might find it difficult to see the connection between its contents and the problems they are struggling with in the classroom. There is a deep suspicion of theory unless its relevance to improvement of practice is clear and unmistaken. The message throughout seems to be that educational theory, and research in particular, should be addressed, through empirical enquiry, to the problems of policy and practice.

In the rest of this chapter, I want to argue against both the purist view of philosophy of education (the validity of which lies in its distance from the practical deliberations of the teachers and the policy makers) and the notion of an educational practice to which philosophical thinking is seen to have no relevance. We live in a world of ideas. These ideas shape thinking about practice (whether that be the practice of the teacher or the practice of policy makers) in unacknowledged ways. One function of philosophy is to make those ideas explicit, to subject them to criticism, and to influence practice, not by providing alternative theories or bodies of knowledge for the guidance of practice, but by ensuring that the assumptions behind practice are tenable and coherent.

I shall do this through reflection upon the independent and comprehensive Nuffield Review of 14–19 Education and Training for England and Wales, a one million pounds project, funded by Nuffield Foundation, whose final report will be published in 2009.

Nuffield Review

Immediately, three concepts need clarification: 'review', 'comprehensive' and 'independent'.

First, as a review, it aims to give an account of the present and changing 14–19 system – its achievements and its failures, the policies which shape it and the practices which embody (or do not embody) those policies, the relationship of the system to the wider needs of society, and the progression from it to higher education, further training and employment. But already there are problems which enter into philosophical territory. What counts as an appropriate description of the system? What 'performance indicators' should be adopted to give that account? What counts as 'evidence' in arriving at a conclusion? To answer these questions, one needs to address prior questions about educational aims because, for example, the 'performance indicators' (one being the number of young people who achieve five 'good' GCSEs) make unquestioned assumptions about the values which underpin the system. Change the aims and you have different performance indicators and different standards by which success is judged. And the identification and justification of those aims takes us into the difficult territory of ethics. The Nuffield Review, therefore, has started with the question, 'What counts as an educated 19-year-old in this day and age?'

Second, the comprehensiveness of the review is based on the assumption that the different aspects of the 14–19 (namely, the quality of learning and its assessment, the curriculum and the framework of qualifications, the choices available and the guidance given, the different providers of formal learning and the opportunities for informal learning, the funding arrangements of the system and the progression routes through it, the economic needs and the level of training required to meet those needs) all interrelate. A holistic approach is required such that the conclusions to be reached are affected by each element interacting within the system as a whole. A holistic approach, also, must respect the logical limitations of any central recommendation or directive to predict and thus to influence, as intended, the many interactions which take place inside and outside the classroom. Is not the *certainty*, with which Government constantly intervenes, the product of the failure to recognize this simple logical point? Above all, however, an understanding of the parts and of their interrelationship is permeated by the underlying and often unquestioned values which constitute the aims of education. 'Quality of learning', what counts as a valid 'assessment of learning', the 'standards' by which the learning and the school performance are to be judged, the concept of 'teaching', all embody particular traditions of education which in turn reflect different values at a very fundamental level. What would at first appear to be an essentially empirical investigation turns out to be deeply philosophical.

Third, the Review seeks to be independent. But independent of what? Certainly, it is independent of Government, and indeed frequently challenges the Government's account of educational aims and performance. But can any account be independent of prejudice or of influences unrealized and unacknowledged? The answer must in one sense be 'no'. We (each of us) come to any situation with ideas and values which influence our enquiries – which affect what aspects are considered important and what are not. The philosopher Karl Popper argues that there are no sure foundations on which indisputable conclusions can be drawn. But the conclusion to be drawn from this position is not total scepticism. Rather it is, as Popper argued, to give an account with such precision that others might know how to argue against it (see Popper, 1972). It is to subject one's views (values and conclusions) to rigorous and open scrutiny. In this, Popper follows in the tradition of the English philosopher, John Stuart Mill (1859; reprinted in Warnock, 1972), who, in his *Essay on Liberty*, says:

> The peculiar evil of silencing the expression of an opinion is, that it is robbing the human race; posterity as well as the present generation; those who dissent from the opinion, still more than those who hold it. If the opinion is right, they are deprived of the opportunity of exchanging error for truth; if wrong, they lose, what is almost as great a benefit, the clearer perception and livelier impression of truth, produced by its collision with error. (p. 142)

Perhaps this is the most significant aspect of philosophy which needs to permeate educational thinking – the clarification of what one means with sufficient clarity that others will know what would count as evidence against what is said. Only those views which have survived criticism are worth clinging on to – provisionally, of course, since those very conclusions are always open to further criticism in the light of new evidence. But, of course, such a critical attitude can be subversive, and that is one reason why philosophy might be unpopular in the training and further professional development of teachers.

Doing philosophy

Already I have indicated what I mean by philosophy. But philosophy itself is a contested concept. By 'contested' I point to the fact that the meaning is not agreed, that the consequent disagreement cannot be rectified simply by appeal to the Oxford English Dictionary and that the differences in meaning reflect wider and deeper disagreements, often of an ethical nature. One difficulty with an educational review is that 'education' itself is one such concept. Disagreement about its meaning affects profoundly the organization of educational practice and that disagreement reflects differences about what it means to be and to flourish as a person.

On the other hand, though philosophers argue with other philosophers about the nature of philosophy, these very arguments are within a tradition of thinking and questioning. Philosophers, though disagreeing with previous generations of philosophers, argue for their point of view more often than not by pointing to where previous philosophers are seen to be wrong. That critical tradition is one in which they are concerned about the most appropriate way of describing, in the most general sense, the physical, social and moral worlds we inhabit. What counts as being human, and thus to grow as a human being? What does it mean to say that such a human being can act freely and be held responsible for their actions? In what sense might a collection of human beings constitute a community? These are perennial questions of philosophy, but they are at the same time interwoven with the accounts and decisions within education and thus within the concerns of the Nuffield Review.

Therefore, philosophers constantly ask 'What do you mean?' The concepts we use (i.e. the ways in which our minds organize experience) can often be obscure and confusing, though we may well fail to recognize that. Excellent examples of this, and of a philosopher systematically asking 'What do you mean?' are to be found in Plato's dialogues. When Socrates asks Theaetetus what does he mean by 'justice' (a word which Theaetetus uses as though the meaning is obvious and straightforward), Socrates constantly gives counter examples until Theaetetus gives up in a huff, unable to give a definition which embraces all the usages of the term. What he thought was a clear concept turns out to be very difficult to define. And yet a lot hangs on the definition (in some cases literally).

There is need, therefore, to attend to the different ways in which particular words are used, for 'their meaning lies in their use within a language' (see Wittgenstein, 1958). Part of a philosopher's job within the analytic tradition has been to trace those different usages – or (to use a frequent metaphor) to map out the logical terrain. For example, if one attends to how 'education' is employed in our language, one is able to pick out certain logical features (i.e. features of its use which characterize its meaning and from which certain further claims follow). Thus one might distinguish between the descriptive use of the term (e.g. 'the educational system') and the evaluative use (e.g. 'an educated person'). Furthermore, in both uses 'education' refers to some kind of learning which is intended or happening, where that learning leads to deeper understanding of the world (physical and social) in which one lives. But the evaluative sense would indicate that not any sort of developed understanding merits the accolade 'education'. That learning has to be in some sense 'worthwhile'. Educational philosophers, therefore, have attended to how one justifies one activity to be more worthwhile than another.

Obviously, not all concepts are of philosophical interest. So many words within our language are pretty uncontroversial. We talk happily about tables and chairs without any fuss. Any dispute here can easily be resolved through recourse to the dictionary. But other words are controversial. Moreover, those controversies, or disagreements in the use of key words, reflect deeper concerns with which philosophers have traditionally engaged. These might be classified (though not comprehensively) as:

- *ethics* – those studies which are concerned with the basis of our judgements that certain actions are right or wrong or that certain ways of life are more valuable than others;
- *philosophy of mind* – those studies which explore what it means to have a mind, to think, to be conscious and to act freely, and what the connection is between the mental world of thoughts, intentions and feelings and the physical world inhabited by our bodies;
- *epistemology* – those studies which are concerned with what constitutes knowledge, its foundations, the truth conditions for any claim to knowledge and the different kinds of knowledge (propositional and practical, scientific, religious, historical and so on);
- *social and political philosophy* – those studies which are concerned with the nature of society, the appropriate relationship between the individual and the societies to which they belong, and the basis of authority and power within a society.

Of course, the above classification is oversimple – other categories such as 'logic' could be given, and there are important distinctions to be made within each. But they suffice to illustrate my argument about the relevance of philosophy to educational policy and practice. The following subsections are examples of how these philosophical concerns enter into our thinking about education, illustrated by reference to the work of the Nuffield Review.

Educational aims

Any educational system is, by definition, concerned with the promotion of learning. But of the infinite range of things which could be learnt, only certain kinds are selected – for example, in the National Curriculum. How do we decide, then, what kinds of knowledge should be picked out as worth learning, what practical skills should be promoted, what attitudes and dispositions nurtured? In the key Government paper on 14–19 developments (DfES 14–19), we were told that education should help all young people to realize their potential. People nod wisely upon hearing this. But a moment's philosophical reflection upon what we mean by potential should immediately sow seeds of doubt.

First, a glance at the daily newspaper makes it obvious that we have the potential as much for evil as we have for good. There are many potentials which we do not want to be realized. Second, the realizing of potential is culturally bound and will be shaped by the cultural forces to which young people are exposed. Indeed, one might argue that that is one reason for schools – to realize certain potentials and not others, and to do so through the introduction to the wisdom, developed over generations, through which those potentials are realized in a particular way. The philosopher Michael Oakeshott (1972) spoke of education as an introduction to the conversation which has taken place between the generations of mankind in which they come to hear and appreciate the voice of poetry, the voice of history, the voice of science.

Educational thinking, therefore, has to attend to the underlying metaphors through which we come to see the enterprise in a particular way. The Nuffield Review has been critical of the language drawn from management and business, through which educational activities are increasingly described and evaluated – an emphasis on economy-related 'skills' and 'enterprise', the reduction of aims to measurable 'targets', the identification of 'performance indicators' as a basis for 'audit', the perception of the curriculum as something to be 'delivered' rather than taught, and the reclassification of cuts in resources as 'efficiency gains'. The Review, therefore, is doing two things that are relevant here.

First, it is seeing how this shifting language of education is affecting the understanding of 'learning' and its assessment, the concepts of 'standards' and 'teaching', the content of the curriculum, and the source of 'authority' for decision-makers within the educational system. Without philosophical critique, this shifting language goes undetected, as does its impoverishing impact upon educational practice. Second, the Nuffield Review has started with, and constantly returns to, the question 'What counts as an educated 19-year-old in this day and age?' And such a question takes us into the central questions of ethics.

> The Nuffield Review addresses the question: 'What counts as an educated 19-year-old in this day and age?'
> First, jot down four characteristics of such an educated person which you think are essential.
> Second, reflect on how you would argue for these against someone who had a different list.

Culture and community

In the above outline, I mentioned the significance of 'culture' in the aim of helping young people to realize those potentials which are thought to be worth while. But culture is itself a tricky concept. Indeed, it would be interesting to hesitate awhile and to attempt a definition which would encapsulate what you mean. It would be even more interesting to compare such a definition with those who were attempting the same exercise.

Again, we need to attend to the different ways in which the word is used. As with 'education' it has both a descriptive and an evaluative use.

On the one hand, we talk descriptively of 'youth culture', 'working class culture' or even 'gang culture'. Culture in this descriptive sense would capture the background social influences upon how people think and find value in things and in relationships – the meanings which are embedded in a way of life and in language which might not be explicitly recognized by the very people who participate within that culture. There have been some excellent sociological studies which pick out those distinctive cultural features without reference to which one cannot really understand how people within that culture think or behave.

On the other hand, we talk evaluatively of the 'cultured person' or of a 'cultural event' – the latter being seen as in some way uplifting. Culture in this sense embodies socially approved ways of thinking, appreciating and valuing. Once again, such cultural judgements are, within certain milieu (e.g. a group of artists), taken for granted. But the philosophical task is to challenge the received understanding of 'high culture' and to seek justifications for why this activity or that subject of study should be regarded as more culturally worthwhile than another. The educational task cannot be isolated from such cultural debate. What intellectual, aesthetic and moral resources – the consequences of the 'conversation between the generations of mankind' – should inform our thoughts and our sensibilities? And how can there be established a link between the cultures (descriptive sense) of young learners and the cultural traditions which inform the official educational programme?

The importance of this concept, and its implications for education as a preparation for living in the community, is emphasized by many educational thinkers and philosophers.

For example, A. H. Halsey, who had been a powerful influence in the development of the comprehensive system of education, spoke in his Reith Lecture:

> We have still to provide a common experience of citizenship in childhood and old age, in work and play, and in health and sickness. We have still in short, to develop a common culture to replace the divided culture of class and status. (Halsey, 1978)

That link between culture and living together harmoniously and productively seems central to education endeavour – the context in which each can learn from, and contribute to the understandings of, others. According to the American philosopher John Dewey:

> Men live in a community in virtue of the things which they have in common. What they must have in common in order to form a community or society are aims, beliefs, aspirations, knowledge – a common understanding – likemindedness as the sociologists say. (1916, p. 4)

Therefore, it is an important philosophical task to examine what it means to live in a community and to thereby share and to develop a common culture which emphasizes what, as persons, they have in common, whilst respecting much cherished differences.

Write down the communities which you see yourself as a member of, and say

- what makes these your community;
- how they are different from other groups of people with which you interact;
- what you would say is a genuine community school.

Learning and teaching

Central to educating all young people must, by definition, be the effort to bring about or to enhance learning. And, given that success in life requires constant learning, it is now a truism that the educational system should enable young people 'to learn how to learn' – to acquire the 'learning skills'. Furthermore, the Government stipulates 'learning outcomes' by which learners will be graded and schools assessed for educational competence. The measured learning of each pupil becomes the basis of the measured performance of the school – and thus its place in the league tables. And the measured performance of all schools in learning outcomes (e.g. proportionate increase of learners with five or more GCSEs at grades A to C) becomes the basis of the evaluation of 'system performance'.

Rarely, however, is there a pause to ask what it means to say someone has learnt. Those with a philosophical inclination would point to the fact that one does not just learn, let alone 'learn how to learn', but that one learns *something* and that what constitutes 'having learnt' depends on the nature of that something which it is claimed one has learnt. One learns to be practical as well as one learns facts, concepts, principles and theories. Moreover, learning a mathematical principle, say, is quite different from learning historical facts, and very different from learning how to be good or how to ride a bicycle.

'Learning' is what the philosopher, Gilbert Ryle, called an 'achievement word'. Its meaning points to certain standards which have been met, and those standards are internal to the subject matter which is being learnt. Not any playing around with numbers counts as having understood mathematics. That requires the mastery of certain rules, and that mastery can be more or less attained, gradually acquired, and achieved at different levels of understanding. In other words, one needs to attend to the 'logic of the subject matter' – to the mode of understanding, the concepts, the ways of organizing experience, the rules of procedure which constitute particular 'forms of thought' or 'disciplines of thinking'. These are very often encapsulated, within the curriculum, in subjects to make it easier to initiate the learner into this distinctive way of understanding.

Education here, if it is to make sense, inevitably involves philosophical work in the theory of knowledge or epistemology in which the basis and nature of different kinds of knowledge claim are analysed critically. Failure to engage in such philosophical thinking results in the reduction of learning to the ability to memorize and to repeat propositions or formulae – to meet behavioural targets – without the deeper understanding of a particular way of knowing.

That affects profoundly one's understanding of 'teaching' and of the role and status of the teacher. Teaching is the active intention to get someone to learn something, and therefore requires, first, an understanding of how much the learner already understands or can do, and, second, an understanding of that which the teacher wants the learner to grasp. It requires a knowledge of the learner and of the subject matter, and the skill to link the two. That which is to be taught is drawn from what Dewey referred to as 'the accumulated wisdom of the race' or what Oakeshott referred to as the different voices in the 'conversation between the generations of mankind'. The profession of teaching, therefore, is both a guardian of that accumulated wisdom and the means whereby it will be inherited by future generations. In that respect, it is a deeply moral undertaking, ensuring the transmission of the best in our cultural inheritance relevant to personal and social development. The Review, in recognizing these links between education, initiation into different and enriching forms of understanding, and teaching, has questioned the dominance in the current 14–19 developments of seeing teachers as 'deliverers' of the curriculum – such a curriculum (e.g. that of the Diplomas) being invented elsewhere, ready to be transmitted or delivered to often reluctant learners.

Consider how far the curriculum should find a place for the young learner's experience.
Write down examples of how the curriculum for a particular group of young learners might build on the learners' experiences in an educationally enriching way.

Provision

We learn from experience as well as through formal provision of education – something which too often is forgotten. But 'experience' is itself a concept with a philosophical history. Is experience the raw material on which the mind gets working – the perception of colours and shapes and sounds prior to any interpretation? There is a strong 'empirical' tradition in British philosophy which has seen basic experience in this way. To develop the mind therefore is to impress upon it (as though it is an empty slate or 'tabula rasa') those sensations which we want to leave as a permanent impression. But alternatively one might see all experiences as already interpreted as they are accommodated within a mind which is already formed by previous experiences and which is constantly adjusting its mode of anticipating future experiences in the light of the present. For Dewey, therefore, education is this constant transformation of experience, and it is the job of the teacher, being aware of the experiential understanding brought by the learner into school, to help with that transformation – to introduce the learner to further experiences (through science, literature, drama, for example) which will extend the capacity of the learner to 'manage life more intelligently'.

The form of educational provision depends, therefore, on how one understands the meaning and significance of the learner's experience. Is the school a place shut off from the outside world, disconnected from the familial and social experience which has formed the minds of the young learner? Or should it be, as Dewey argued, an extension of that experience, deeply rooted in the community from which the learners come? How far can knowledge and understanding be transmitted to (impressed upon the minds of) the young learner without relevant practical experience, or to what extent should growing understanding be seen as a transformation of experience which is ensured by the school – through practical engagement with the environment, with the community and with experimentation?

Conclusion

Both educational policy and educational practice are understood and pursued through understandings embodied in the language we use. Therefore, where that language is obscure or confused, or where inappropriate metaphors sneak in to change our understandings, there is a need to reflect systematically upon that language. There is a need to make explicit and to examine critically the meanings through which we understand the physical, social and moral worlds we inhabit. So many of the key concepts, through which we talk about education, are contestable, reflecting deeper disagreements about the meaning and aims of education, about the significance of the cultural resources upon which the schools and colleges draw, about what it means to learn and to understand, and about the links between the formal provision of education and the experience, prior or current, of the young learners.

One aim of the Nuffield Review is to show the relevance of such philosophical reflection to the understanding of developments 14–19, and to help, if only a little, to: 'to pass from a piece of disguised nonsense to something that is patent nonsense'.

What this chapter has tried to do (illustrated through the Nuffield Review of 14–19 Education and Training) is to show that

- educational policy and practice embody ideas which too often are only implicit;
- these ideas, when made explicit, are seen to be confused, even misleading;
- such confusion often runs deep – concerning the nature of knowledge, or the justification of what is considered to be worthwhile, or what it means to develop as a person, or how human behaviour might be explained;
- philosophy is the systematic and disciplined way in which these confusions and questions are addressed.

Further reading

The Socratic arguments in the many Plato dialogues are an excellent introduction to philosophical argument and method. Of these there are many editions. Perhaps one of the best and most relevant of these to education students is *The Republic*, in particular Part I and the discussion between Socrates and Theaetetus on the nature of justice. The importance of discussion, conducted in the spirit of doubt (i.e. searching out the possible objections to a received or favourite belief), is argued for clearly in John Stuart Mill's *Essay on Liberty*.

Recent analytic philosophy of education was pioneered by Richard Peters at the Institute of Education University of London. The classic text *is Ethics and Education*, and particularly chapters 1 and 2, where he analyses the concept of education, and chapter 5, where he considers why certain activities might be justified as more worthwhile than others. But a most influential philosopher has been the American John Dewey. His *Democracy and Education*, written in 1916, and the much shorter defence of his views in *Experience and Education*, written in 1938, have influenced generations of teachers and policy makers – as well as annoyed many others (a good example of the perceived consequences, for good or ill, of philosophical thinking). Richard Pring's recent *John Dewey: The Philosopher of Education for the 21st Century?* is a short but expensive introduction to Dewey's philosophical influence. Similarly, with regard to the curriculum, Dewey (1902, reprinted in Garforth, 1966), *The Child and the Curriculum* is an excellent read.

A key influence on educational research, because of the position he argues for on the nature of knowledge, has been Karl Popper. The major work is *Objective Knowledge*, but a good introduction to it is that by Richard Bailey (2000a). Roughly, the argument is that knowledge grows through criticism and falsification of received knowledge and assumptions – the reverse of our normal approach which is to defend rather than to challenge our most cherished beliefs.

Beautifully written papers on learning and education were written by the philosopher, Michael Oakeshott, collected together in a book edited by T. Fuller. See particularly the paper on 'Learning and Teaching'.

Useful website

The Nuffield Review has a large collection of papers and research covering all aspects of 14–19 education and training, including philosophical papers on the aims of education. See www.nuffield14-19review.org.uk.

What Is Education For? 3

Roger Marples

Chapter Outline

Introduction

Every year the British government spends tens of billions of pounds on education with, for the most part, the approval of the tax-payer. However, if asked what they thought such a colossal expenditure was *for* it is a safe bet that the answers would vary enormously; indeed it would be surprising if there were any general consensus amongst the vast majority of those who were most directly affected – pupils, parents and teachers. Given the fact that children are meant to be in school for a minimum of 11 years, one would have hoped that before a National Curriculum had been constructed for them to pursue, there would have been some attempt on the part of government, or at least that branch of government responsible for a public system of education, to formulate a coherent and plausible set of overall *aims*. Although it is true that the revised National Curriculum begins with a set of clearly specifiable aims, these were written *subsequently* to the actual content of that curriculum, with little or no consideration as to the relationship between them (DfEE/QCA, 1999).

We are all affected by the behaviour, attitudes and values of school leavers. It follows that schools, with their profound influence on the shaping of young people's belief systems and dispositions, have a major impact on the kind of society in which we have to conduct our lives, and it is therefore incumbent upon both teachers and those who are responsible for formulating the content of the curriculum to do their best to ensure that pupils are equipped with the wherewithal to make the sort of contribution to society that a liberal democracy has a right to expect. Such a task is far from straightforward, given the complexity and varied nature of a modern industrial society. The Victorians were convinced of the desirability of two radically different kinds of schooling, whereby the working classes spent most of their time learning how to read, write and sort things into dozens, with the patronizing intention of teaching children to appreciate their position, while their middle class counterparts were provided with a diet of almost unrelieved Latin and Greek, with the very different intention of preparing them for positions of leadership at home and throughout the Empire. It is now generally accepted that schools today should be concerned with something very different indeed. Part of the aim of this chapter is to spell out what this might justifiably amount to.

What is 'education' and must an educator have an aim?

Both of these questions engaged the attention of one of the most distinguished philosophers of education of the twentieth century, namely Richard Peters who, in a hugely influential book (Peters, 1966) argues that education is logically (or conceptually) connected to what is deemed to be 'worthwhile', the corollary of which, he believes, is that its value is intrinsic in the sense that it is not derivative from something else, such as a meal ticket towards getting a job. Peters would therefore take great exception to the question posed in the title of this chapter; once we understand what it is to be educated we shall, he insists, be forced to acknowledge that it is an end in itself and not a means to something else. As he puts it: 'To ask questions about the aims of education is . . . to get clear about and focus attention on what is worth while achieving. It is not to ask for the production of ends extrinsic to education which might explain their activities as educators' (ibid., p. 28). According to Peters, 'being educated' entails that: (i) one has a body of knowledge and a degree of understanding involving a conceptual scheme by reference to which what one knows is more than a collection of disjointed facts; (ii) such knowledge cannot be 'inert' in the sense that it can be hived off as it were, and thereby fail to characterize one's way of looking at things, for 'education' implies that a man's outlook is transformed by 'what he knows'; (iii) one has what he calls a 'cognitive perspective' whereby one does not have an impossibly limited conception of what one is engaged in; (iv) unlike being trained, an educated person is not merely competent at performing a particular task, rather her competence is linked to a much wider belief system than someone *merely* trained (ibid., pp. 30–4).

The fact remains that even if it is true that education need not necessarily serve any instrumental purposes, we might well have reason for educating people for reasons other than that it is good in itself. Having specified what he takes 'education' to be, Peters goes on to argue that education is the process of *initiation into intrinsically worthwhile activities*, or those activities in which one might engage for their own sake. At first sight this is an appealing notion. After all, a child is not born with a conceptual framework enabling her to make sense of the world; she has to *learn* what things are and what they mean. Peters explains what is involved with his customary elegance:

> A child is born with a consciousness not yet differentiated into beliefs, purposes, and feelings. . . . The objects of consciousness are first and foremost objects in a public world that are marked out and differentiated by a public language into which the individual is initiated . . . Differentiation develops as the mastery of the basic skills opens the gates to a vast inheritance by those versed in more specific modes of thought and awareness such as science, history, mathematics, religion and aesthetic awareness. . . . Each has its own family of concepts peculiar to it and its own distinctive methods of validation. . . . for all who get on the inside of such a form of thought . . . the contours of that public world are transformed. The process of initiation into such modes of thought and awareness is the process of education. (ibid., pp. 49–51)

The questions to which this gives rise are both numerous and difficult. They include: (1) Why should we accept the definition of education provided so far? (2) How are we to determine what is 'worthwhile'? (3) Even if the intrinsic value of certain forms of knowledge and understanding can be demonstrated, does anything follow about the extent to which the actual curriculum should be confined to their study, or even include them at all?

What are your thoughts about these questions?

In the years following the publication of *Ethics and Education*, Peters worked closely with his colleague Paul Hirst and together they proposed that education's principal concern should be the development of mind for its own sake, relying very much on the notion of 'liberal education' articulated and defended by Hirst in an earlier publication (Hirst, 1965). There are, of course, many ways of specifying what such an education might entail. Charles Bailey usefully characterizes it by its capacity to liberate a person from the here and now, by involving pupils in what is fundamental and general and intrinsically worthwhile in order to promote the development of what Hirst calls the 'rational mind' or the capacity to think (Bailey, C. 1984, p. 29). *Knowledge and understanding* for its own sake is so frequently suggested as the principal aim of education that it merits rather more detailed consideration. Apart from anything else, it raises questions relating to the sort of knowledge with which schools should be concerned.

In the light of what Peters has to say about initiating pupils into intrinsically worthwhile activities, how would you set about trying to demonstrate to someone that the study of history or science was more 'worthwhile' than playing computer games or watching Big Brother?

Knowledge for its own sake

According to Hirst – or at least the Hirst of the 1960s and 1970s – knowledge is subsumable under seven different forms. These are: mathematics, physical sciences, knowledge of persons, literature and the fine arts, morals, religion and philosophy. What distinguishes one form from another, according to Hirst, is the fact that (i) each has its own unique set of concepts , for example, 'number', in mathematics, 'gravity', in science, 'figurative drawing', in art, 'god', in religion, 'wicked', in morals and so on, (ii) each form has its unique logical structure, (iii) each form has its own tests for truth – for example, the truth of the proposition that $2 \times 8 = 16$ is established in an entirely different way from that required to determine the temperature at which water boils at sea level. Hirst does not say that such 'forms' should be equated with school subjects and he allows that certain subjects, geography for instance, may well have a place on the curriculum that are themselves something he calls 'fields' – geography employs mathematical concepts as well as concepts from history and the physical sciences but it is not a distinct form of knowledge.

In order to justify his defence of the idea that the forms of knowledge should form the basis or content of a genuinely liberal education, Hirst employs a complex and highly contentious argument similar in many respects to Peters' justification of how certain things (and only certain things) are worthwhile in themselves. His reasoning is as follows:

> If the achievement of knowledge is necessarily the development of mind in its most basic sense, then it can readily be seen that to ask for a justification for the pursuit of knowledge is not at all the same thing as to ask for the justification for, say, . . . making them orderly and punctual in their behaviour. . . . To ask for the justification of any form of activity is significant only if one is committed already to seeking rational knowledge. To ask for a justification of the pursuit of rational knowledge itself therefore presupposes some commitment to what one is seeking to justify. (Hirst, 1965, p. 126)

While there is indeed something logically peculiar in asking the question 'Why pursue knowledge?' while refusing to accept that in so doing one is thereby committed to whatever it is for which one is seeking a justification, it is far from obvious, that this argument is sufficient to demonstrate that the forms of knowledge as outlined by Hirst, should be pursued in schools. After all, some might argue, schools should be principally concerned with the teaching of skills such as how to get on with people, swimming or speaking Spanish. Rather than filling children's minds with propositional knowledge (knowing *that* such and such is the case), children should leave school with skills that are likely to be of use to them in later life (they should know *how* to do such and such). In whatever way the advocate of knowledge for knowledge's sake might meet this objection, there is a hidden assumption on which such a viewpoint rests and that is that knowing things is of some *benefit*. As we shall see, a strong case can be made for the importance of all kinds of knowledge and understanding if one is to stand any chance of living a fulfilling life in a society such as ours, but until we are clear as to what there is about such knowledge that renders it significant, in the sense that it is indispensable to a person's long-term interests, we cannot simply assume that it is the only thing of any value in a child's education, or indeed that it should be regarded as having supreme importance. If we are to take seriously the aims underpinning the current National Curriculum, it is unclear, without further argument, how a knowledge or subject-based curriculum is expected to realize such aims.

Some philosophers of education have expressed reservations not only about Hirst's analysis of knowledge, but have cast serious doubts on the extent to which we are entitled to restrict the notion of liberal education to something as narrow and restrictive as being initiated into forms of understanding which are primarily intellectual (see Martin, 1981). There is more to a person than her intellect. She has an emotional life, engages in all kinds of physical activities, and is confronted with all sorts of practical problems; she does not exist in some kind of ivory tower, pursuing the truth in the manner of the proverbial professor. And what about those who, for whatever reason, fail the initiation test? Are we to consign them to join the queue with other barbarians at the gate? Knowledge for knowledge's sake may well withstand the charge of elitism but it certainly has an elitist whiff about it. For this reason it is doubtful that it will suffice as an answer to our question as we go into the twenty-first century. We therefore need to consider other claims and to address some of the recent debates relating to the competing merits of liberal versus vocational education before returning to the question of what constitutes an appropriate education for a *whole person*. If, as will be argued, schools should be concerned with the education of *persons*, we need a rather more generous interpretation of 'relevance' than that provided so far.

Education for work

It is not uncommon to hear people justify schooling as a means to obtaining qualifications, as a passport to a 'good job'. If pressed, they will often equate the notion of good job in monetary terms whereby a high salary enables one to purchase lots of things as a means to becoming happy. Apart from the questionable assumption that owning lots of things is likely to make one happy, there is the additional presupposition that happiness is the ideal state to be in and something to which everything else is but a means. (We shall pursue this line of thought later in the chapter, in order to expose its shortcomings.) Surely, they insist, if schooling is to have any relevance at all it has relevance in so far as it prepares people for the real world – the world of employment where they can earn a living. Book learning is all very well but it doesn't exactly butter the parsnips.

While it would be naïve to pretend that all pupils, especially those in the later stages of secondary education, willingly engage in study for its own sake, we should hesitate before concluding that some kind of vocational training, motivating as it might well be, is the universal panacea for the disgruntled student or those who are charged with the task of educating her. While there is no doubt that if we were to have a separate provision for the academic sheep and the vocational goats from, say, the age of 14, the lives of many teachers would be less stressful and more students would find their educational diet more 'relevant'. Unfortunately, such a solution is not only facile, it is fraught with dangers.

To begin with, the solution is open to all kinds of manipulative possibilities. How, for instance, are the vocational 'goats' to be identified? Someone may well be turned off by science and history and be an utter nuisance in class but it does not follow that she would be better off *as a person*, by preparing for a job of work. First, there are questions to do with the *kind* of work for which she is expected to be trained – is it boring or useless work, in the sense that she is helping to make something for which nobody has any real need as well as having deleterious consequences for the environment or the economy of a developing country? Does it prevent or frustrate opportunities for the development and exercise of imagination or her opportunities for personal fulfilment associated with family life, or the cultivation of friendships, appreciation of the arts and natural beauty not to mention any talents or enthusiasms she might have for sport, music, cookery, gardening, or philosophy? To presume that people can be graded like apples at such a young age, before they are in a position to appreciate much in the way of significant alternatives upon which rational choice depends, especially when their critical powers of evaluation are substantially underdeveloped, is to assume too much. Again, so much work that is done in our society is undertaken with the sole intention of making profits for those who are already privileged and wealthy. Unless we conceive of vocational education in more liberal terms than that associated with vocational training, we are, in conspiring to get people to accept with equanimity the non-egalitarian and oppressive features associated with so many jobs in modern Britain, selling children short.

None of this is to deny that work may well, be an essential component of a fulfilling life for some people. Indeed, some philosophers have argued that it is an essential component of the good life. According to Richard Norman, work:

> forms the common core of people's lives, which sets the pattern for their general character. . . . It is their work above all that defines them in the eyes of others . . . what you are is primarily what you do, and what you do is primarily a matter of what work you perform [such that] no one could now find satisfaction in a life which did not contain its component of meaningful work. (1983, pp. 177–9)

I admit to once finding this immensely persuasive but I have been persuaded otherwise as a result of reading John White's work on the role of education in relation to work (White, 1997), in which he not only makes some immensely important distinctions including that between (i) autonomous work (where it is one of one's major goals to produce something) and heteronomous work (where it is not), (ii) work in which one willingly engages from that done unwillingly, (iii) paid work and voluntary work. It is reasonable to suppose that many people would give up work if they won millions on the lottery. While there are those who would continue to work because they find it intrinsically rewarding and fulfilling, it is not obviously the case that work, even autonomous work, must be seen as a necessary ingredient of a fulfilling life. (Norman does not talk about autonomous work but 'meaningful' work. That they are not one the same thing can be seen by reference to the fact that I might well work at something autonomously in the sense that I am not being forced to do it, but on my own terms regard it as totally meaningless.) There are so many things I might take delight in – cross country running, chess, playing the saxophone, wine-tasting or enjoying good conversation. Why, in addition to these all-absorbing pursuits, do I need to find time to work in order to flourish? The fact remains that in this society many school leavers are likely to end up in work that is tedious, boring and repetitive, but have to take it out of necessity even though it is not something they would see as a major goal in life. All this is something of which schools are all too aware.

Teachers could respond in a variety of ways – from burying their heads in the sand, pretending that it is their business to educate, nothing more nothing less, to actively preparing pupils for the world of work. But what would such preparation entail? It is all too apparent that many youngsters will find themselves in heteronomous work with limited prospects. What would count as an appropriate form of preparation? It may well require that teachers find themselves in the disagreeable position of having to convey the importance of values to which so many employers are attached, such as deference and obedience, values which they themselves might find morally repugnant. One could hardly call it preparation in the requisite sense if, as workers, they proved to be dysfunctional in the work place. And how is such kow-towing compatible with the laudable educational aims associated with critical thinking, personal autonomy, self-respect and an enthusiasm for activities done for their own sake, or are these aims appropriate only for the academic sheep?

An altogether different approach would be to conceive of vocational education as part of a genuinely liberal education, something which has engaged the attention of a number of philosophers of education since John Dewey who questioned the legitimacy of the distinction between the theoretical and the practical (Dewey, 1916). More recently, Richard Pring has tried to show how the supposed dichotomy between preparing for a life that is intellectually rich on the one hand and a life that includes a vocation on the other may be reconciled by what he calls 'vocationalizing the liberal' (Pring, 1995). He is highly critical of vocational *training* and rightly so. Someone who is merely trained need have no comprehension of the purposes for which she is being trained and when successfully trained may well be incapable of exercising any judgement (moral or otherwise) about the value of that for which her training has prepared her; she is merely *competent* at such and such. It was the desire to see people trained in the skills required by industry and the business community that led to the soon to be discredited Technical and Vocational Education Initiative in the 1980s. By re-examining the liberal ideal by reference to what it is to be fully human, Pring not only defends this as the right of everyone, it necessitates bringing the educational ideal of intellectual excellence 'to the vocational interests of young people, educating them through their perception of relevance, helping them to make sense of their social and economic context, enabling them to be intelligent and questioning in their preparation for the world of work' (ibid., p. 190). Vocational education can be liberating and provide opportunities for people to gain access to the forms of knowledge 'through which a person is freed from ignorance, and opened to new imaginings' (ibid., p. 198). One may well come to appreciate something from an aesthetic, a scientific or even a moral point of view through the practical world of building, carpentry or motor mechanics. Whatever one's view on the matter, Pring certainly provides a powerful challenge to those who would see liberal and vocational education as incompatible.

It is time to explore more deeply what is required of schools if they are seriously to answer the question 'what is it that *persons* are entitled to expect from a period of compulsory schooling?' We have had reason to doubt that it is nothing more than knowledge and under-standing for its own sake, and there are obvious problems with conceiving of criteria of relevance in purely vocational terms. If we return to the aims specified in the *National Curriculum Handbook* we see that in addition to the aims listed above, the curriculum should: '. . . pass on enduring values, develop pupils' integrity and autonomy and help them to be responsible and caring citizens . . . and secure their commitment to sustainable development . . . It should promote [their] self-esteem and emotional well-being and help them form and maintain worthwhile and satisfying relationships . . . It should develop their ability to relate to others and work for the common good . . . and equip them to make informed choices at school and throughout their lives . . .' (ibid.). There is much more here than simply equipping pupils with knowledge or preparing them for a job of work. It is impossible in a short introductory chapter to explore this in any detail, but it is worth homing in on something mentioned here, namely that of 'well-being' as an umbrella term under which notions such as self-esteem, the ability to choose, concern for others and such like, may get a purchase. It is worth looking at the notion under a number of guises.

To what extent, if at all, should schools be concerned with preparing pupils for the world of work?

Education for well-being

Well-being and happiness

At a parents' evening many years ago, the mother of one of my pupils said that she did not mind how her son performed at school as long as he was happy. But teachers cannot just go along with this. While it may well be relatively easy to distinguish happy people from those who are not, without further argument it would be wrong to conclude that there was no more to personal well-being or flourishing than being happy. For the early utilitarians such as Jeremy Bentham and John Stuart Mill the good life amounted to a happy life whereby one enjoyed 'an existence made up of few and transitory pains, many and various pleasures' (Mill, 1861). One might take issue with this particular account of happiness but it does capture the *subjective* nature of the phenomenon; what makes one person happy may leave others unhappy. To account for well-being in terms of the quality of one's own subjective experiences is particularly problematic. For example, as Robert Nozick has demonstrated (Nozick, 1974), we could envisage an experience machine whereby one could experience anything one wanted – that one has friends, is in control of one's life, is virtuous and knowledgeable. But can one really said to be flourishing if *in reality* one is friendless, conditioned like a Brave New World zombie or pig–ignorant? Surely, there is a distinction to be made between merely believing that one is flourishing and actually flourishing. If that is not objection enough to what might be termed the 'mental state account' of well-being, the underlying assumption that one could somehow *aim* for happiness is itself implausible. Those who are fortunate enough to find happiness in their lives do so as a result of aiming for something else which results in their being happy with (at least some) aspects of their lives, such as their relationships, place of residence and so on. If I had helped my pupil to develop meaningful relationships, acquire enthusiasm for history, equipped him with the knowledge and insights enabling him to choose between a variety of significant alternatives he might have stood a fair chance of living a happy life, but happiness is not the sort of thing to which I could have steered him, and even if this were possible it is not clear whether I should have concentrated on his long-term happiness or focused on what was likely to make him happy on a particular occasion.

Well-being and desire-satisfaction

In order to overcome the difficulties associated with equating well-being with a mental state, an alternative account construes it in terms of desire-satisfaction. Such a view has been defended in a variety of ways.

The theory has an intuitive plausibility in that it appears to decry paternalist accounts of well-being which assume that flourishing consists in pursuing one kind of life in particular, requiring teachers to veer children towards it. To this extent it is compatible with the values associated with a liberal democracy whereby individuals should be allowed to pursue their own version of the good life, providing that in so doing they do not frustrate other people's attempts to pursue theirs. One of the most obvious problems with this account concerns the difficulties associated with determining which of our numerous and all too often conflicting desires we are expected to satisfy, and this is why exponents of the theory tend to emphasize the necessity of being able to structure one's desires in some kind of hierarchical order; one has to press further than just asking 'what do I want?'; one has to ask questions such as 'do I *really* want it – not just now, but long-term?' Concern for pupils' well-being therefore, means that we need to get them to recognize what is involved in *genuine* choice. It is not merely plumping for something, but instead requires the capacity to *reflect* on the value of that which is chosen. Hence, White's one time characterization of it as '*post-reflective-desire satisfaction*' (White, 1982).

Other difficulties with this account are, perhaps, less obvious and include the fact if it were correct then my well-being might be promoted unbeknownst to me, which is odd to say the least. For instance, I might desire that my charitable donations contribute to the welfare of others and yet never discover the extent of that benefit. My desire will have been satisfied, but in what sense has that had an impact on *my* welfare if I have no idea as to where, and on whom, it was spent. And what if my desire for something was based on a false belief, or is a result of the manipulation or over-bearing influence of others? In what ways might I be better off by satisfying such desires? These and other problems have led a number of philosophers to restrict the desire-satisfaction account to *informed-desires*. Let us see if this fares any better.

In a more recent book, White characterizes well-being as the satisfaction of those desires one would have, were one in possession of information enabling one to appreciate the implications of satisfying a particular desire (White, 1990). The attraction of the account lies in the fact that in so far as one has a clear understanding of the objects of one's desire, one is less likely to be confronted with unresolved conflict, and certainly less likely to fall victim to one's desires. But satisfying one's *informed* desire may well be incompatible with one's ability to flourish. While knowing that smoking kills, I may well continue to satisfy my desire for tobacco.

To confine rational choice to the endless pursuit of desire-satisfaction, however well-informed, seems to me to be spurious for a number of reasons. First, I reflect not only about the extent to which my *desire* might be satisfied, but also think how its satisfaction might satisfy *me*. I may feel indifferent or even disgust in having satisfied a particular desire which, at the time, appeared to have a deep significance in my scheme of things. There is something highly questionable, therefore, in White's claim to the effect that 'reflectiveness . . . subserves desire-satisfaction' (White, 1982, p. 14), and he gives up too soon in supposing that 'one cannot . . . say what one's well-being *is* as distinct from what one *thinks* it is' (ibid., p. 55). Desires don't just descend on us out of the blue; they have a rationale. We prefer *x* to *y* in virtue of the fact that we acknowledge the *desirability* of the former and in virtue of something other than simply desiring it. Again, the underlying assumption that I always reflect in order to find out what I most want, is simply false. Sometimes I reflect in order to discover what it is that I *need* – what is in my *long-term interests*. And it is this that provides the clue to what is an altogether richer account of personal well-being.

Education and well-being: beyond desire-satisfaction

We have already seen how the official documentation relating to the aims of education stresses the importance of things like personal autonomy and the caring citizen, the implication being that such character traits are desirable and necessary in order to flourish in our society. In other words they are something in which individuals may be said to have a real interest. Now while my interests are subjective in the sense that they are mine, they are not subjective to the point of being entirely idiosyncratic. If, on the other hand, a desire-satisfaction account of well-being were acceptable, we should have no reason to doubt that I could have a legitimate interest in anything whatsoever. Another way of putting this is to say that unless a person's real interests were met, she would be harmed in ways that would not necessarily occur if her desires were frustrated. It is therefore incumbent upon us to show how the values associated with autonomy and caring are not only important enough to feature as worthy aims of education on the grounds that they are quite properly essential components of a flourishing life, but that a proper understanding of what is involved in attempting to promote them, results in an account of well-being far removed from the confines of a desire-satisfaction account.

First, what is to live autonomously – to be in the driving seat of one's own life where one's beliefs and actions are self-determined? The following would seem to be necessary requirements:

- a reasonable degree of self-knowledge whereby one is able to recognize the forces of socialization by reference to which one's beliefs and desires are formed and, if necessary, the courage and strength of will to resist them and thus act in accordance with one's *own* evaluations;
- the ability to relate one's present choices to one's past and future in order to provide some kind of shape to one's life thereby distinguishing it from the life of the infant which is largely episodic;
- the ability and opportunity to choose between a significant array of options.

These conditions seem to be the very least of what is required; as to whether they are sufficient need not detain us. What is worth emphasizing is the fact that discussions of autonomy in an educational context are all too frequently confined to intellectual autonomy and ignore the importance of emotional autonomy. After all, one's emotional reactions may well be stereotypical and unreflective just as one's beliefs and actions may be predictable and other-directed.

It would be difficult to envisage how one might conceivably flourish in a modern industrial society such as our own, unless one were autonomous in such important areas of one's life as choice of occupation, spouse or religion. As Joseph Raz says: 'For those of us who live in an autonomy-supporting environment there is no choice but to be autonomous: there is no other way to prosper in such a society' (Raz, 1986, p. 391). If we want school leavers to make a positive contribution to society they must, of necessity, be taught how to reflect on something other than what it is they most want; they need the capacity, as the well as the disposition, to critically reflect on the different ways society might be structured and governed, and the extent to which they might be manipulated and oppressed. Lacking the requisite degree of autonomy, they are more likely to fall victim to the will of others, where the opportunities to live lives that are authentically their own are missing.

While personal autonomy may well be an indispensable feature of the good life for those growing up in contemporary Britain, it is easy to forget that individual well-being is not something completely separable from that of others. Who the 'others' are will depend, to some extent, on the context. They may be one's family or friends but could equally well be one's country or fate of the planet. My interest in my own well-being is not something that can be articulated as something independent of any *mutual* interests I might have. Take friendship for example; something which has been recognized since Aristotle to be a particularly valuable feature in a good life. It cannot possibly thrive on the basis of a purely self-interested motive. Friends act, at least in part, for the sake of each other. Our mutual well-being is something we share; the well-being of each is dependent on that of the other. Once this is acknowledged, teachers are faced with the not inconsiderable challenge of getting children to *care*, or to be sensitive to the needs of others including themselves. Only in this way will they come to appreciate that individual well-being is far from being the concern of the rational egoist hell-bent on satisfying her own desires. This is why some form of moral education, beyond a mere concern for the ability to understand moral concepts, has to feature prominently in a system of schooling. As Anthony O'Hear puts it: '. . . it is only when we perceive and feel we are in a community of persons . . . will appeals to our sense of fairness or sympathy or shame or guilt in our dealings with others be at all relevant . . . Moral behaviour is not so much a matter of an isolated rational agent acting on freely chosen principles, as a development of one's sense of a shared humanity' (O'Hear, 1981, pp. 129–30).

The implications for what schools are for are considerable. At the very least it requires a determination to help children acquire some understanding of where their well-being might lie, together with the respects in which it is bound up with the well-being of others, all of which necessitates their possessing a very great deal of knowledge and understanding. Suffice it to say that White is surely correct to insist that knowledge aims can only play a legitimate part in educational programmes if they are seen to be logically derived from more deeply underlying values (White, 1990, p. 115). Exactly what knowledge and skills are required is not something that can be pursued here but the interested reader will find answers, radically at odds with the existing subject-based curriculum, in a recent publication of his which has the virtue of being both short and very approachable (White, 2006).

Further reading

Brighouse's (2006) *On Education* is a remarkably succinct and very clear introduction to what is involved in being educated. Hirst's (1974) *Knowledge and the Curriculum* is also useful, although Hirst would no longer wish to subscribe to much of what is said here (for a clear exposition of his current view on the aims of education see his chapter in Marples, 1999). Speaking of which, *The Aims of Education* is a collection of essays written by distinguished philosophers of education across several continents, the final chapter of which contains a critique, by John White, of the views of all the contributors. Pring's (2004) *Philosophy of Education: Aims, Theory, Common Sense and Research* is a wide-ranging collection of essays on many aspects of philosophy of education. Standish (2006) is a scholarly and thought-provoking view on the aims of education. Finally, Wringe's (1988) *Understanding Educational Aims* is one of the very best introductions to the aims of education with chapters on many of the issues raised here.

What Should Go on the Curriculum?

Michael Hand

Introduction

A major preoccupation of philosophers of education over the last fifty years has been the question of what should go on the school curriculum. In this chapter we shall look at some of the answers that have been offered, and some of the objections those answers have provoked. As will quickly become clear, the differences between rival curriculum theories run deep, and the prospect of anything resembling a consensus of philosophical opinion in this area remains, for the time being, remote.

Notably less controversial than the question of what should go on the curriculum has been the question of what a curriculum is. Few have paid much attention to the concept marked by the word 'curriculum', and the accounts produced by those who have are broadly similar. Paul Hirst defines 'curriculum' as 'a programme of activities designed so that pupils will attain by learning certain specifiable ends or objectives' (Hirst, 1974, p. 2); on John Wilson's slightly fuller analysis, the word is 'only properly used for planned, sustained and regular learning, which is taken seriously, which has a distinct and structured content, and which proceeds via some kind of stages of learning' (Wilson, 1977, p. 68). If, for the purposes of this chapter, we think of a curriculum simply as *a planned programme of learning*, we shall do no serious injustice either to ordinary usage or to the tacit assumptions of those whose curriculum theories we shall be discussing.

There is, however, another and more contentious philosophical matter to which we must attend before coming on to the main business of the chapter. Logically prior to the question of what *should* go on the curriculum is the question of what *could* go on the curriculum. What, that is to say, are the limits of the class of possible curriculum content, from which actual curriculum content must be selected?

What could go on the curriculum?

At one level, the answer to this question is straightforward: the things that could go on the curriculum are just the things that can be learned. If a curriculum is a planned programme of learning, it follows that the range from which the content of curricula must be drawn is the range of what human beings can acquire by learning. But this answer is not very satisfying. What, we now want to know, are the limits of the class of things that can be learned?

One thesis to which some philosophers of education have been attracted here is that the range of what can be learned is identical with the range of what can be known. Learning, on this view, is always a matter of coming to know something. So D. W. Hamlyn writes:

> At all events, on our ordinary conception of learning it would, I suggest, be impossible to suppose that someone could have learned something if he had not in some sense acquired new knowledge, whatever form that knowledge may take (and it may of course include skills as well as factual knowledge). (Hamlyn, 1973, p. 180)

What is there to be said in support of this view? Well, on the face of it at least, learning that something is the case is equivalent to coming to know that it is the case, and learning how to do something is equivalent to coming to know how to do it. Moreover, the phrase 'learn that *p*' shares an interesting logical feature with the phrase 'know that *p*': it is a necessary condition of the application of either phrase that *p* is true. I cannot learn that Sydney is the capital of Australia any more than I can know that it is, for the simple reason that Sydney is *not* the capital of Australia.

But the equation of what can be learned with what can be known may not be as defensible as it looks. For one thing, the truth criterion governing 'learn that *p*' plainly does not govern 'learn *to think* that *p*': the fact that Sydney is not the capital of Australia is no logical impediment to my learning to think that it is. But if I have learned to think this – that is, if I have come by learning to believe a falsehood – what exactly is the knowledge I am supposed to have acquired?

For another thing, while 'learn that *p*' shares with 'know that *p*' the condition that *p* is true, it is less clear that it shares the condition that *p* is believed for good reasons. To *know* something I must have good reasons for believing it to be so, but it may be that I can *learn* it in the absence of such reasons. Imagine a child who has learned a series of facts by rote, who has come to believe a set of true propositions but has not acquired any sense of how they are known to be true. Here we should feel uneasy about saying that she knows these facts, or at least obliged to put the word 'knows' in inverted commas; but we should surely have fewer qualms about saying that she has learned them.

And it is not only in the area of propositional learning that the proposed connection between learning and knowing looks shaky. In the following passage, Wilson argues that there are many things we learn to do which do not appear to involve the acquisition of any sort of knowledge:

> But what sort of thing have I 'come to know' in those (very many) cases where I have clearly learned to do something, yet have not acquired any new *propositional* knowledge? It is natural here to rely on the much canvassed notion of 'knowing how'; but there seem to be clear counter-examples even to this. I may learn, just by practice, not to look down when climbing mountains, to keep my temper, not to show surprise, and so forth. In these and many other cases there is little or no 'how' to learn or know; one just has to set oneself the task and practise doing it. In fact it seems we only speak seriously of knowing how to X when some kind of propositional knowledge *is* involved, in however shadowy a way: knowing how to fly an aeroplane or solve a quadratic equation, not (or not so easily) knowing how to walk or talk or turn a somersault. If there is no question of attending to some proposition, or at least of following some kind of rule, the 'how' is otiose . . . Depending on what one learns to do, there are different gaps between learning how to do X and learning to do X: gaps not to be filled by anything we could properly call knowledge. The most obvious gap is a lack of motivation: I may learn *how* to behave politely – that is, I have the required factual knowledge and skill – but not learn *to* behave politely, because I do not want to. It is also, I think, possible to drive a wedge between know-how and ability: there seems to be a clear sense in which someone familiar with the proper method knows *how* to solve an equation or fly an aeroplane, even if he cannot in fact solve it or fly it (perhaps the equation is too hard for him, or he always gets giddy in the cockpit). Here again we might well say that he has learned how to do these things, but has not learned *to* do them. (Wilson, 1979, pp. 72–4)

Key Questions

1. In this passage Wilson offers a number of examples of cases where we would speak of learning but not of coming to know. How plausible do you find these examples? Is he right that not all cases of learning are cases of coming to know?
2. Is there anything you think ought to be on the school curriculum that involves learning but not the acquisition of knowledge?

Wilson's own proposal is that the class of what can be learned includes both the things human beings can know and the various ways in which they can *exercise control*. We should, he thinks, 'say that "learn" means, unequivocally, something like "acquire knowledge or control by paying relevant attention"' (Wilson, 1979, p. 74). This broader delimitation accounts well enough for the sort of cases he considers: learning by practice to keep my temper and not to look down when climbing mountains are well-described as cases of acquiring control over my emotions and bodily movements. But it may be that the range Wilson defines is still too narrow. Consider the various virtues that human beings can be said to acquire by learning. Some virtues, to be sure, are plausibly characterized as forms of self-control: courage and temperance, for example, clearly have something to do with controlling oneself in the face of powerful fears and appetites. But what of such virtues as compassion and justice? Learning to be compassionate or just is not obviously a matter of coming to know something, but neither does it seem to be a matter of acquiring self-control.

The question of what *could* go on the curriculum, then, is a trickier one than it first appears, and one to which further philosophical attention is badly needed. Perhaps, however, enough has been said here to indicate that the range from which the content of the school curriculum must be selected is a good deal broader than is often supposed.

The academic curriculum

We turn now to our central question, and to the first and most influential of the curriculum theories advanced by philosophers of education. According to this theory, the basic components of the school curriculum should be academic subjects or disciplines. The primary responsibility of schools is to initiate children and young people into forms of theoretical inquiry.

Why? The classic and most fully articulated justification of this view is the one offered by R. S. Peters in his seminal book *Ethics and Education* (1966). Peters' justification rests on two claims: (i) that initiating people into theoretical activities is just what the word 'education' means, and (ii) that theoretical activities are worthwhile.

The first claim is defended by analysis of the concept of education. Peters declines to offer a definition of 'education', but instead identifies a number of criteria to which processes must conform in order to qualify as educational. The upshot of his analysis is that an educational process must involve initiation into those 'differentiated modes of thought and awareness' that are 'characterized both by a content or "body of knowledge" and by public procedures by means of which this content has been accumulated, criticized and revised' (Peters, 1966, p. 50). It must, in other words, involve teaching the academic disciplines.

On its own, this conceptual claim will not suffice to justify the academic curriculum. For it remains open to those favouring curricula of other kinds simply to give up the word 'education'. If I hold that education necessarily involves initiation into theoretical activities, but that such initiation has little or no worth, I am free to propose that schools operate under some other banner than 'education' and focus their energies on teaching things that *are* of worth.

That is why Peters needs to advance and defend his second claim: that theoretical activities are worthwhile.

Theoretical activities are those activities that have truth as their end. They are worthwhile, says Peters, because truth is valuable, and he sets about proving the value of truth by means of two transcendental arguments. A transcendental argument is one designed to show that its conclusion is presupposed by, or is a condition of the possibility of, some widely accepted kind of experience, judgement or practice. What Peters contends is that a commitment to truth is presupposed by serious engagement in practical discourse. A person who professed a serious interest in a practical question, such as 'Why do this rather than that?', but who denied caring about the truth, would be guilty of self-contradiction, of ignoring or failing to recognize the logical implications of her interest. Since we can hardly avoid engaging in practical discourse, as this would involve 'a resolute refusal to talk or think about what ought to be done' (Peters, 1966, pp. 115–16), we have little choice but to care about the truth.

Peters' two transcendental arguments pick out different logical connections between engagement in practical discourse and commitment to truth. First, the person who seriously asks 'Why do this rather than that?' must, in order to answer her question, find out what this and that involve. She is committed to investigating the nature of this and that and coming to understand them well enough to assess their relative merits and make an informed choice between them. When she carries out these investigations, she will find herself 'embarking on those forms of inquiry such as science, history, literature and philosophy which are concerned with the description, explanation and assessment of different forms of human activity' (Peters, 1966, p. 162).

Second, the fact that a person is seriously asking a practical question shows that she has already adopted a certain kind of stance towards life. She has made some assessment of her predicament in the world and undertaken to think and act in ways that are responsive to reasons. It is not simply that, having committed herself to 'choosing rather than plumping' (Peters, 1966, p. 121), she is obliged to try to understand the options before her; it is that her commitment to choosing rather than plumping is itself grounded in a desire to make sense of the world. This is how Peters articulates the argument:

> . . . in so far as [a man] can stand back from his life and *ask* the question 'Why this rather than that?' he must already have a serious concern for truth built into his consciousness. For how can a serious practical question be asked unless a man also wants to acquaint himself as well as he can with the situation out of which the question arises and with the facts of various kinds which provide the framework for possible answers? The various theoretical inquiries are explorations of these different facets of his experience. To ask the question 'Why do this rather than that?' seriously is therefore, however embryonically, to be committed to those inquiries which are defined by their serious concern with those aspects of reality which give context to the question which he is asking. In brief the justification of such activities is not purely instrumental because they are involved in *asking* the question 'Why do this rather than that?', as well as in answering it.
>
> . . . the attitude of passionate concern about truth . . . lies at the heart of all rational activities in which there is a concern for what is true or false, appropriate or inappropriate, correct or incorrect.

Anyone who asks seriously the question 'Why do this rather than that?' must already possess it; for it is built into this sense of 'serious'. It is impossible to give any further justification for it; for it is presupposed in all serious attempts at justification. (Peters, 1966, pp. 164–5)

Key Questions

1. Is it true that seriously asking 'Why do this rather than that?' presupposes a 'passionate concern about truth'?
2. If it is true, does it show that theoretical activities are worthwhile?

The kind of curriculum for which Peters argues is, of course, precisely the kind of curriculum currently found in British schools. The formal education of most British children – indeed, of most children in the world – consists very largely of initiation into theoretical activities.

But there are some serious problems with Peters' defence of the academic curriculum. Take first the conceptual claim about education. Contrary to what Peters says, it appears that the word 'education' can be applied to a wide variety of programmes of teaching and learning without contravention of the rules governing ordinary usage. John Wilson argues plausibly that the strongest conclusion conceptual analysis can yield is that education is going on when 'human learning above the natural level is being deliberately promoted in accordance with some general or overall policy' (Wilson, 1979, p. 33); and this clearly leaves open the question of what should go on the curriculum.

Peters' transcendental arguments have attracted a number of criticisms, the most important of which is that they merely defer the justificatory problem from why we should value truth to why we should seriously ask practical questions. John Kleinig writes:

It only trivialises education if it is argued that a commitment to certain activities deemed to be educationally valuable is presupposed by the justificatory question. For such an argument does not tell us why education is justified except in the sense that it is necessary to answering justificatory questions. What is needed is an account which will display for us the importance of justificatory questions. (Kleinig, 1982, p. 87)

The worry here is that the transcendental arguments do not amount to a justification. They logically connect commitment to truth with serious engagement in practical discourse, but they do not explain why we should go in for either.

Moreover, even if the transcendental arguments are successful in demonstrating the worthwhileness of theoretical activities, it does not follow that these activities should be the basic components of the curriculum; for there may be other activities that are equally or more worthwhile. There is nothing in the transcendental arguments to suggest that truth is the supreme value, and Peters elsewhere explicitly denies that he takes this view:

> I do not think, and never have thought, that the values surrounding the concern for truth are the only ones in life. I am not sure, either, whether I think that they are of over-riding importance. There is also the consideration of interests – especially of those who suffer, justice, love, and the more hedonistic or 'vital' values constitutive of people's interests. (Peters, 1977, p. 37)

If justice, love and pleasure are also valuable, then activities that have these things as their ends must also qualify as worthwhile. Why, then, should academic disciplines take precedence over other worthwhile activities when it comes to the selection of curriculum content?

The fortress of the academic curriculum, by virtue of the long shadow it casts over the educational systems of the world, has about it an air of impregnability; but the philosophical foundations on which it rests are rather less firm than one might expect.

The vocational curriculum

The most familiar alternative to the view that the curriculum should comprise forms of theoretical inquiry is the view that it should comprise the forms of practical activity by which young people will, in due course, earn a living. According to defenders of the vocational curriculum, the first task of schools is to equip children and young people, not with expertise in academic disciplines, but with the skills, understandings and critical capacities they will need in their professional and everyday lives. Richard Pring writes:

> For any young person, assistance with how to live one's life, in which the sort of job one does plays such a significant part, is the most important of all educational experiences – clarifying the style of life judged worth living, identifying the training and work that will enable one to live that life, questioning the ends or values embodied within it, acquiring the necessary skills and competences. (Pring, 1995, p. 190)

In arguing that the building blocks of the curriculum should be forms of practical activity or areas of practical concern, vocationalists are emphatically *not* arguing for a curriculum based on skills rather than knowledge. Much philosophical work in support of the vocational curriculum has been concerned with exploding the myth that knowledge and understanding are the preserve of the academic disciplines. It is true that theoretical activities, unlike practical ones, are *defined* by the aim of generating knowledge; but participants in practical activities draw upon and apply knowledge in all sorts of ways, and indeed generate it for themselves, in the pursuit of their practical ends. Becoming a competent and reflective practitioner in a vocational or professional field typically involves significant levels of theoretical understanding and intellectual engagement.

In the following passage Pring identifies some of the 'false dichotomies' underpinning the assumption that vocational curricula must be narrowly concerned with developing skills:

> There is a mistaken tendency to define education by contrasting it with what is seen to be opposite and incompatible. 'Liberal' is contrasted with vocational as if the vocational, *properly taught*, cannot itself be liberating – a way into those forms of knowledge through which a person is freed from ignorance, and opened to new imaginings, new possibilities: the craftsman who finds aesthetic delight in the object of his craft, the technician who sees the science behind the artefact, the reflective teacher making theoretical sense of practice. Indeed, behind the liberal/vocational divide is another false dichotomy, namely, that between theory and practice. Theory is portrayed as the world of abstractions, of deep understanding, of the accumulated wisdom set down in books, of liberation from the 'here and now'. Practice, on the other hand, is identified with 'doing' *rather* than 'thinking', with the acquisition of skills rather than knowledge, with low level knowledge rather than understanding. Intelligent 'knowing how' is ignored, the practical way to theoretical understanding dismissed, the wisdom behind intelligent doing unrecognised. . . . There is another false dualism. Certainly, the concepts of 'education' and 'training' do not mean the same – education indicates a relatively broad and critical understanding of things, whereas training suggests the preparation for a relatively specific task or job. But, despite the different meanings, one and the same activity could be both educational and training . . . For example, the student teacher can be trained to plan the lessons, to manage the class, and to display the children's work. But the training can be so conducted that the student is educated *through* it – in becoming critical of what is happening, in understanding the activity, and in coming to see it in a wider educational context. (Pring, 1995, p. 189)

Key Questions

1. Pring classifies as 'false dichotomies' the distinctions between liberal and vocational, theory and practice, and education and training. How persuasive are his arguments? Should we abandon these distinctions in our thinking about education and the curriculum?
2. Do all jobs and practical activities offer ways into 'those forms of knowledge through which a person is freed from ignorance and opened to new imaginings', or only some of them?

Arguments like Pring's effectively undermine the suggestion that vocational education cannot be intellectually ambitious. But this is not the only sort of objection one can advance against the vocational curriculum. A more serious objection, I think, is the problem of how to decide which vocations or occupations pupils are to be prepared for. In which of the many hundreds of jobs and careers available to school-leavers today should schools offer vocational courses and qualifications, and, perhaps more importantly, how are individual pupils to be selected for one vocational course rather than another? However such decisions are made, it seems likely that many young people will eventually choose careers other than the ones for which their education has prepared them; or, if constrained to pursue the careers for which they are qualified, will feel bitterly betrayed by an education that has deprived them of vocational choice.

Considerations such as these tempt one back towards the thought that an academic education, concerned to impart a broad and general range of knowledge and understanding, is preferable to a vocational one. This was John Stuart Mill's view of the matter:

> . . . men are men before they are lawyers and if you make them capable and sensible men, they will make themselves capable and sensible lawyers . . . what professional men should carry away with them from an University is not professional knowledge, but that which should direct the use of their professional knowledge, and bring the light of general culture to illuminate the technicalities of a special pursuit. (Mill, 1867, cited in Pring, 1995, p. 184)

Defenders of the vocational curriculum have proposed a solution to this problem, but one that has seemed to many to be unsatisfactory. Their solution is to retreat from advocacy of vocational education per se to advocacy of what they sometimes call 'prevocational education'. The purpose of prevocational education is not to prepare young people for particular occupations but to equip them with the information they need to make intelligent occupational choices. So Christopher Winch writes:

> Prevocational education . . . is concerned with two sub-aims. First, the preparation of young people for the understanding of work and the economy (in this sense it is an extension of cultural literacy) and second, through the provision of generic vocational programmes, which give the opportunity to make more informed choices about work for those contemplating entering an occupation or going into an apprenticeship or further education at the end of the compulsory phase [of schooling]. (Winch, 2000, p. 32)

The aims of imparting a general understanding of the economy and of enabling young people to make informed choices about work are unexceptionable: what worries critics of prevocational education is the suggestion that these things are best achieved through 'generic vocational programmes'. The problem here is that it is not clear what generic vocational programmes are supposed to be. We have a good idea of what it means to initiate young people into such theoretical activities as mathematics, history and literary criticism, and into such practical activities as banking, plumbing and civil engineering: we know what it is to do these things well or badly, to understand them or misunderstand them. But the sort of broad occupational domains addressed by generic vocational programmes (standard examples are 'media', 'manufacturing' and 'leisure and tourism') are not activities one can master or fail to master. One can master the individual occupations that make up the domains, but this is the concern of vocational rather than prevocational education. By distancing itself from academic disciplines on the one hand and vocational practices on the other, prevocational education seems to leave itself with nowhere to go.

Moreover, prevocationalists are perhaps too ready to dismiss the potential of the academic curriculum to deliver the desired outcomes of economic understanding and informed choices about work. Winch claims that the prevocationalists differs from the 'modern liberal' in that 'the former is much more prepared than the latter to spell out what the choices involved in making plans for a future life are and what the means to attaining them are, while the modern liberal is more inclined to think about ends in an unconstrained way, as if the future adult will be an isolated person of leisure' (Winch, 2000, p. 31). That 'modern liberals' who advocate the academic curriculum are guilty of this charge is open to question, and, even if some of them are, it does not follow that the academic curriculum must be silent on 'the choices involved in making plans for a future life'. The academic disciplines of economics and sociology may be at least as well placed as the generic vocational domains of media and manufacturing to yield economic understanding and informed choices about work.

The virtue-based curriculum

A different sort of challenge to the academic curriculum is the one posed by defenders of what we shall call the virtue-based curriculum. According to this challenge, the problem with Peters' position is not so much that he is wrong to regard theoretical activities as worthwhile, as that questions about the worthwhileness of activities are the wrong ones to be asking. The question with which we should begin when constructing the school curriculum is rather 'What sort of people do we want children to be?'. And the kind of answers to which this question gives rise will not be lists of worthwhile activities, but lists of personal qualities or virtues.

Here is one such list, set out by John White in *The Aims of Education Restated*:

> The educated person is a person disposed to act in certain ways rather than others. He possesses the general virtue of prudence, or care for his own good (as well as subordinate virtues like courage and temperance). This, being in an extended rather than a narrow sense, includes within it the more specifically moral virtues like benevolence, justice, truthfulness, tolerance and reliability. It includes both the lucidity needed to sort out clearly the complex conflicts of value which face him, and the wisdom needed to reflect on these conflicts and try to resolve them within as broad a frame of relevant considerations as possible. The educated person, prizing autonomy, will be independent-minded himself and sympathetic to independent-mindedness in others. His ability to detach himself from narrow ends and to enter imaginatively into others' points of view makes it inconceivable that he be the kind of humourless person we can all number among our so-called 'educated' acquaintances. As well as all this, one may expect him to be a person of vitality, throwing himself with enthusiasm into the prosecution of his chosen life-plan and the myriad particular activities which it contains. Virtues like these – prudence, courage, temperance, benevolence and the other moral virtues, lucidity, independence of mind, wisdom, humour and vitality – are the hallmarks of the educated person. (White, 1982, pp. 121–2)

Key Questions

1. How persuasive do you find White's description of the educated person? Are any of the virtues on his list controversial, or are these qualities we would all like our children to possess?
2. Is it a fair criticism of White's position to say that the world would be a poorer place if we all possessed the same qualities of character?

White contends both that we should be able to reach agreement on the virtues we would like people to possess and that the teaching of these virtues is the proper business of schools. Let us set the first of these contentions to one side and look more closely at the second. Are virtues the sort of things it is possible to teach? And are schools the right places in which to teach them?

I see no reason for scepticism about the teachability of virtues. Teaching, in this context, is simply the deliberate facilitation of learning, and, as we have already noted, virtues must certainly be counted among the things that can be learned. The more interesting question is whether we can reasonably expect them to be learned in schools. Some philosophers of education are doubtful about this. Graham Haydon, for example, argues that there is 'a strong case for concentrating on what schools can do best, which is . . . to teach things of a broadly cognitive nature' (Haydon, 1997, p. 131). Cultivating virtues, he thinks, is one of the things schools are ill-equipped to do well:

> . . . despite the recent attention given to the development of virtues as an educational aim, it is by no means clear how the aim is to be pursued or how far it can be achieved. Too often there are only rather vague references to the ethos of the school, the example set by teachers, and the good character of teachers themselves. And these may be relatively small influences in a child's life. Since, in speaking of the development of virtues, we are speaking of a person developing a certain 'mind-set' which is more than just cognitive, which also involves some of the person's deepest desires and feelings, we have to wonder how much teachers can do. (Haydon, 1997, p. 124)

Haydon's objection is a forceful one. Virtues are indeed intimately connected with deep desires and feelings: one finds compassion, if at all, in the presence of sorrow, courage in the face of fear, and love in the company of powerful attraction. Schools and classrooms, one is inclined to think, are necessarily inimical to the expression and exploration of the emotions in relation to which virtues are developed. They are too public, too formal and too regulated to be appropriate sites for the baring and shaping of souls. What advocates of the virtue-based curriculum owe us, then, and what they have conspicuously failed to provide, is an account of the sort of classroom activities, lessons and courses by means of which the desired virtues are to be cultivated.

White is frustratingly cagey on this matter in *The Aims of Education Restated*. He is slightly (but only slightly) more forthcoming elsewhere: 'We need to know the most appropriate vehicles for realizing the aims and should not assume that these will always be discrete subjects – let alone the current subjects of the National Curriculum. Topic-based or integrated courses; various practical activities; periods of free private study; wider groupings such as "the arts" rather than music, visual arts and literature as separate subjects, are all in the ring' (White, 2004, p. 28) The suggestion here is that the shift from knowledge-oriented to virtue-oriented education might be effected by experimenting with topic-based and integrated courses and wider subject groupings. But this seems implausible. The usual argument for moving away from discrete subjects to interdisciplinary and thematic work is that understanding is fragmented by artificial boundaries between subjects. It is one thing to claim that breaking down subject barriers will lead pupils to a more integrated, holistic understanding of the world, quite another to claim that it will somehow make them virtuous.

The idea that curriculum theorizing should start with the question of the sort of people we want children to be has undoubted intuitive appeal, but the virtue-based curriculum remains severely compromised by the failure of its defenders to set out a persuasive account of what it might actually look like on the ground.

Conclusion

We noted at the outset that there are deep differences of philosophical opinion on the question of what should go on the curriculum. What will now be clear is that this is, in part at least, a consequence of the fact that all the leading curriculum theories in philosophy of education are vulnerable to rather compelling objections. Notwithstanding the considerable quantity of philosophical ink spilt on the matter, satisfactory answers to the most basic normative questions about the curriculum are yet to be advanced, and the need for further philosophical work remains pressing.

Further reading

Useful general discussions of what should go on the school curriculum are to be found in Carr, 2003 (chapters 9–10), Barrow and Woods, 1988 (chapters 2–3) and White, 2004. The last of these includes chapters on each of the subjects of the National Curriculum for England, focusing on their justifiability and their fit with overall curricular aims. On the academic curriculum, it is interesting to compare Peters' justification with that of his sometime collaborator, Paul Hirst. Hirst's justification is set out in Hirst, 1974 (chapter 3), and his version of the transcendental argument can be found on p. 42. On the vocational curriculum, a challenge of a rather different sort to the one outlined in this chapter is developed in White, 1997. And on the virtue-based curriculum, David Carr's discussion of why and how we should 'educate the virtues' in Carr, 1991 is well worth a look.

Can We Teach Ethics?

James C. Conroy

Introduction: to do and to be

The title of this chapter is deceptively simple and of course the answer to the question might be an equally simple yes or no. Indeed it would be very helpful if the answer were so straightforward. All we might have to do to make people good is teach them how to be good and, lo and behold, they would be good. But it would appear that, even after they have attended school where, at least in part, the purpose is to teach them to be good, lots of students, young people and older adults continue to behave badly. How are we to account for this? Well it could be that teaching goodness is like teaching mathematics, some people get it and others don't or again, it could be that some teachers are better than others when it comes to teaching students how to be good. Maybe that is all there is to be said on the matter. Yet no society is going to be content with such answers – Why not we might ask? Why not accept that some people are good and some are bad and consequently lock up, punish or kill the bad ones? Arguably in previous generations that is precisely what communities did. Indeed today there are political and religious communities who continue to act in something like this way. However, in liberal societies, what counts as good or bad is itself not so straightforward. There is little enough agreement as to what is right or wrong, good or bad, action. Does this matter? Should we teach everyone to be moral, after all, we don't have to teach everyone everything?

Maybe we don't wish to see learning morality as having an exact equivalence to learning mathematics. Most societies can cope if some, perhaps even significant numbers, of its people are not entirely competent in solving quadratic equations or working out the relationship between a force and the breaking point of a particular material. Arguably, as long as people, such as engineers, who might need to know these things, do indeed know them, then there is not much of an issue. After all the majority of the population are unlikely to need knowledge of mathematics of this kind after they leave school. But, can societies cope if most of the citizens leave school unable to act in a moral way? We are unlikely to experience social or political disintegration if lots of people don't know or understand differential calculus but we are likely to experience precisely such collapse if the majority of people don't know how to act morally or, worse still, actively behave immorally.

Sometimes, the shape of language can beguile us into thinking that when we teach people, 'to be good' that we are doing the same kind of thing as when we teach calculus. The sentences 'I am teaching 2B calculus' or '2B are learning how to do calculus' can look the same as 'I am teaching 2B morality' or '2B are learning how to do morality'. Of course, on closer examination, while the two statements share a syntactical form they certainly don't share the same sense of teaching and/or learning. In the case of calculus we are teaching students how to perform particular kinds of operations, which they can then apply to particular construction or other problems. In the case of morality, we can properly re-construct the sentences to read, 'I am teaching 2B to be moral' or '2B are learning to be moral'. To do something and to be something would, on this account, be different kinds of things. To do X is not to be X. We wouldn't say 'I taught Matilda to do moral', but we might say, 'I taught Matilda to be moral', the verb, *to be* is the tricky chap in all this talk because it refers to our being, how we are in the world, how we stand in relation to others, indeed, how we stand with respect to ourselves. Here we can see that being is a much more expansive notion than doing and refers to how we live, or, at least, how we should live. If we were to ask, which is more difficult to teach, 'how to be good or how to do calculus' what might the answer be? Technically calculus might appear more difficult but imagine trying to teach someone to be good!

A lack of agreement on what is good

There are of course a finite number of ways to teach calculus but it is not quite so clear in the case of goodness. Indeed, recent decades have seen the very notion of goodness challenged, or at least the notion that there is a single thing called goodness. The post–Second World War period has witnessed a shift in the way we think of morality. Prior to this there might well have been differences between individuals as to what they saw as 'goodness' but in the period between 1945 and the present something else happened. The arguments about goodness, which might have been conducted in the corridors and classrooms of universities or in seminaries and educational establishments for clergy or, again, in the chambers of parliament between philosophers, academics, educators, clergy and politicians spread much more widely to involve and implicate the whole population. Arguments once discussed by elites appeared to move onto the street. No longer were people prepared to unquestioningly accept the rules laid down by others intended to regulate social behaviour; now they could make up their own minds.

But this perceived change in attitude masks two things. First, there is really nothing new about such debates though the terms of reference may have shifted somewhat. Secondly, there is a breaking point where the loss of any common or shared moral agreement destroys the very fabric of society consequently threatening all within its bounds.

Let's begin then with the first. Before we can begin to answer the question posed at the opening, 'Can we teach people to be good?' we need some notion of goodness itself. Human beings have wrestled over these questions certainly for several millennia. For the Hebrews what was good was that laid down by God, most obviously in the Decalogue (or Ten Commandments). But, from the nineteenth century onwards the reading of the Hebrew scriptures has been conditioned by a belief that most of these stories reflected things that happened in the course of human activity, which were then given a theological meaning and employed by the community as a means of exerting social control. Thus, if we were to look at the version of the Ten Commandments in the Book of Exodus chapter 20, we can see a list of injunctions including one which prohibits the Israelites from worshipping false Gods.

> I am the Lord your God, who brought you out of the land of Egypt, out of bondage,
>   You have no other gods before me
>   You shall not make for yourself a graven image, or any likeness of anything that is in heaven above, or that is in the water under the earth; you shall not bow down to them or serve tem; for I the Lord your God am a jealous God, visiting the iniquity of the of the fathers upon the children to the third and fourth generation of those who hate me, but showing steadfast love to thousands of those who love me and keep my commandments.

Clearly the commandment not to worship false gods comes from a period of history when the existence of God or gods was not in question, and when they were deemed to engage quite explicitly in the moral, social and political affairs of human beings. The Jews were a group of disparate tribes who were brought together under the leadership of Moses so that they might escape enslavement in Egypt. They would have brought with them a range of religious beliefs and practices.

How might these beliefs and practices have contributed to the shaping of the commandment to worship only the God of Israel?

An equally important ethical text from the Hebrew Bible that concerns Abraham and his son, Isaac, begins with Abraham having rested for some time in the land of the Philistines. After some time,

God tested Abraham and said to him, 'Abraham!' And he said, 'Here am I.' He said, 'Take your son, your only son Isaac, whom you love and go to the land of Mori'ah and offer him there as a burnt offering upon one of the mountains of which I shall tell you.' So Abraham rose early in the morning, saddled his ass, and took . . . his son Isaac; and he cut the wood for the burnt offering, and arose and went to the place of which God had told him . . . On the third day Abraham lifted up his eyes and saw the place afar off. [He] took the wood of the burnt offering and laid it on Isaac his son and he took in his hand the fire and the knife . . . And Isaac said to his father, Abraham . . .'Behold, the fire and the wood; but where is the lamb for the burnt offering?' Abraham said, 'God will provide himself the lamb for a burnt offering'. . .

When they came to the place of which God had told him, Abraham built an altar there, and laid the wood in order, and bound Isaac his son, and laid him on the altar upon the wood. Then Abraham put forth his hand and took the knife to slay his son. But the angel of the Lord called to him from heaven, and said, 'Abraham, Abraham!. . . Do not lay your hand on the lad or do anything to him . . . for now I know that you fear God, seeing you have not withheld your son . . . from me. Abraham lifted up his eyes and looked, and behold, behind him was a ram . . . And Abraham went and took the ram, and offered it up as a burnt offering instead of his son . . .

Can it be ever be morally acceptable to play such a cruel joke on someone in order to teach them a better way of behaving?

What is of particular note here is the ethical suggestion that it is better to obey the commandments of God than preserve the life of one's son. This would seem to suggest that goodness is following the will of God, even where the action appears to be in conflict with one's instincts because later in the passage Abraham and his children unto generations receive God's blessing. Blessings are to be bestowed on the righteous. Of course, as in the first scriptural example above, and this is an important point for anyone using textual material to assist in the teaching of morals, the context of the story is all-important. The context for this particular story is at least partially set by the practice, then not uncommon, in Near Eastern ritual practice to make and offer human sacrifice to appease the gods. This story represents an invitation to the hearer to turn away from these practices; that is why God provides an animal to take the place of Isaac. Of course a clear implication of the story is that the Israelites are indeed more moral than their neighbours and that this is partly a consequence of their greater insight into the nature of God, humanity and their relationship.

Do you think a religious belief which bans human sacrifice is morally superior to one that doesn't? If so, why? If not, why not?

Although the relationship between a scriptural or other moral text, its historical circumstances and the twenty-first century hearer or reader is, as we can see, quite complicated many teachers still draw on the insights which these passages can hold. Hence it is not uncommon to see religious texts used in assembly and collective worship in schools to offer moral example or reinforcement.

> Do such stories continue to have any place in the conduct of moral education in a school?

There are arguments on both sides with some suggesting that these stories are nothing more than a reflection of their historical culture, which have little resonance with the decisions we want or need to make. Others will argue that these stories are the distillation of long traditions of wisdom and that it would be foolish to ignore their powerful message. In yet other religious traditions there are those who would suggest even today that their religious texts embody the moral will of God and that the human situations in which they are to be found simply reinforce the claim that God acts in the world of human beings.

Historical changes in moral thinking

Increasingly the claim that God acts in the world in the way described above has proved difficult to sustain as a common or universal belief and its difficulties go back to the European Reformation when, for the first time, large numbers of Christians get access to the Judaeo-Christian scriptures in their own language. These people no longer need someone else (usually a priest) to translate or interpret the text for them since they can now enjoy direct access. And, once they can read a text for themselves, surely they can begin to interpret it for themselves. This is an important shift because it suggests that the individuals can read, interpret, think and act under their own guidance and don't necessarily need someone else to tell them how to do these things.

Over the next 200 years the power of the individual to reason her (or more generally at the time, his) way to moral decision and action evolve until we reach the eighteenth-century Enlightenment where philosophers across Europe start to give increased prominence to individual moral reason. In the domain of morals the most well known of these figures was Immanuel Kant whose book, *The Foundations of the Metaphysics of Morals* became and remains an important source for moral educators everywhere. In it Kant argues that it is human reason that enables us to make moral choices; an act is good, not because it says so, nor because it is contained within sacred writings nor indeed because someone else has told us that it is good. Rather, it is good because we can rationally justify to our neighbour that it is good. He himself puts it this way,

> . . . it is better in moral evaluation to follow the rigorous method and to make the universal formula of the categorical imperative the basis [of moral action]: Act according to the maxim which can at the same time make itself a universal law . . . Always act according to that maxim whose universality as a law you can at the same time will. This is the only condition under which a will can never come into conflict with itself, and such an imperative is categorical . . . the categorical imperative can also be expressed as follows: Act according to maxims which can at the same time have themselves as universal laws of nature as their object. Such, then, is the formula of an absolutely good will.
>
> It is not enough to ascribe freedom to our will, on any grounds whatever, if we do not also have sufficient grounds for attributing it to all rational beings. For since morality serves as a law for us only as rational beings, morality must hold valid for all rational beings, and since it must be derived exclusively from the property of freedom.

What do you think Kant meant here by the following terms?

- 'rational'?
- 'good will'?
- 'imperative'?

For Kant people act in particular ways in order to bring about certain kinds of things, hence, if I want to finish writing this chapter before Wednesday I will need to stop watching television and get back to my laptop. The imperative or command here is 'to stop watching television' but it isn't a moral imperative, it is a hypothetical imperative. If I want to do X then I need to do Y in order to achieve it or bring it about. There might indeed be a 'good' here though it is not a moral but a prudential good; in other words, if I really want to get the chapter finished then it would be prudent to get up and go and work. These kinds of goods are often deemed to be moral goods in schools. So it is that in some schools, and in order to avoid congestion and conflict, students may be required to operate according to a one-way system. Often in the rules laid down by the school and the disciplinary actions of teachers this prudential good is transformed into a moral good. This is an understandable slip from one category into another but Kant argued that moral goodness is different. Thus, if an action is to be regarded as truly moral then it would have to be regarded as the right thing to do in any similar circumstances and not just on those occasions where it was going to produce some kind of looked for or particular end (in the case above, that people can move around efficiently). It is also an action the worth of which is to be considered independently of the particular people carrying it out. This is what Kant means by 'universal'. In other words, anyone, given the same circumstances, would do the same thing even if it meant hurting a friend, or, worse still, have some negative consequences for one's personal life.

Imagine if you will, trying to persuade 5-year-old Freddie, in his first year in primary school, that he should not hit Matilda who has just eaten his sweets.

- Should you persuade him that hitting Matilda is wrong in these circumstances?
- How are you going to persuade him that this is wrong?
- Would hitting Matilda be wrong in any circumstances?
- What are you likely to say and do in order to persuade him?

Now, let's turn to Peter, who is 15 and has just sneaked behind his friend John's back in order to have amorous relations with Petunia. John beats the daylights out of him in the playground.

- How would you persuade John that such 'violence solves nothing!'
- What are you likely to say and do in order to persuade him?
- Are the cases different?
- Would the conversation be any different between these two cases?
- Would you offer John and Freddie different reasons for not hitting those who have upset them?
- Do we expect 15-year-olds to reason differently from 5-year-olds?

It was one thing to answer such questions prior the nineteenth century when there might have been some disagreement about how we were to know what was moral or indeed what we should focus on when teaching children to be moral but there was very little disagreement about the existence of objective moral truth which we could teach. Indeed, so sure was Plato that there was an objective truth about how people should love that he thought ethics a more objective or pure discipline than mathematics. Of course, getting to 'see' moral truth in all its absoluteness was a tricky kind of a journey and it wasn't always clear that even where people saw the truth that they could live with it! But this was all to change, and in classrooms today, as we noted at the beginning, we are the inheritors of a legacy which questions the very existence of any binding objective (or normative) law which determines or should determine how we are to conduct ourselves. Let's go back to the question in the introductory section and imagine that moral education is like science education. Would this make life for the teacher a little simpler? At the level of primary or secondary schooling there is little enough disagreement about the speed of light or that it refracts in water or that sound travels in waves which oscillate at a certain frequency but as we have already said moral education is not quite of that type. There is disagreement about the basic claims that there is such a thing as absolute right and wrong and this disagreement is mediated to children in myriad ways every day. Indeed the moral culture of the school and the home may be entirely at odds. And this potential opposition is not just a matter of disagreement as to how we teach such matters but more fundamentally whether or not the things schools try to teach in moral education (responsibility, loyalty, courteous behaviour) are the kinds of things to which society as a whole subscribes. If there is little continuity and congruity between the values of the school and the home, and indeed sometimes between the values of one school and another, or yet more problematically, between one classroom and another then teaching moral education as a set of substantive claims that x is good and y is bad becomes ever more problematic. Before we attempt a response to this challenging question we might want to ask, 'how has this state of affairs come about?'

Towards the end of the nineteenth century a range of views emerged which were opposed to seeing morality as bound to and founded on a religious worldview. While, as we have seen in our discussion of Kant, there had been some credence given to the claim that God was not the ground of morality in the course of *The Enlightenment* a century earlier, particularly by philosophers like David Hume, this had not, even a century later, received widespread acceptance or agreement. The last quarter of the nineteenth century saw the emergence of psychological (Sigmund Freud) and sociological (Emile Durkheim) claims that God was no more than a projection. In the case of Freud, God was the reification (or objectification) of the fraught and jealous relationship between son and father; in the case of Durkheim, God was the reification of the *conscience collective (a kind of social glue),* which bound society together to assure communal survival and security. If God was to be regarded as a projection then the claims that morality was determined by God as part of the nature of things had to be up for question. So it was that the beginning of the contemporary educational problem for moral educators emerged in sharp relief, 'what and how are we to teach morality in a world where what has traditionally been thought of as good is constantly being challenged?' Important though these thinkers (Freud, Durkheim etc) have been for the way we think about morality, hence moral education, they have not been as significant as the less well known German philosopher, Friedrich Nietzsche (b.1844). Central to Nietzsche's thinking was the belief that the energy that drives human beings forward to achieve ever greater things is not (as the Christian scriptures or Kant believed) love of neighbour but a desire to dominate. Religion, devised to serve and preserve a priestly class, made people ethically weak because it always wanted to drag them back to an older, more conservative world. In this world moral education would be a matter of obeying ancient laws embedded in the mists of history, which for practical purposes was intended to convey their absolute nature as the foundations of our very existence. Look at this passage from Nietzsche's, *Twilight of the Idols* (1895, cited in R. J. Hollingdale, 1968):

> Nothing is rarer among moralists and saints than integrity; perhaps they say the opposite, perhaps they even believe it. For when faith is more useful, effective, convincing than conscious hypocrisy, hypocrisy instinctively and forthwith becomes innocent: first principle for the understanding of great saints. (§. 42)

What do you think Nietzsche meant by the slightly puzzling observation that hypocrisy becomes innocent?

If everyone who claims that there is morality and consequently moral education is a hypocrite, what are they trying to hide?

From whom are they trying to hide it?

What would be the consequences for teaching moral education if we were to follow Nietzsche's teachings?

While Nietzsche might be deemed rather too negative and cynical by many, he nevertheless, more fully than anyone else at the end of the nineteenth century, poses a robust challenge to the idea that the teaching of those who lead – priests, teachers, politicians and others – is motivated by an attachment to, much less an understanding of, some set of absolute and enduring moral truths such as had been subscribed to by philosophers for over two millennia. This of course does not make his analysis unproblematic. If we were to uncritically accept his view that human exchange should be subjected to the 'will to power' (the belief that we should pursue our own goals of self realization irrespective of consequences) might this not lead to social disintegration and the collapse of social projects such as education, which are, at least partly concerned with the moral purpose of redistributing certain kinds of resources with potential advantages for an individual or groups flourishing? These are indeed complicated questions. What is undisputed is that this shift in the way we historically think about morality has had a pretty substantial impact on moral education, even where teachers might be completely unaware of Nietzsche, Freud or Durkheim or the other philosophers of the nineteenth and twentieth century who shared or developed their views. It has become much more difficult for a teacher to say with any degree of certainty that such and such behaviour is good or bad, right or wrong. Yet teachers continue to want to do precisely this and governments continue to press them to be ever more concerned with teaching children what is considered to be morality. Of course neither teacher nor government are immune from the charge that they are inclined to confuse convention and morality. There are lots of conventions, which, having evolved through the ages, take on the aura of moral absolutes but they are not necessarily such. This does not mean that there is no such thing as morality nor does it suggest that moral education is a redundant exercise. Rather it points to the likelihood that morality may find its expression in why people commit particular kinds of actions rather than in the particular actions themselves. This returns us to Kant's claim that moral education is a rational activity where what is moral is determined by reason rather than action.

It is precisely this concern that is taken up in the 1960s by American psychologist, Lawrence Kohlberg (1984). Kohlberg drew heavily on Kant's claims that the moral person was one who could offer justifiable rational arguments for choosing one course of action over another. He was also influenced by developmental psychologist, Jean Piaget who marked out and analysed what he saw to be children's cognitive development. Now, it is pretty self-evident that an infant doesn't come fully loaded with the ability to reason but Piaget took this common sense notion and described particular stages through which a child has to go before she can come to think in abstract, conceptual terms. Blending the rationalism of Kant and the developmentalism of Piaget (1965), Kohlberg is generally seen as being the key twentieth-century figure in creating a school of moral developmental psychology. For his followers the goal was, and remains, to fully understand how to best cultivate moral behaviour in human beings. For Kohlberg this was no academic exercise. What motivated him was that series of events in the middle of the twentieth century which included the holocaust and the Korean War. How was it, he wanted to know, that people, who in normal circumstances appeared perfectly moral according to the social conventions of their time and culture could behave in ways that, to the outsider, could be described as grossly immoral? It was a question that perplexed many psychologists and philosophers in the second half of the twentieth century including Hannah Arendt who escaped from Nazi Germany and France during the Second World War and made her way to the United States. In a small but very important book entitled, *The Banality of Evil*, Arendt (1963/1992) discusses the trial of Adolf Eichmann, who was the officer responsible for ensuring the smooth running of the logistical system which transported prisoner, mostly Jews, to concentration camps such as Auschwitz. Arendt comes to the conclusion that evil actions are not the prerogative of peculiarly wicked people. Rather, she suggests, many ordinary people placed in the particular extraordinary historical and cultural circumstances in which Eichmann found himself might well have done exactly the same thing and rationalized it as 'simply following the rules'. This idea of 'following the rules' is at the heart of Kohlberg's analysis wherein he argues that there are broadly three phases of moral justification (though each one of these has two sub elements), pre-conventional, conventional and post-conventional. Each of these phases reflects a form of justification for action. The pre-conventional phase encompasses justifications that rely on either a symmetry between what is immoral and what is punishable (an adult telling me x is wrong makes x wrong) or on a concern to protect the self (if I do it to you, you are likely to do it to me). These conventional stages give way as a person grows (morally) to justify actions conventionally. Here she sees something as wrong because it fails to get approval from others (say adults). This in turn leads to the heart of convention. Something is wrong because the social system prohibits it. While at the earlier stage of conventional morality society is very concrete (my mum or dad or teacher approves/disapproves of this) here society is construed in more abstract legalistic terms as the entity which determines how individuals should conduct themselves. Conventional moral justification may give way to post-conventional morality, which begins to construct a yet more abstract view of the ideal society; that is a society where the particular values in a society are themselves subject to larger or prior moral principles. Justice is central here. At this, stage 5, it is possible to conceive of someone refusing to obey the rules of society on the grounds that the rules are themselves unjust. In other words one can take a rather more bird's eye view of a society's conventions. The final stage of this developmental sequence reflect Kohlberg's belief that some special human beings can stand above the melee of every day life and evaluate even the most sophisticated socio-moral systems from the perspective of the pure moral choice (i.e. one untainted by what's in any way in one's own interests).

> Go back to the two different cases outlined above and suggest the stage of development in each of the two cases. If the two boys are at different stages in their moral development does this mean that we should treat them differently? If there aren't any differences, suggest why not. If you think that there are differences can you identify and list these?

Many teachers, and a great deal of curriculum material developed for schools since the 1970s, have been influenced by this thinking and indeed whole syllabi for children were written which attempted to turn Kohlberg's philosophical and empirical reflections into pedagogies. Moreover, so smitten was Kohlberg himself with the idea that people would become increasingly moral if only we could get them to understand and apply the overriding principle of justice to socio-moral situations that he established what came to be known as Just Community Schools in New York and elsewhere. The aim was to articulate and reinforce the centrality of justice to a person's moral development and this was to be achieved not only in having conversations about justice (in other words formal teaching about moral reasoning) in the classroom but also in situating the practices of the school in a milieu of rational social justice.

> If we were to teach students that rational argument is the most just thing to do in any circumstances, is it likely to be sufficient to make them moral people?
>   Might there be any other considerations we might have to take into account in teaching moral education?

Kohlberg's work has been subject to a lot of revision and modification with many arguing that there are other things apart form rational justice that we need to teach if we are to culti-vate good or moral persons. These include care and compassion, consistency, moral resilience to name but a few. An appeal to justice might not be enough. In any event the exercise of justice is an extremely complicated matter. After all it is possible to reprimand one child for throwing a pen across the room and not reprimand another child for good reasons though it might appear to the outsider that the different treatment of two students is unjust. The action of the teacher might be based on subtle insider knowledge of the students in question, the class and context and dictate quite different responses. This exercise of discipline, sanction and reprimand can of course constitute a meaningful moral learning experience for students but probably only if there is consistency, discussion and explanation. Even then the learning here is of a more implicit kind. As social institutions schools are required to be moral places and teachers are obliged to cultivate and promote those moral attitudes that are themselves likely to be conducive to the creation of the good society. But, yet again the cultivation of morality is not unproblematic. Precisely because schools are social institutions they are likely to reflect, at least to some degree, the pre-existing mores of society. For example, when society no longer saw corporal punishment as desirable or morally defensible teachers had to stop using it to discipline students. Of course the reverse may also be true.

Take some time to think of a social development which may have negatively impacted on the moral culture of the school?

It is interesting to examine some of the ways in which the teacher is portrayed in the popular media. Not infrequently teachers are depicted as slightly dysfunctional and somewhat weak characters whose interests are dictated by the politics and relationships in the staffroom rather than the needs of students in the classroom! Of course working out whether or not these televisual and related images actually impact on the moral climate of the school is an empirical rather than a philosophical question. But, underpinning any empirical consideration is the concern to understand what should be the relationship between the state, the wider society and the institutions they establish as agents for nurturing children into adulthood. There are also importantly related questions as to how far schools have to take responsibility for the moral education and development of children. Should they, for example, be morally superior to society as a whole? These and a host of questions remain.

One recent response to this 'modern' insecurity about whether or not we can teach that x is wrong and y is right has seen a return to one of the very earliest figures in moral theory, Aristotle. David Carr has spent much of his career arguing that teachers should focus not on particular moral beliefs but on cultivating 'virtue'. He draws on Aristotle's very famous work, 'The Nicomachean Ethics' and its modern development in the thought of Alasdair Macintyre where the Greek philosopher argues that the object of moral education is the cultivation of virtue. Instead of focusing on this action or that action we should focus on people's disposition to act in particular ways. This generally means that we should teach students to avoid excessive behaviour but strive for a mean or a middle way. Hence, we should be neither foolhardy nor cowardly but courageous, neither profligate nor mean-spirited but generous and so on.

> How do you think we are to do this?

For Aristotle the only way to cultivate virtue is to act virtuously; practice is everything. Virtue is, in this sense habit-forming. If I keep acting virtuously I will become virtuous. Equally, if I keep acting immorally I will become immoral. We do not become virtuous merely by talking about it but by practising it. This takes us back to the question about whether or not the focus of moral education should be teaching of lessons in the classroom or the creation of a moral climate in the school. It is clear that government would like schools to create moral students. They are inclined to see schools as capable of doing so even where the climate is against them. It is not however clear that governments themselves always act in moral ways and the influences on students are confined to neither the classroom nor the school. Consequently, we are likely to educate children morally to the extent that our society is moral!

Further reading

There are a great many classic texts which you can read on the major thinkers in moral education and they come in a number of editions. These include Aristotle's *Nicomachean Ethics* and Kant's *Foundations of the Metaphysics of Morals*. The particular Nietzsche passage here is from R. J. Hollingdale's (1968) edition of Twilight of the Idols *and* The Anti-Christ.

While I would always recommend reading the whole text, there is a useful reader which covers many of the major thinkers in the field. It is entitled *The Moral Life: An Introductory Reader in Ethics and Literature* (Pojman, 1999). One recent study which discusses a number of issues surrounding the politics of moral education is Stephen Law's *The War for Children's Minds* (2006). He suggests that liberalism is in danger and attacks public figures such as Rabbi Jonathan Sacks for conflating liberalism and relativism and trying to undermine enlightened autonomy. An interesting book, it might overstate the case since children are much more likely to be prey to the relativism and self-obsession of consumerism, a very particular expression of liberalism. There is a lot of material on Kohlberg and Piaget and the field of moral development (Kohlberg, 1984; Piaget, 1965).

Hannah Arendt's (1992) essay on the trial of Eichmann offers a very interesting insight into some of the moral issues of the twentieth century.

Useful websites

The single most important journal in the field is the *Journal of Moral Education*, which brings together scholarly work from psychology, philosophy, sociology, cultural studies and education. It can be accessed at http://www.informaworld.com/smpp/title~content=t713432411

An overview of developmentalism in moral education can be found at http://tigger.uic.edu/~lnucci/MoralEd/overview.html

It is worth looking at Nel Noddings' work which sees moral education as intimately tied to the cultivation of a care ethic. A short essay on her philosophy may be accessed at http://www.infed.org/thinkers/noddings.htm.

Do Children Have Any Rights?

Harry Brighouse and Paula McAvoy

Introduction

Liberal societies are founded on the principle that human beings have certain rights that ought to be protected by the government and respected by fellow citizens. These rights protect our interest in being self-governing persons who enjoy the freedom to live our own conceptions of the good life. The place of children in this understanding of human beings has been a challenge to sort out within liberal theory. Consider the following case. In 2007, King Middle School in Portland, Maine approved a policy, which allows students free access to an on-campus health care centre. Among the services provided by the clinic are prescriptions for birth control. It is the centre's policy not to notify parents when a student requests contraceptives.

This case illustrates the difficult position of children in liberal society. Some may want to say that 13- and 14-year-olds have rights to privacy and to their bodies just like any other person, and perhaps a right to self-determination in sexual matters. Others might argue that as children, they are dependent upon others and so are not full rights bearers. Further, parents may claim to have a right to know what their children are doing and to raise a family without excessive interference by the state, or even to control their children's sexual behaviour. This tension between the interests of children, the interests of parents, and the interests of the liberal state creates the puzzle of children's rights.

Review the academic programme at King Middle School and the policies of the health centre.

- King Middle School: http://king.portlandschools.org/
- King Student Health Center Policies:
  http://king.portlandschools.org/files/ourschool/health/King%20Student%20Health%20Center.pdf

Does the school seem to adequately attend to the interests/rights of children?

The choice theory of rights

To solve this puzzle, we must come to an agreement about what rights are and why they are important. One theory that has a great deal of purchase in the public discourse is known as the choice theory of rights. A good deal of confusion about the claim that children have rights depends on the tacit assumption that the choice theory is the correct theory. Here is H. L. A. Hart, the most prominent defender of this theory of rights in the last century, elaborating the equal right to freedom, which, he thinks, underlies all other rights:

> Any human being capable of choice (1) has the right to forbearance on the part of all others from the use of coercion or restraint against him save to hinder coercion or restraint and (2) is at liberty to do any action which is not coercing or restraining or designed to injure other persons. (Hart, 1955, p. 175)

This is a very intuitive idea about rights attributions: rights are essentially guarantees of various freedoms to direct one's own life, but not those of others. In addition, they give one control over other people in the sense that one can prevent others from encroaching on one's own freedom. Hart also claims that as rights bearers we can waive our rights, or put another way, choose not to invoke our rights when we feel a more important value ought to govern a situation. On this theory the inappropriateness of considering children rights-bearers is obvious: crucially, this is because they are not competent choosers, are vulnerable, and are dependent. Children (especially young children) cannot make good choices about whether to claim or waive their rights. They cannot, in other words, exercise the discretion that rights–as–freedom give in ways that enhance the quality of their lives. Children 'lack the requisite autonomy, in the moral much more importantly than the merely physical sense of the term. Their will is unformed or deformed, their judgement deficient or impaired' (Goodin and Gibson, 1997, p. 187). The idea is, of course, not that children are literally unable to choose: from a fairly early age one can ask a child which one of two or three things they want to do, and they will formally make a choice. But children often do not grasp the ramifications, for them or for others, of the choice they make. This is true even of very simple decisions (what and whether to eat for lunch; how long and with whom to play after lunch; how early to go to bed), let alone decisions about whether to waive or claim their rights. Hart himself accepts this implication: 'these considerations should incline us not to extend to animals and babies whom it is wrong to ill treat the notion of a right to proper treatment' (Hart, 1955, p. 181).

So, if the choice theory is correct, children do not have rights. Whether adolescents, or older teens, have rights depends on whether they have achieved the requisite level of capacity for self-governance, something which in the West teenagers seem to be very optimistic about having done, but which others may be more sceptical about. To return to King Middle School, a choice theorist has no basis for saying that the children have the right to private information concerning, and supply of, contraceptives. But nor does the choice theorist have grounds for claiming a parental right over this matter – because in the choice theory rights are rights to govern one's own life, not the lives of others. So, for the choice theorist, rights do not comment on the case.

The interest theory

Theorizing about rights has not been dominated by the choice theory, but by an ongoing debate between the choice theory, and another, different, theory which is usually called the interest theory. Joseph Raz describes the theory very succinctly:

> Definition: 'X has a right' if and only if X can have rights and other things being equal, an aspect of X's well-being (his interest) is a sufficient reason for holding some other person(s) to be under a duty.
>
> The Principle of Capacity to Have Rights: An individual is capable of having rights if and only if either his wellbeing is of ultimate value or he is an 'artificial person.' (Raz, 1984, p. 195)[1]

Raz leaves open what it is for an individual's well-being to be of ultimate value, but another interest theorist, Neil MacCormick (1982), is more committal, and explicitly (and plausibly) argues that children do have rights to, at least, care, nurture and love. MacCormick rejects the will theory on the grounds that neither children, nor the people who take care of them may waive these rights:

> . . . it is not the case that the child or someone deemed to be acting on the child's behalf has an option of enforcing the duty of care and nurture, which option may or may not be exercised according to arbitrary choice. If the child needs greater care than it is being provided, there is no discretion

to be exercised, that greater care must be provided. Of course, there is discretion in judging any
question of 'need', but it is discretion of a kind not contemplated by the will theory. (ibid., p. 158)

Rights bearers, then, need not have well-developed capacities for choice, but are beings whose
interests demand moral respect – beings like ordinary human adults, ordinary human children, and, perhaps, some animals. On this account, rights are not only justified by their role
in protecting choice, but by their role in giving people opportunities for their lives to go well.
Since children's well-being is, like that of adults, of ultimate value, children are clear candi-
dates for rights-attributions. There is no need on this theory for children and adults to have
the same rights, because the rights that are ascribed to children depend on what will best
protect *their* interests. This helps to explain why the rights enshrined in the Universal Declaration of Human Rights are so different in form and content from those enshrined in the
Convention on the Rights of the Child.

> Read the text for the Convention on the Rights of the Child. Does it promote choice rights or
> interest rights? Does the King health care policy support this understanding of children's rights?
> Why/why not?

Is there an argument for the interest theory of rights over the choice theory of rights?
The quoted passage from MacCormick comes from an extended argument that the interest
theory is superior because it supports children having rights. In our context, that argument
would be circular. There is certainly no consensus among philosophers; indeed, this dispute
has been raging as long as philosophers have thought about rights, so we are unlikely, here,
to provide an argument that will convince opponents. We can, however, state a view which
we find plausible, and that seems to support the interest theory. It seems to us that the purpose of social and moral institutions is to make people's lives go better than they otherwise
would, rather than to protect individual choices. But once we are enmeshed in a social matrix,
we make different choices than we would outside, or in a different, social matrix, and our
capacities for choice are different. Given our assumption about the purpose of social institutions, and the subsequent observation, it seems artificial to restrict to choices the very strin-
gent protections and guarantees that rights protect. Having choices, when one has developed
the capacity for making good judgements about one's life, is very important for well-being,
but if advancing well-being is the point of social institutions, other important contributors to
well-being seem worthy of protection.

How does the interest theory of rights apply to the King case? Things get complicated
because not only does the interest theory have the resources to recognize children as rights-
bearers; it also has the resources to recognize parents' as having rights over their children.

If adults have an interest in being able to have a certain kind of relationship with children, and reliably enabling people to have such a relationship requires assigning them rights over their children, then the interest theory will say that parents have precisely those rights over children (see Brighouse and Swift, 2006, for an argument for parents' rights along these lines). Of course, if children and adults have equal moral standing (as we believe that they do), then their rights, prima facie, have equal standing. But because children are dependent and vulnerable, and because parents, unlike children, have voluntarily entered the relationship, it's natural to think that children's rights have priority.

That all children have a right to quality health care is clear under the interest theory because health care furthers every child's current and future well-being. This, an interest theorist would argue, is a moral right, that translates into a legal right that obligates adults and the state to ensure that all children are cared for. So when it comes to prescribing contraception without parental consent, the issue is not whether or not children have explicit rights to freely choose to engage in sex, or have the same right to privacy that we grant to adults (they clearly do not), but whether or not this policy furthers the child's well-being and, whether or not it does, whether it undermines the parental interest in having a relationship of a certain kind with their child.

Let's suppose that children command our moral respect, or have interests that are of ultimate value, and that the interest theory of rights is true. This tells us that children might be rights-bearers, but not that they are, nor what rights, if any, they have.

> Both the Universal Declaration of Human Rights and the Convention on the Rights of the Child say that a child has a right to an education, but that the parent has a right to control that education. Should parents really have so much power over their children?

Why might children not have rights?[2]

We want to evaluate two arguments against children being rights-bearers made by Onora O' Neill which are, we think, made from within the interest theory of rights. O'Neill grants that children have positive rights (obligations owed to them by others), but she argues that the language of fundamental rights does not adequately secure all, and indeed obscures much, that is owed to children because taking 'rights as fundamental in looking at ethical issues in children's lives we . . . get an indirect, partial and blurred picture' (O'Neill, 1988, p. 187). Instead, she asserts that children are owed something more, what she calls: fundamental obligations.

How could this be? She points first to the distinction between perfect and imperfect obligations, arguing that the latter cannot be captured by rights talk:

Sometimes we are required to perform or omit [some type of action] for all others. Sometimes we are required to perform or omit this type of action for specified others. Sometimes we are required to perform or omit an act for unspecified others, but not for all others . . . (O'Neill, 1988, p. 189)

The first two requirements are perfect obligations because they require universal compliance and therefore correspond to rights. The third case is an imperfect obligation because, although agents have no latitude over whether to perform or omit the pertinent act, we do have some discretion over who should be the beneficiary of that performance or omission. For example, the obligation to be kind to strangers is not the obligation to be kind to all strangers, or to be kind to specified strangers, only to be kind to some. No particular stranger has a claim on our kindness. If Clement is in a hurry to get back to his wife's bedside as she gives birth, he falls down on no obligation by refusing a lift to a stranger who needs to get to the other side of town.

How does this relate to children's rights? Much of what children need in order to acquire what is due to them falls into the category of imperfect obligation (O'Neill also notes that there are, of course, perfect obligations to children like refraining from abusing all children). That is, little right that they have comes from any particular person, or from all people. As O'Neill puts it:

We may have a fundamental obligation to be kind and considerate in dealing with children–to care for them–and to put ourselves out in ways that differ from those in which we must put ourselves out for adults. This obligation may bind all agents, but is not one that we owe either to all children . . . or merely to antecedently specified children. (190)

What children need are 'special relationships' with adults who take on the necessary roles to secure a child's well-being like parents, teachers, and social workers. These adults take on a role that carries an ethical obligation to children. O'Neill believes that the duties associated with the role are not captured by rights, but require a much deeper set of obligations:

Those who do only what the children they interact with have a (universal or special) right to will do less than they ought. They will fulfill their perfect but not their imperfect obligations. In particular parents or teachers who meet only their perfect obligations would fail as parents or teachers. (ibid., p. 191)

These 'cold, distant or fanatical parents and teachers . . . wither children's lives' by failing to provide children the experiences that make life rich and meaningful (ibid., p. 192).

This argument certainly impugns thinking of what is owed to children *solely* in terms of rights. But it does not impugn rights talk with respect to children altogether. It seems reasonable, for example, to think that each child has a right to some level of education. Who has the obligation to deliver on that right? The obvious thought is that, since it is a right to something which is itself highly socially contingent, all of us have an obligation to maintain an institution which assigns duties in a way that secures the right. This is the role of the state in modern societies: it is the guarantor of last resort, with a duty to ensure those institutional arrangements that most reliably insure that every child gets the appropriate level of education. This may require that it provide schools itself, or may just require that it provide schooling, for those children whose parents either cannot or will not pay for the education themselves. Similarly, it seems reasonable to think that each child has a right to a high level of care. Parents have the obligation to provide this, but if the parents fall down the state must step in: it is, again, guarantor of last resort.

O'Neill is right that any parent who refrains from doing anything more than the child has a right to, will be failing to discharge all the obligations of parenthood. The child will be better off, and the relationship more fulfilling, if the parent regards the child with love and care, not as merely someone who has rights against her. But this morally full relationship is compatible with seeing the child as having some specific rights which one is required to observe, and which one is in a uniquely suitable position to protect.

In other words, children are better off when parents do not view a child as someone they own, but someone who they are nurturing toward independence. This does not mean that at all times the child's 'right' to nurturing trumps the adults' interests. It is good for a child to have music lessons, but providing them might take way money being spent on a parent's education toward a more fulfilling job. A parent is not obligated to provide all things that are merely 'good for' a child, but ought to do so some of the time. But, a rights-respecting parent would not stop payment on her child's health insurance in order to pay for her own education.

O'Neill also makes a second, more political, critique of the idea of children's rights. She notes that a central purpose of the grand declarations of rights, from the Declaration of the Rights of Man to the Universal Declaration of Human Rights, is to 'empower the powerless' (ibid., p. 210). Rights cannot have this function for children, because the vulnerability and dependence of children is not an ameliorable artifice of unjust social institutions: it is a natural feature of their biological condition. The way for children to overcome their dependence and vulnerability is not to assert their rights but, as O'Neill puts it, to 'grow up' (ibid., p. 204).

Again, she is right. But, children's rights may have a different important political function. Rights talk exhorts the disadvantaged to assert their equality, but it *also* reminds the privileged to withdraw their assertions of superiority. The call for women's rights doesn't just encourage women to claim their rights, but also encourages men to grant them, to think of women as people whose interests count as much as their own. Human rights documents say this to the powerful:

> You may indeed have inherited superior power. But this fact does not authorize you to use that power to your own advantage. In some cases you must attempt to relinquish that power.

But in others, in which it cannot be relinquished, you must understand that the person in your power is a rights-bearer, one whose interests count for as much as yours.

This function has great significance for children's rights. It draws the attention of governments, welfare agencies and parents, to the independent standing of the child, and the centrality of her interests in determining policy, intervention, and her upbringing respectively. In an era when talk of children's rights is more or less taken for granted this may seem trivial, the more central task being to determine what those interests are and to act on them; but it is very new that children's interests have systematically been taken seriously by governments and welfare agencies and that the patriarchal legacy of the pre-modern age has been seriously challenged.

Children's interests

Recall that O'Neill argues that the language of rights may not be the best way to protect the interests of children. We have argued that while rights will not sufficiently capture all that is due to children, identifying some rights are nevertheless important – especially for clarifying the duties of institutions attending to children. If the interest theory is correct, in order to identify children's rights, we must first identify their interests.

One natural thought is that children have an interest in becoming effective adults. And surely, most do. There has been a tendency among moral and political philosophers thinking about childhood to, indeed, regard children as proto-adults and to see their interests primarily in those, future-oriented, terms. But let us suppose that a child does not grow to adulthood, for some tragic reason. Does this mean that she has no interests (and therefore no rights)? It doesn't – she has interests in the present day, and these are sufficient for us to think that she has some rights. But whatever these interests are, other children, more fortunate because they will actually reach adulthood, share them as well. There are goods available in childhood which are not available in adulthood, and the value of which is not reducible to the role they play in human development. Children have a unique capacity for spontaneous joy; childhood is a stage in life in which it is possible to have the pleasure of being carefree and enjoying unstructured time without being irresponsible or fearful of the consequences. There are, in other words, distinctive goods of childhood the value of which is not reducible to their function for human development (MacLeod, forthcoming).

Children have other interests, which although highly functional for their future development, are also valuable for them in the present. They have an interest in food, shelter, loving care and attention, friendship and other kinds of meaningful connection with other children, acquaintance with adults who are not their parents, some sort of integration into their community, etc. Of course adults also have these interests, which lie at the basis of some of their rights, on the interest view. But for adults, because they generally have a better sense of what will serve their well-being than any other agent does, we think they should have a great deal of control over how and whether these interests are met. Young children are in a different condition, and do not have an interest in controlling as much of the conditions of their lives as adults do. If you like, they need love, not control over determining whom to be in a loving relationship with.

This leads us to a third category of children's interests. Adults have what are commonly called agency interests. Like the choice theory of rights, agency interests recognize that adults have the capacity to control how things go in their lives. Children lack this capacity. This does not mean that they do not have agency interests, just that their agency interests are complex. Children combine three features, which make them unlike adults. They are profoundly dependent on others for their well-being, because they cannot meet their own needs (emotional, physical, developmental), or negotiate the obstacles in the social world in such a way that their needs will be met. They are also (for this reason) profoundly vulnerable to the decisions of others. Even if those on whom they are dependent are highly reliable with respect to their welfare, whenever something goes wrong it is normally because the decisions of another have failed. Finally, children, unlike other persons who are dependent and vulnerable, have the capacity to develop the capabilities to meet their own needs. That they exhibit these three features makes children unique (The very old, the severely cognitively disabled, and domestic animals share the first two conditions of children but not the third. People in comas share these three characteristics. But what must be done to develop their capabilities is quite different – the aim is to restore normal functioning, not to develop it). The first two features suggests that their agency interests in the short term will be very different from, and much more limited than, those of adults. But the third feature, future capacity, suggests that they have a powerful interest in the conditions and resources needed for them to develop into the kinds of beings that have the agency interests. They have, in other words, very strong interests in developing the skills, personality traits and knowledge base that will enable them to negotiate the physical and social world independently in the future (when they become adults).

Before continuing to talk about rights, let's think about the King case in the light of the foregoing comments. Whereas adults have very strong agency interests in self-determination with respect to their sexual activity, children do not, even in early adolescence. Their capacity for judgement in these matters is (normally) not yet well developed, and (normally) they lack both the self-knowledge and the ability to read others well that underwrites the interest in self-determination in these matters. For the vast majority, their future agency and well-being are also at issue, but in a complex way. Sexual activity puts their physical and emotional health (and therefore, also, their future agency) at risk in a way that non-activity does not. On the other hand, as proponents of the King policy will point out, many of them will engage in such activity, and will thereby put their health and future agency at risk regardless: armed with proper information and resources those who would engage in sexual activity anyway are less at risk than they would be without the information and resources. A supporter of the policy could argue that in the current social matrix, protecting a sexually active child against

STDs and teen pregnancy might be the best for promoting well-being in an otherwise undesirable circumstance.

Conclusion: so, do children have rights?

To summarize the previous section, children have three kinds of interest: interests in attaining the goods that are specific to childhood, welfare interests that resemble those of adults, and agency interests that are quite different from those of adults. What rights, then, might they have? We want to suggest that they fall into three broad categories, very roughly corresponding to the broad kinds of interests we have identified. The correspondence is very rough because each right typically protects more than one interest, and the interests can come from more than one category.

First are rights that protect the interest in the goods distinctive to childhood. The rights to play, to use their imagination, and to an environment in which friendships with peers can develop – all serve these interests, even if they also serve others. Similarly, whereas the main justification of the right to an education, as we shall see, is best made in terms of the future interests of the child, children have a right that their education be carried out in a manner consistent with them not being made deeply miserable. The right not to be bullied may or may not serve one's future interests, but the central reason we should uphold is that children have a right, right now, not to be made unnecessarily miserable.

Second are rights that protect the welfare interests children have in common with adults like access to a home, to shelter, to a family, to food, and to restful sleep. Whereas the agency rights of adults support only that the government ensure that everyone who wants these things can get them, since children lack the requisite capacities for agency. However, it is appropriate for the government to establish strong institutional guarantees that they will actually have all of these things, whether they, or any other person, want them or not. For some of these rights correlative duties are usually assigned to parents, who must endure penalties if they routinely fail to deliver. For others, like, the right to restful sleep, it is very difficult to enforce a legal duty on parents, so it has been common to rely on social norms to protect this right. The right to education is justified in part by reference to one's future welfare interests: one has a right to an education adequate to participate effectively in the economy as an adult, so that one can, in adulthood, secure the means to a livelihood.

Finally, there are rights that protect one's future capacity for agency. It is common to include the right to education in this category, and to specify the content of the education one has a right to by reference to, among other things, future agency interests. For example, one strand of thought says that children have a right to an education that will facilitate or promote their personal autonomy (Callan, 1997; Brighouse, 1998), and that will facilitate their being competent democratic citizens (Macedo, 2000; Gutmann, 1989), by reference to the interest in future agency. But other rights also protect future agency – if children have a right to be loved (Liao, 2007) that is not only because it is good for them while they are children (although it is partly for that reason) but also because children who are not loved are at very high risk of not being capable agents as adults.

Let us return, finally, to the King case. We think that rights *are* at stake in this policy, but they are not the rights of choice. Children do not have the right to engage in sexual activity, nor do parents have the right to control a child's sex life. The question for policy makers is whether or not this policy protects a child's interests in the short and long terms. In this case, it is not immediately clear. We can imagine children who will not talk to their parents because of the policy, and would be better off if they do. We can also imagine students who will have sex, and are better off because of the information and protection that they received from the clinic. Policy makers have to consider the interests of different types of children in different, imperfect contexts, and this inevitably means that we have to make trade-offs.

Recall MacCormick's comment that children cannot waive rights, nor can adults waive their obligations to children. If a middle school decided to implement a policy like King's, they would be, in some cases, usurping power from parents with respect to how they wish to raise their child. Because the parents provide much of what is owed to children, the school must be sure that the policy is not creating a net loss in care for children. It would be unconscionable for a school simply to open a clinic and hand out contraceptives to any 13-year-old who requested it given that sex at that age is not in the child's best interest. The school's first priority should be to develop children who make good decisions and do not need contraceptives. The second priority should be to make the best of the worst case by providing care to those who are engaging in sexual activity. If both aims are to be realized, the school must recognize obligations to all children. First, the clinic must take-on a paternalistic role for all who use the clinic and even more so for those who request contraceptives. This includes, but is not limited to, getting to know all the children and then providing counselling prior to receiving contraception and follow-ups to make sure the student is getting support. The school staff must also consciously create a positive ethos within the school that promotes: healthy friendships, supportive student–adult interaction, and provides students with multiple ways to feel challenged and successful. Second, the school must provide students with a comprehensive and honest sex and health education programme that includes helping students to critique and question the sexual messages that they receive in the media and from their peers and even, perhaps, from their parents. This is not an exhaustive list, but sheds some light on how focusing on children's interests for a fulfilling childhood and adulthood causes policy makers to think more holistically, and justly, about the needs of children. In a dysfunctional school this policy could be dangerous, in a healthy school it could be the best choice for securing the rights of children.

Further reading

There is now a great deal of philosophical literature on children and childhood, so this guide to further reading is really just the tip of an iceberg. Cohen (1980) gives a trenchant defence of a child liberationist view, on which children have the same basic rights as adults; Purdy (1992) is an equally powerful argument for paternalistic authority over children. Brennan and Noggle (1997) provide a child-centred defence of parents' rights, and Schapiro (1999) develops a Kantian account of the nature of childhood. Archard (1993) is a comprehensive discussion of children and their rights which, unusually for philosophical literature, also sets the philosophizing in the context of the historical and cultural studies literature about childhood; Archard and MacLeod (2002) is an excellent collection of papers by philosophers about the status of children. Gutmann (1989) and Brighouse (2006) explore the responsibilities society has toward children's education, with some discussion of policy matters. Wringe (1981) is hard to get hold of, but is well worth reading as a philosophically intelligent, but institutionally grounded, discussion of children's rights in the context of education. Postman (1982) is not a work of philosophy, but of cultural studies; it is a pessimistic reading of the way that childhood is experienced in contemporary wealthy societies, and is full of insight, and worth reading among other things for the view of the value of childhood that Postman advances.

Ambitious readers will seek further reading on rights, themselves. Hart (1955) is the contemporary classic on the choice theory of rights; for a more recent version of that theory, see Wellman (1985). Raz (1984) is a very precise and clear statement and defence of the interest theory of rights; Raz (1986) is a magisterial contribution to political philosophy, elaborating in full detail the view of freedom of which the interest theory of rights is an integral part. Waldron (1984) contains several classic philosophical papers on rights.

Useful websites (Accessed on 13 July 2009)

UNICEF:

  http://www.unicef.org/crc/

Text for the Convention on the Rights of the Child:

  http://www2.ohchr.org/english/law/crc.htm

Universal Declaration of Human Rights:

  http://www.un.org/Overview/rights.html.

Notes

1. 'Artificial persons' are legal entities such as corporations which are recognized as rights-bearers for the sake of efficiently assigning responsibilities and liabilities. For our purposes we shall ignore this part of Raz's condition.
2. This section draws on Brighouse (2002).

7 Can Schools Make Good Citizens?

Tristan McCowan

Chapter Outline

Introduction

'Civic' or 'citizenship' education has not had a strong historical presence in the curricula of UK schools, as it has in other countries, such as France and the USA. Yet with the coming to power of New Labour in 1997, the subject came dramatically into favour. A report (QCA, 1999) was commissioned by the Education Secretary David Blunkett, chaired by the academic and long-term campaigner for political education, Bernard Crick. The Crick Report, as it became known, paved the way for the entry of the subject into the National Curriculum in 2002.

Yet, while many have welcomed the arrival of citizenship in schools, there have been critics and sceptics on both sides of the political spectrum (e.g., Flew, 2000; Gamarnikow and Green, 1999; Gillborn, 2006; Tooley, 2000). The teaching of citizenship in schools is problematic for a number of reasons. First, there is no consensus over what 'good citizenship' is, and, therefore, over the aims of citizenship education. Secondly, there is uncertainty as to the types of educational activities and experiences that might be effective in promoting citizenship, and indeed doubts as to whether schools can have an influence at all.

This chapter addresses these contested questions. First, the concept of 'citizen' itself will be discussed. Next, there will be an outline of the different ways in which 'good' citizenship can be conceived. Lastly, the chapter will address the diverse ways in which citizenship can be promoted in schools and elsewhere, and the extent to which these may be effective.

What is a citizen?

Citizenship refers to membership of a 'polity', or political unit of some form. The word 'citizen' has its origins in the Latin *civis,* a resident of a city, on account of the predominance of city-states (Athens, Sparta etc.) in the ancient world, rather than the nation-states (e.g. 'Greece') of today. The term is principally associated with membership of a *republic* (those of us who are 'citizens' of the UK being, technically speaking, *subjects* of the monarchy).

In practice, there are two related uses of the term citizenship:

1. Official membership of a state ('I'm a Canadian citizen', 'I have dual citizenship')
2. Fulfilling expectations associated with membership of a state ('We must encourage young people to be good citizens').

In the first of these meanings, either one is a citizen or one is not. It refers to a legal status, and a set of rights guaranteed by the state (though they may not always be upheld in practice). With the latter meaning, however, we can speak of 'good' or 'bad' citizens, or 'effective' or 'ineffective' citizenship: this is no longer a simple legal status but a question of individual and collective identity, virtue and action. The question posed in this chapter ('can schools make good citizens?') relates to the second of the two uses.

The 'Life in the UK' test that foreign nationals now have to take if they wish to settle in the country is a requirement for obtaining citizenship in the first sense. The Citizenship component introduced in the National Curriculum is aiming to develop those qualities associated with the second sense in young people who already have the status of 'citizen'. However, it is clear that the expectations we might have of citizens and the types of qualities or activities we might want them to display can vary dramatically. The next section will assess these different conceptions.

Conceptions of citizenship

What does the phrase 'good citizen' bring to mind? Commonly we think of activities such as turning out to vote at general elections, putting rubbish in the bin, helping elderly people across the road and staying on the right side of the law. Yet what about protesting against global poverty, campaigning for the rights of a discriminated group or refusing to obey an unjust law? Some people, at least, consider the latter to be things that a good citizen might do. It is clear that conceptions of citizenship are not uniform across society.

When we describe someone's political position, we usually use terms such as 'right-wing' or 'left-wing'. 'Right' and 'left' here relate first and foremost to the notion of 'equality', that is, those on the left believe that people should be equal and those on the right believe that equality is either undesirable or unviable. We can also distinguish between different views on liberty. At one extreme, there are authoritarians believing that individuals should be controlled by or subordinated to the state, and on the other, anarchists believing that the state should have minimal or no influence.

These categories, however, are insufficient for understanding the complexities of citizenship. We cannot distinguish neatly between ideal right-wing and left-wing citizens: for instance, free marketeers can be either patriotic or internationalist, as can socialists. Further distinctions are needed in order to understand the contested nature of the notion.

There is a very large body of literature on conceptions of citizenship (some of these works are listed at the end of the chapter). Much of this writing is recent, as the idea of 'citizenship' has gained popularity in both political philosophy and philosophy of education since the 1980s. One distinction commonly found is that between *liberal* and *civic republican* approaches (e.g. Kymlicka, 2002; Heater, 1999). In the former, the citizen is seen as the holder of a set of rights. In T. H. Marshall's (1950) well-known analysis, these are of three types:

- Civil (e.g. the right not to be imprisoned without charge)
- Political (e.g. the right to vote and stand for office)
- Social (e.g. the right to healthcare)

The citizen according to this conception is guaranteed protection and assistance by the state, and in return must respect its laws and the rights of others. Citizens can participate in politics and public life if they want, but they are not obliged to do so. In civic republicanism, on the other hand, this type of participation is essential. Being a citizen means having an active involvement in collective decision-making, whether at a local or national level. An example of civic republicanism is the ancient Athenian democracy, where all citizens (i.e. all free men – women and slaves were not included) participated in discussions and law-making. However, while a number of modern commentators call for 'participatory democracy' of this sort (e.g. Barber, 1984; Pateman, 1970) in practice most states today follow the liberal rights model.

Terry McLaughlin (1992) made an influential analysis of citizenship as a continuum from 'minimal' to 'maximal'. This continuum of interpretations related to four features: identity, virtues, political involvement and social prerequisites. In relation to the first of these, McLaughlin (1992, p. 236) states:

> On 'minimal' views, the identity conferred on an individual by citizenship is seen merely in formal, legal, juridical terms. . . . On maximal views, however, this identity is seen as a richer thing . . . Thus, the citizen must have a consciousness of him or her self as a member of a living community with

a shared democratic culture involving obligations and responsibilities as well as rights, a sense of the common good, fraternity and so on.

Another way of viewing citizenship is according to four dimensions: rights and duties; universality and difference; the local, the national and the global; and criticality and conformity (McCowan, 2006).

Rights and duties

Citizenship is very commonly described in terms of rights and duties (or responsibilities). Conceptions of citizenship differ in the extent to which they prioritize either one or the other. In the categorization outlined above, we can see that the liberal approach emphasizes rights, and the civic republican approach responsibilities. While some fight for greater attention to be paid to human rights, others complain that an overemphasis on rights has led people to forget their duties to others in society.

However, it is not only a question of balance but also of *which* rights and duties. In nineteenth century Britain (for the restricted part of the population that was considered to have full citizenship at least), there were substantial political and civil rights, but a largely free market system operated with little social welfare. In contrast, the Soviet Union in the twentieth century provided for substantial social rights, but few civil and political ones.

Universality and difference

Most conceptions of citizenship are *universal* in the sense that they see it as applying in the same way to all people. Societies across the world have changed considerably since the ancient Athenian democracy, and now it is rare for adults to be denied formal citizenship on the grounds of gender or race, for example. However, the status of *formal* citizenship does not always guarantee that citizen's rights will be upheld *in practice*. A number of movements emerged in the twentieth century decrying injustices against specific groups – such as people with disabilities – even when the individuals in question in a formal sense had full citizenship.

In addition, many thinkers – foremost amongst these feminists (e.g. Arnot and Dillabough, 2000; Yuval-Davis and Werbner, 1999) – have gone further to argue that there is something wrong with the very *universality* of conventional notions of citizenship. Unterhalter (1999, pp. 102–3) states that:

> . . . governments, through an appeal to an abstract concept of the citizen, stripped of all qualities save subjective rationality and morality, have been able to maintain and perpetuate social divisions based on gender, race ethnicity, sexuality and disability.

These theorists argue that *difference* must not only be tolerated, but recognized and allowed to flourish.

The local, the national and the global

In the modern world, citizenship is strongly linked with the nation-state. We are all (or almost all) citizens of a particular country, and it is in this national context that our rights and responsibilities are located. However, the challenges to the nation-state posed by globalization, and the need for solidarity and political action beyond national borders, has led some to call for a 'global' citizenship (see Delanty, 2000). Since there is no global state, this is citizenship in a *moral* rather than a *legal* sense. In conjunction with the expansion to the global level, there has also been a movement inwards to the local, captured in the slogan 'think global, act local'.

Criticality and conformity

Thomas Hobbes in his book *Leviathan* (1651/1996) proposed that an all-powerful state was necessary to reign in the destructive impulses of humanity. Later in the seventeenth century, John Locke (1690/1924) argued against him, saying that the people should have the right to judge their governments and remove them if necessary. Today, tensions remain between, on the one hand, the needs of unity and allegiance, and, on the other, that of a critical citizenry. The US philosopher William Galston argues against criticality, proposing that civic education should not require children to question their situation. He states:

> [R]igorous historical research will almost certainly vindicate complex 'revisionist' accounts of key figures in American history. Civic education, however, requires a more noble, moralizing history: a pantheon of heroes who confer legitimacy on central institutions and constitute worthy objects of emulation. (1989, p. 91)

Many commentators disagree, however. Will Kymlicka (1999, p. 82) states that:

> The ability and willingness to engage in public discourse about matters of public policy, and to question authority . . . are perhaps the most distinctive aspects of citizenship in a liberal democracy, since they are precisely what distinguish 'citizens' within a democracy from the 'subjects' of an authoritarian regime.

Given this range of issues on which concepts of citizenship can differ, it is clearly challenging to pin down the notion of a 'good citizen'. What we think a 'good citizen' is depends on our fundamental moral and political values, our ideas on the way society should be organized and on what human life is for. That does not mean, of course, that any one conception of citizenship is as good as another: we might put forward strong arguments that, for example, having an interest in political life is better than not doing so, both for the individual and society.

This multiplicity of conceptions has a clear bearing on our ability to answer the question, 'Can schools make good citizens?' It might be that they can make good citizens according to some conceptions and not according to others. It is very hard to show the relationship *generally,* that is independently of a specific conception. For the purposes of the subsequent discussion, therefore, I will make a broad stipulation of a 'good citizen' in a democratic society, one that has wide (but not by any means universal) acceptance. In the broadest possible terms we can say that citizens should be aware of, defend and exercise their rights (civil, political and social); respect, defend and enable the rights of others; and participate actively in the public sphere to further the common good as far as possible. Yet, can schools help form these citizens? And, if so, how?

Making citizens

As discussed above, there is a remarkable amount of recent literature on citizenship education. However, most of this is focused on the *aims* of citizenship education, or on the question of whether it should be compulsory in schools. Much less is written on the educational processes involved. Yet the question of *how,* if at all, citizenship can be developed through education is also highly problematic.

Knowledge, skills and values

The types of attributes that can be developed through education are often divided into the elements of knowledge, skills and values (although different varieties of these are seen, such as 'understanding' in addition to knowledge, 'capacities' in addition to skills, and 'attitudes' or 'dispositions' in addition to values). In relation to citizenship, these might consist of knowledge of political processes and current affairs, skills of analysis and communication, and values of fairness and respect for persons.

Yet, how can education develop these qualities in people? *Skills* can be developed through practice, either of the desired activity itself (e.g. flying a plane) or through a simulation (e.g. using a flight simulator). In citizenship education, simulations such as mock trials or pupil parliaments are often used to develop particular citizen capacities. *Knowledge* can be developed through reading and discussion – although the retention of that knowledge, and a more than superficial understanding of it, depends on more complex pedagogical processes. 'Traditional' forms of civics focus heavily on the knowledge element, particular that of government procedures and institutions.

The most complex of the three aspects, however, is values. Teachers can try to develop these through *exhortation*, that is, coaxing or coercing pupils into adopting certain values or dispositions. This is an uncertain business, particular in the context of a society in which many young people reject and sometimes rebel against the school system. An alternative approach is *exemplification*, by which pupils adopt values through seeing them practised by their teachers or perhaps embodied in the institution of school. This approach is surely more promising, but there is no way of predicting exactly what the responses of the pupils will be.

Values can also be adopted through critical reflection and understanding, but again the outcome of the reflections are hard to predict. The problematic nature of the very aim of instilling pedagogical values can therefore be seen. It would clearly be undesirable for values to be imposed on pupils, or absorbed by them without autonomously endorsing them. And yet, respecting learner autonomy makes the process highly uncertain. The difficulty of transmitting values is at the heart of the significant problems of promoting citizenship through education.

Neutrality and bias

Another pressing issue that citizenship education initiatives must address is the need for impartiality. If democratic citizenship is the aim, then indoctrination and the imposition of particular beliefs must be avoided. Furthermore, if our 'good citizens' must be critical and autonomous (rather than conformist, as discussed above) they must have had the experience of navigating through contested and controversial topics, rather than having a single view fed to them. Yet, is it really possible to avoid bias in teaching citizenship? Are there occasions on which it might be positively undesirable?

Much of the past opposition to the introduction of citizenship education in the UK has been based on the problems of maintaining political neutrality (e.g. Flew, 2000; Scruton et al., 1985; Tooley, 2000). Yet Bernard Crick (1999, p. 344) argues that:

> Neutrality is not to be encouraged: to be biased is human and to attempt to unbias people is to emasculate silence. Bias as such is not to be condemned out of hand, only that gross bias which leads to false perceptions of the nature of other interests, groups and ideas.

The Crick Report also proposes the inclusion of controversial issues, even when these may challenge core moral and religious values of the students. It advocates three possible ways in which teachers can approach neutrality when dealing with controversial issues:

- 'neutral chairman': allowing the pupils to express their diverse views
- 'balanced': presenting alternative viewpoints to those already expressed
- 'stated commitment': making one's views explicit, but encouraging pupils to decide for themselves (QCA, 1998).

There might be occasions, furthermore, when we would think a teacher entitled, and perhaps even duty-bound, to avoid neutrality. If, for example, a pupil is making racist or sexist remarks in class, an intervention from the teacher would seem appropriate and important. However, it is not clear where the line is to be drawn. Thinkers associated with *critical pedagogy* (e.g. Giroux and McLaren, 1986) drawing on the ideas of Paulo Freire (1972) assert that the teacher should at all times be committed to a political vision of justice and equality, so as to counter the hegemonic forces of capitalist oppression. Others argue that educators should avoid *substantive* positions (i.e. those presenting a particular political view) and instead adhere to *procedural* principles such as fairness, respect for reasoning and toleration (e.g. Crick and Porter, 1978).

James Tooley (2000, p. 145) states in relation to the Crick Report that:

> It is pretty easy to spot a tad of political bias creeping into the report at every stage. After all, '. . . ethical trading, peace-making and peacekeeping', and 'poverty, famine, disease, charity, aid, human rights', all seem to be recognizably the building blocks of a discernible political creed, one focused on the problems of underdevelopment, the evils of global capitalism and how the United Nations can put it all right. There is nothing wrong with holding such political creeds, of course, only one worries about how teachers will be able to teach such controversial issues without bias creeping in. [Original emphasis]

Is Tooley right in saying that the National Curriculum framework has a left-wing slant? Might it be possible to teach these issues without 'bias creeping in'? Is there anything wrong with 'bias' on these issues?

Sites of citizen learning

We come now to the heart of the question. Can schools really make good citizens? The answer depends on what we mean by 'school'. When we think of learning in schools, we normally think of classroom activities, but it is clear that with an area like citizenship, experiences in the corridors and playgrounds, relations with teachers and peers, and perceptions of and participation in school decision-making more broadly are likely to be as important. In addition, there may be many sites outside school in which young people can develop their citizenship – in fact, these may be *more* influential than school.

Ofsted (2005) reports have shown citizenship to be 'the worst taught subject at secondary level'. Problems are seen to have been posed by the delivery of citizenship through other subjects, rather than as a lesson in itself. Being a separate subject in a GCSE qualification will certainly enhance its standing in the school curriculum. Yet is citizenship an academic discipline at all, to be approached in the same way as History or Physics? Is it appropriate to assess and grade Citizenship as occurs with other subjects? Might there be advantages to a cross-curricular approach?

Classrooms

As discussed above in relation to knowledge, skills and values, there are many ways in which citizen qualities can be developed in the classroom. Through discussion and teacher explanations, knowledge can be acquired on political institutions and their functioning, and understanding gained of key concepts. Simulation activities can be used to develop experience in arenas to which children and young people do not normally have access, such as courts of law, councils and parliaments. General academic skills, such as literacy (or ideally 'critical literacy' – Halstead and Pike, 2006) are also important.

There is another quality emphasized in the literature – deliberation – that classrooms may be well positioned to develop. 'Deliberation' is engagement in reasoned discussion with others, presenting one's views in a way that is comprehensible and respectful, and allowing all to have their voices heard. It has become a popular concept amongst philosophers (see, for example, Enslin et al., 2001) searching for ways to reconcile the diversity of modern societies with the need for a shared public sphere. John Rawls (1971, 1993), for example, argues for the use of 'public reason', through which issues are discussed on the basis of principles that all can share, rather than, in Brighouse's (2006, p. 68) words, 'appeals to revelation, to the authority of purportedly sacred texts, to naked self-interest, and to personal and unreproducible experience'.

The multi-cultural classrooms of state schools in countries like the UK and USA seem ideally placed to develop the skills and dispositions of deliberation necessary in a diverse society (see Gutmann, 1987). However, not all accept that it is possible, or desirable, to let go of deeply held beliefs like religious revelation in political interaction. This is certainly the case in recent elections in the USA, where the Christian fundamentalist vote has been pivotal.

The school as a whole

Yet, despite these possibilities, there are strong reasons for believing that citizenship is learnt as much outside the classroom as inside it. To a large extent, this is because of the importance of what is sometimes called the 'ethos' of the school – in McLaughlin's (2005, p. 311) words, 'the prevalent or characteristic tone, spirit or sentiment informing an identifiable entity involving human life and interaction'. These features of school life are sometimes referred to as the *hidden curriculum*. In the school context, two areas in particular are likely to shape our attitudes and actions as citizens: the relation between teachers and students, and the decision-making systems in the management of the institution. The extent to which students feel themselves respected by their teachers, have their opinions listened to and see themselves valued in their individual and group identities (or alternatively, learn through fear of punishment, subordinate their views to those of the teacher or textbook and are ridiculed or humiliated) will clearly affect their development as political actors. The work of the US philosopher of education John Dewey (1916) made the link in this way between the *processes* of schooling and the development of democracy, arguing for an enquiry-based, problem-solving approach.

Secondly, schools as institutions can be run in more or less democratic or inclusive ways. The current school system in the UK allows some choice to pupils in terms of their daily activities, but gives them little say in the running of the school and even less in the content of the curriculum (even teachers and parents have only very indirect influence here). School councils and the like have been encouraged in recent times in order to enhance pupil participation in the running of schools. Even setting aside the question of whether children have a *right* to have a say in decision-making that affects them, there are strong arguments in support of participatory bodies like these in terms of pupil learning: as an opportunity for developing the abilities of deliberation, for considering conflicting interests and exercising responsibility, and for developing democratic attitudes and values (the limitations of UK school councils in practice notwithstanding).

Seen in negative terms, citizenship education is very unlikely to succeed if students perceive a contradiction between the message and the medium, that is, if people are taught to be democratic and inclusive in an undemocratic and exclusive manner. A *harmony* between ends and means will enhance the potential of an initiative for developing democratic citizenship (McCowan, forthcoming).

In addition, the relationship between school experiences and later life is not a straightforward one. We cannot be absolutely certain that democratic schools will create democratic people. Neither can we be certain that an open classroom will create critical thinkers. Radical thinkers like Karl Marx, Antonio Gramsci and George Orwell emerged from education systems that were largely inimical to this type of thought, so by the same measure, uncritical, anti-democratic people may emerge from open, democratic settings. In response, it could be argued that there is a moral imperative to run schools in a democratic fashion, whatever the consequences. (And despite the lack of certainty, our intuition tells us that democratic schooling is, at least, *likely* to produce democratic citizens.)

> The way that a school is run, and the way a child sees her place in it, may influence the traits developed. I am emphatically not suggesting that schools should be internally democratic; children are children, and it is appropriate for adults to exert a certain amount of paternalistic power over them. But it may well be important that the school be seen to be set up for the benefit of all who inhabit it. It might be important, for example, that teachers exhibit a certain level of collegiality and solidarity, and that they and principals treat non-teaching staff with respect, as well as treat children with similar dignity and respect (Brighouse, 2006, p. 73).
>
> What distinction is Brighouse making here between being 'internally democratic' and treating people with 'dignity and respect'? In what circumstances might it be right for schools not to be democratic? What benefits might showing respect for pupils and staff bring?

The wider society

Yet even taking into account this broader perspective of school learning (i.e. one that acknowledges ethos and relations), is school really the most effective or most appropriate place for young people to learn to be good citizens?

Children and teenagers spend only a portion of their lives in schools, and a great part of the general moral development that underpins their values as citizens takes place in other arenas, or has already taken place in the family context by the time they start school. Yet even in relation to specifically political learning, non-school arenas are important. It can be argued that just as you cannot learn to ride a bicycle without actually riding one, so citizenship cannot be learnt without exercising it. John Stuart Mill (1861/1991), the nineteenth-century British philosopher, argued that people could best learn citizenship through the holding of public office and participation in public activity such as jury service. While these particular activities are not generally available to those of school age, other experiences of political life may be (campaigning, participation in public debates etc.). In this way, the Crick Report advocates 'community involvement' as one of its three strands.

However, it is important to distinguish between 'volunteering' and 'political participation' here. While both are aimed at bringing positive change in society, volunteering is based on the principle of charity, and political participation on the principle of justice. If we are concerned about homelessness, a charity perspective will aim to mobilize resources from those who are wealthy and have time to dedicate in order to provide the necessary housing. From a justice perspective, this is both uncertain (it is not clear how long this provision will last) and potentially disempowering (making people feel they are 'charity cases' rather than bearers of rights). Instead, attempts will be made to bring new laws, or enforce current legislation, so as to uphold all people's right to a home.

In this way, young people can be involved in volunteering activities (helping at an old people's home, setting up a local nature reserve etc.) or political activities (campaigning, letter writing, protest, participation in public debates etc.). In practice these activities cannot always be sharply distinguished, as many charitable organizations (such as Oxfam or Actionaid) do engage in political campaigning, even if they are not politically affiliated. However, 'citizenship', by definition, involves those aspects that are political rather than purely charitable.

We can justify the participation of young people in these activities on the basis of the actual results brought about. Yet, beyond the effects of the participation, there are benefits in terms of the learning of the participants. First, knowledge of issues and skills of discussion, decision-making and political action can be gained. While simulations within schools can also develop these skills and knowledge, the learning is likely to be enhanced by the real context of participation. Moreover, there are aspects that can only be gained from real rather than stimulated participation. The lack of participation of young people in political processes can, at least in part, be attributed to their sense of inability to bring change. In many ways, their apathy is therefore not due to laziness, but due to a rational decision that participation is not worth the effort. A sense of efficacy of political participation can only be gained through an actual experience of bringing change. Clearly, not all of the experiences engaged in by young people will actually be positive in terms of the results. In cases where they are not, young people can still develop valuable understanding of the conditions in which forms of participation can and cannot bring change.

Conclusion

Brighouse (2006) and others (e.g. Rooney, 2004) argue that citizenship in schools cannot be a panacea for problems that have their roots essentially in the limitations of our political system. It is clearly wrong to place the responsibility for the problems of citizenship solely on the shoulders of teachers and schools. Nevertheless, as has been discussed above, schools do have an important role, affecting our development as citizens in all sorts of ways, some obvious and some more subtle. Attention, therefore, needs to be paid to the effects of schooling on citizenship, whether or not this involves a subject called citizenship. Yet it is equally clear that schools are not the only influence on this development. A simple answer to the question posed in this chapter, therefore, is that schools can make good citizens, but only in conjunction with other arenas in society.

However, we are thrown back to our original discussion of what is meant by 'citizenship'. It is impossible to answer the question of whether schools can make good citizens without first addressing what we mean by 'good citizen'. (Unfortunately many discussions on education in the media, and even in academic circles, do not make this initial step.) If the notion of a 'good citizen' is a law-abiding and patriotic subject willing to sacrifice herself for the nation, then study of a noble 'pantheon of heroes' through history and literature in schools is likely to be effective. From this perspective, school councils and circle time will certainly seem irrelevant. If, however, our aim is to create citizens able and willing to critique the current system and change it for the better, than attention must be paid to the relations and management of schools as well as its content.

Still, the central tension of citizenship education remains. Does not any attempt to instil a *specific* form of citizenship on pupils through education – one that has been predefined by others – go against the principles of democracy and respect for persons who are supposed to inspire the undertaking in the first place?

Further reading

Chapter 7 of Kymlicka (2002) provides a comprehensive overview of general debates on citizenship in political philosophy. Implications of these debates for education are explored in Callan (1997) and Brighouse (2006) [chapters 4, 6 and 7], particularly with regard to the tension between the competing demands of liberty and democratic participation in a liberal society. Bridges (1997) brings together a range of studies on education and democracy, addressing themes such as nationalism, the family, markets and autonomy. Lockyer et al., (2003) focuses more closely on citizenship in the National Curriculum, discussing the complexities and flaws of the provision, while Bailey (2000b) draws out the implications of citizenship for individual National Curriculum subjects.

Useful websites

Association for Citizenship Teaching, a professional organization for teachers of citizenship:

http://www.teachingcitizenship.org.uk

Citized, resources for teacher education in Citizenship:

http://www.citized.info/

Citizenship Foundation, an Independent charity promoting democratic participation:

http://www.citizenshipfoundation.org.uk/

Should the State Control Education?

Judith Suissa

Introduction

Think about the following remarks:

> 'The government should spend more money on education.'
> 'Alfie has just turned 5; he'll be starting school in September.'
> 'We're moving to a better area because we want our children to have the best possible education.'

We frequently encounter statements like these in our everyday conversations, and they make perfect sense to us. Yet behind them all are some assumptions common not just in popular discourse, but in a great deal of academic work on education. These assumptions are as follows:

1. That education is a process that mainly goes on in schools.
2. That these schools are controlled by the state.

However, neither of these is necessarily true. For most of history, children's education and upbringing was largely the responsibility of their parents. While the form and content of the education children received varied enormously amongst different cultures, social classes and historical periods, it was generally up to parents and communities to decide exactly how to educate their children. For much of history, children learnt a trade or craft through a system of apprenticeship. Although schools have existed in some form for a very long time, they were often available only to privileged and wealthy members of society, and in many countries, until quite recently, were controlled by religious authorities.

It is only in the second half of the nineteenth century that the state became directly involved in the provision of education in most Western countries. Many historians link this process to the rise of the modern nation state and the associated processes of industrialization and urbanization. The story of the way in which various social, political and economic factors contributed to changes in the provision of children's education is a complex one, yet by the beginning of the twentieth century, across most of the industrialized world, the model of state controlled, free, compulsory schooling had become widely accepted. Indeed, the fact that statements such as the opening ones seem so unproblematic to us is evidence of the way in which the association between the state and education has become entrenched in our thinking.

The model of schooling that has recently come to characterize education in most of the Western world, involves,

> the attempt to standardise curricula, school architecture, teaching practice and school behaviour; the regularisation and enforcement of school attendance of all children of what came to be understood as school age, and the enforced non-attendance of those deemed too young; the undermining of parents' custodial role over their offspring; the gradual loss of control by local communities, individuals, parents – and eventually the teachers themselves – over what went on in the school; and a considerable expansion of social space controlled (in theory at least) by the state. (Miller, 1989, p. 2)

Historians differ in their accounts of the story behind the eventual acceptance of state education. It seems plausible to accept, with Miller, that it was a combination of complex factors, and to recognize that, in many instances, the causality goes both ways – with state education both influencing and being influenced by issues to do with family structure, patriarchy and employment patterns. One clearly cannot understand the rise of state education without some understanding of the growth of the modern, capitalist nation state. But it is important to separate out questions about the *causes* of a phenomenon from questions about the *reasons* for it. In other words, while it may be true that the spread of industrialization and the mass migration of people towards urban centres created a need to provide trained workers for the economy, and thus played a causal role in the establishment of universal state schooling, one can still ask questions about whether the state's need for a skilled workforce constitutes a good *argument* for supporting state education. It is also important to separate out questions about what defenders of state schooling claim it *should* be doing – what it is *for* – from questions about what it is *actually* doing. Answering these questions is never a straightforward matter of collecting data, but – like most issues in education – involves critical judgement and discussion of moral and political values.

Even the familiar argument that compulsory, free state schooling was an essential step towards increased educational opportunities and widespread literacy, is challenged by a wealth of historical evidence documenting the prevalence of independent working-class educational initiatives in literacy and adult education (see Johnson, 1979) and the wide uptake of places in private schools even amongst the poorest sectors of the population in Victorian England, long before the 1870 Education Act. So it is important to bear in mind that, as Miller suggests, 'State schooling was at one and the same time imposed on working people, resisted by them, and fought for and used by them' (Miller, 1989, p. 6).

So, arguments about the advantages, disadvantages, uses and abuses of state education are never straightforward. But sometimes, looking beyond our own historical and political reality to a period when state control of education was by no means taken for granted, can help us to unpick some of these arguments and the assumptions behind them, and to think clearly about the values behind many of our ideas about education.

At the time that the idea of state schooling was becoming accepted, the intellectual ground around it   and, indeed, around the form of the modern nation state itself – was still very much contested. There were those who argued forcibly for the practical and political advantages of state education, and some of these arguments have survived in the narratives we often tell ourselves about why state schooling is a good thing: children have a right to a broad education that will enable them to function fully as adult members of society; they should be protected from the world of labour; they should not be prey to indoctrination by religious authorities; they should not be denied educational opportunities because of their parents' financial situation. And indeed, there is no question that the establishment of free, compulsory state schooling in many countries has played a vital role in ending the widespread practice of sending children out to work in factories and fields in order to contribute to the family economy. However, at the same time that these important advantages of state schooling were being defended, dissenting views were expressed from various political perspectives against the very principle of the state being directly involved in children's education. Some of these positions continue to play a role today in critiques of schooling, and they often take the form of an argument about what it is that schools *actually* do. Thus, a common critique is that while state schools are presented as a progressive force, freeing children from work and offering them a liberating, broad education, in fact what they are doing is a form of social control: oppressing children by institutionalizing them and instilling certain values and patterns of behaviour in them. Theorists differ as to the extent to which they think a sinister agenda of social control is, or was, a conscious motivation behind the establishment of state schooling. But from a philosophical point of view, the interesting question is the values behind this argument about the oppressive nature of schooling.

The argument from autonomy

On one view, a strong commitment to individual autonomy leads to the conclusion that society is not morally justified in intervening in the educational development of the individual.[1] Thus any form of education imposed on the child constitutes a form of oppression. This is the view defended by libertarian thinkers such as A. S. Neill and John Holt, and it is often traced back to Rousseau, who, in his classic eighteenth-century educational treatise, *Emile*, outlined his vision of the ideal education of a young man brought up free from the corrupting influences of the wider society.

In his important political treatise, *The Social Contract*, Rousseau famously declared: 'Man is born free, yet everywhere he is in chains', thus laying the ground for the view of children as naturally good. As philosophers of education have discussed, there are serious questions as to the extent to which Emile is genuinely free to follow an unhindered course of individual educational development. But the 'growth metaphor' associated with this view – the idea that the child is like the young sapling, who, provided with the right conditions for growth: water, sunlight and air, will grow into a tree – is an enduring one that has featured over the years in libertarian, progressive or 'child-centred' traditions of education. (For an interesting discussion of this metaphor and its educational influences, see Darling, 1994.) However, this position is not concerned particularly with the role of the state in education, but with the idea that *any* intentional intervention in the educational process is morally problematic. Thus A. S. Neill, the founder of the famous Summerhill School and one of the most well-known proponents of libertarian education, was committed to the view that children should be allowed to determine their own values, becoming self-regulating, autonomous individuals, and that nobody – including parents – had the moral right to try and direct this process. 'Children will turn out to be good human beings if they are not crippled and thwarted in their natural development by interference' (Darling, 1982, p. 68).

Thus, presumably, Neill would not have had any principled objection to the state setting up and funding schools, provided they were all places rather like Summerhill, where children were essentially free to determine the form and content of their own education. The problem, for such theorists, is not the fact that the state as such is involved in education, but the fact that the form and content of this education – and indeed the decision as to whether, when and where it takes place – is determined by an agent other than the child herself.

In order to grasp the significance of this point, it may be helpful here to distinguish between three levels of state intervention. Tooley, drawing on Barr (1993), points out that 'there are three levels at which states can intervene in education: provision, funding and regulation' (Tooley, 2003, p. 427). Provision refers to the level of supplying buildings and paying teachers' salaries; funding refers to the direct use of public funds to offer free school places to children; and regulation refers to the laws governing, for example, compulsory attendance, school-leaving age, the curriculum, and assessment mechanisms and qualifications.

So, for example, it would be perfectly possible in theory for a state to fund schools, but not to intervene at all in the regulation of the curriculum, the structure of the school day, and so on. Some theorists have argued for a kind of voucher system, which would enable children to purchase educational services from a variety of providers, some of which may be regulated by the state, but the choice amongst which would, ultimately, be left to individuals. On this view, inevitably, it is parents who are charged with the responsibility for making choices about educational provision for their children.

Key Questions

In 1999, Ofsted threatened to close down Summerhill following an inspection that questioned the value of the school's libertarian educational philosophy. The teachers and students fought a legal battle, which they won. You can read about this battle, the history of the school, and recent Ofsted and press reports on the school website: http://www.summerhillschool.co.uk/

Would you send your child to Summerhill?
Do you think schools like Summerhill should be supported in a liberal society?

Parents and communities versus the state

Unlike libertarians, who are more concerned with the form of the educational process itself rather than with questions regarding state intervention in its provision, many of those who advocate greater freedom from state intervention at the level of educational regulation assume that children need some sort of guidance in order to flourish. However, they argue that it is not up to the state to determine the form and nature of this guidance. Some proponents of this view believe that parents are the only people morally justified in deciding on the aims and content of their children's education. They might, then, support various forms of home-schooling, or independent schools set up and run by parents and communities.

But even if one disagrees with Neill's view that children will turn out to be good human beings if they are largely left to their own devices, there is still a great deal of disagreement as to just what the 'interference' in their natural course of development should consist of. What is it that children *need* in order to 'turn out to be good human beings'? And who has the right and the duty to determine this? It is often acknowledged that, as future members of a society, children need to be inducted into the values and skills appropriate to that society. If the relevant society happens to be a liberal state, then the argument is often made that there are certain minimal skills, abilities and values that children need in order to grow up to be adults capable of fully flourishing in this state.

In examining these arguments, however, it is important to bear in mind the distinction between different levels of state intervention mentioned above. Thus, even accepting that the aims of education ought to be determined by the wide community in which a child is growing up – that, in the liberal democratic state, they should be, as John White has argued (White, 2005), democratically determined by the political community – does not necessarily lead to support for state intervention at the level of provision and funding. The state could simply lay down a set of agreed qualifications required of all children before they be allowed to participate in the liberal democratic political community, but leave it to individual parents to decide when and how to obtain such qualifications.

> What do you think children need in order to flourish as adult members of contemporary British society? Could you compile a list of appropriate skills and knowledge? Who should determine such a list? Do you think it would be possible to arrive at a broad consensus over what should be included in it, and what should be excluded?

Interestingly, the idea that it is parents, not the state, who have the primary moral right and duty to educate their children, is one that goes back to J. S. Mill, often regarded as the father of modern liberalism. Mill, in his classic work, *On Liberty* (1859) was concerned to establish the limits of the legitimate use of power on the part of society over the lives of individuals. His central idea is summed up in the Harm Principle, which states:

> The only purpose for which power can be rightfully exercised over any member of a civilized community, against his will, is to prevent harm to others.

Individuals, in other words, should be free to act as they wish so long as their actions do not interfere with others' freedoms. Decisions as to the form and content of children's education should, according to Mill, fall within this sphere of individual liberty, for the reason that the diversity and free experimentation amongst different life-styles that he saw as so essential to human flourishing would be undermined by a uniform system of education. The state should only step in, he argued, in cases where parents were incapable of fulfilling their duties with regard to their children's education:

> A general State education is a mere contrivance for moulding people to be exactly like one another . . . An education established and controlled by the state should only exist, if it exists at all, as one among many competing experiments, carried on for the purpose of example and stimulus . . . (Mill, pp. 117–18)

The requirement that all citizens achieve a certain level of education in order to function as competent adult members of society was, according to Mill, to be met by requiring everyone of a certain age to pass a public examination 'confined to facts and positive science' (ibid., p. 119).

Some parents may wish to hire a private tutor, some may want to take advantage of schools set up by communities or the Church; some may keep their children at home until the age of 10 and cram all the preparation for the exams in later; it was no concern of the state, so long as all children achieved the basic level of competency. 'If the government', Mill argued, 'would make up its mind to require for every child a good education, it might save itself the trouble of providing one. It might leave to parents to obtain the education where and how they pleased, and content itself with helping to pay the school fees of the poorer classes of children . . .' (ibid., p. 117).

There is something appealing in the idea that one can lay down a minimal list of the capacities and knowledge required to function in society. Yet in pluralistic, technologically advanced societies, this is not straightforward. Positions such as Mill's raise questions as to whether there can be such thing as 'facts and positive science'. The contents of curricula and the pedagogical processes involved in teaching them are, inevitably, imbued with values, whether implicitly or explicitly, and judgements about what to include – and what not to include – in any 'minimum' curriculum that are based on normative positions and arguments.

Faced with the apparent impossibility of reaching any consensus as to what such a 'minimal' education would consist of in modern, multi-cultural societies, it may be tempting to revert to the view that it should be up to parents and communities to determine the form and content of their children's education. Such positions, however, run into difficulties when it appears that the values and ways of life that parents are passing on to their children are at odds with those underlying the very structure and legitimacy of the liberal state.

Arguing from within a commitment to liberalism as a political and moral framework, many contemporary philosophers of education have thus developed rigorous theoretical positions of the aims of education in a liberal state, looking closely at connected questions to do with parental rights and duties, the rights of children, the requirements of citizenship and the relationship between the liberal state and communities.

Whereas for Mill, the minimal education required was pretty sketchy and thin, contemporary liberal theorists have argued that in a liberal democracy, which depends for its legitimacy on citizens' capacity for democratic participation, it is essential that future citizens develop the capacities necessary to sustain this political framework and to flourish in it as individuals. There is a diversity of opinions amongst contemporary philosophers even within the liberal tradition as to how 'thick' this minimal requirement should be. As Strike points out, 'a view of liberalism in which the socialization requirements of citizenship were so substantial as to preclude an adequate range of views of the good life would fail to do what liberalism chiefly intends to do: that is, to make it possible for people to live according to their own views of the good' (Strike, 1999, p. 50).

Nevertheless, some theorists have defended fairly thick accounts of precisely the kind of education necessary to enable individuals to pursue their own 'views of the good' within a broad commitment to liberal values.

Most contemporary liberal theorists would be uneasy with the removal of state regulation of education, arguing that the liberal state depends on the value of autonomy, and that only a neutral public education can guarantee that children develop autonomy and appreciate its significance. This view is connected to the central liberal principle of legitimacy, according to which the state is legitimate only if it can be justified to the various diverse communities and individuals who belong to it, all of whom may hold different conceptions of the good. This idea is developed in Rawls' theory of political liberalism (see Rawls, 1971, 1993).

So many liberals, committed to the central value of autonomy, would argue that the state would be justified in intervening to prevent parents or communities from educating their children into ways of life that hindered their ability to develop autonomously. Disputes around such issues illustrate the ways in which questions about education often reflect questions about the meaning and limits of individual freedom.

One famous case that highlighted these issues is '*Wisconsin v. Yoder*'. In this landmark legal case, a group of parents from an Amish community in the USA refused to send their children to school beyond the age of 14, arguing that attending a state high-school would be a threat to the continuity of the Amish tradition, religious beliefs and way of life. The State of Wisconsin fined the parents and ordered them to send their children back to school but they appealed to the US Supreme court, who ruled that the state's application of the compulsory school attendance law violated the parents' constitutional right to free exercise of religion.

This case raised several important philosophical questions. Do parents have a right to bring their children up into a particular religious way of life? Are there restrictions on the kinds of ways of life we would regard as acceptable in this context? What, if any, are the rights of children? Joel Feinberg, looking at these questions, has defended the notion of the 'child's right to an open future'– arguing, on the basis of the liberal commitment to autonomy, that children have the *right* to an education that does not close off options for meaningful lives, as 'an education that renders a child fit for only one way of life, forecloses irrevocably his other options' (Feinberg, 2006, p. 82). Interestingly, Feinberg agreed with the majority decision in Wisconsin, arguing that the children in question had already been exposed to an autonomy – promoting 8 years of primary education, during which they had acquired basic literacy and other skills that would equip them for life in society, even were they to choose to leave the fairly closed, traditional rural world of the Amish community. Had the parents insisted, on the grounds of their religion, on removing their children from all state education, the child's right to an open future would have trumped the religious freedom rights of the parents. However, one could still question to what extent the Amish children in question are really 'free' to leave their community, and what this would mean. Likewise, there are complex philosophical questions around what degree of 'openness' is desirable or even possible when it comes to children's upbringing. For an interesting discussion of the idea of the child's right to an open future, see Mills, 2003.

Do you agree with the court's decision in Yoder?
What would you have decided?
Do you think that the individual right to religious freedom extends to the right to pass on religious beliefs and ways of life to one's children?

Marketizing education

What about the argument that we should remove all levels of state intervention in children's education? One contemporary theorist who has offered such an argument is James Tooley (2000) who, in his book *Reclaiming Education*, argues for a complete withdrawal of the state from the role of funding and provision of education, retaining only a very minimal regulatory role.

Tooley is not a libertarian thinker; he does not believe, like Neill, that children should just be left alone to grow up, or that any planned intervention in their natural course of development constitutes a form of oppression. Thus he shares the liberal intuition that children need some kind of guidance in order to grow up into flourishing adults. Likewise, he shares the liberal view that, as future citizens of a particular political framework, children need to acquire certain skills and capacities. As he puts is, everyone has a right to 'a sufficiently good education for them to function adequately in the economy they will face as adults'. What he rejects is the assumption that the state is the best or the most efficient way to provide this.

Citing examples of private initiative in other areas – for example, the supermarket chains that supply most of our food – Tooley argues that the mechanism of the market is a more efficient way to ensure the provision of this 'sufficiently good education'. Of course, many of the questions that we asked above about Mill's idea of an education 'confined to facts and positive science', can be asked about Tooley's ideas about just what an adequate minimal education consists of. Most critics of his position, however, have focused on another aspect of this debate: the link between educational opportunities and socio-economic positions.

Many liberals, especially those on the 'egalitarian liberal' end of the spectrum, believe that the state has an important role to play in minimizing socio-economic inequalities amongst its citizens. One argument for state control of education, then, is that requiring that all children have access to state-funded, state-regulated schools is the best way to guarantee that they all enjoy equal educational opportunities, which in turn will guarantee relatively equal socio-economic opportunities.

Thus calls for a complete privatization of the education system have prompted criticism from many liberal philosophers of education concerned that this would undermine the goals of equality of opportunity. The classic argument for this position is drawn from Rawls, and states that 'educational inequalities due to family background circumstances or family choices are unacceptable' (Brighouse, 2000, p. 118). The fear is that if educational provision was entirely left to individual choice and was supplied by private initiatives, 'more advantaged parents would secure a better education for their children leading to even greater socio-economic inequalities' (ibid.).

Tooley, however, argues that market mechanisms *would* be better able to guarantee fair and equal educational opportunities. It is important to recognize that the question here is largely an empirical one, and there is certainly no disputing the empirical point, often made by Tooley, that so far it does not look as if state education in Western societies has done a great job in eradicating or even minimizing socio-economic inequalities. However, the crucial point is that the empirical evidence amassed by Tooley to suggest that, in certain situations, private initiatives *can* guarantee an adequate minimal standard of education, does not constitute enough support for the argument that they *will*, and therefore is not sufficient to justify removing state control. As Brighouse notes, for the justice requirement to be met, it is essential to *guarantee* that private initiatives comply with it. And it seems fairly plausible that, given existing socio-economic inequalities, guaranteeing this will require some level of state regulation.

Tooley argues that in the same way that the existence of different big brands of supermarkets across the country, for example, guarantees 'consistent quality' in the products available to shoppers who choose to use these supermarkets, so private suppliers of education, driven by the pressures of the market and the demand for brand consistency, would provide consistent quality of educational services. Yet as Brighouse points out in his criticism of this analogy, 'brands go where it is profitable to go, and not where it is unprofitable' (Brighouse, 2000, p. 62). So relying on the profit motive of private companies is not, most liberals agree, likely to ensure that all children benefit from fair and equal educational opportunities. While many people may agree with Tooley that modern states, so far, have not done a very impressive job of reducing socio-economic inequality through publicly funded schooling, they would suggest a range of other ways to make educational opportunities more equal; for example, by abolishing private schools, or increasing government funding in deprived areas.

> Do you think that there is already a degree of privatization/marketization of education in Britain today?
> Should we allow more private educational initiatives in the education system?
> What would be the advantages and disadvantages of such a move for parents?

What all these discussions indicate is that the question as to whether or not schooling would be *better* in terms of the adequacy and fairness of its provision, if the state were to be removed completely from the equation, depends at least partly on the socio-economic status quo.

Interestingly, what both Tooley and most liberal thinkers have in common is a certain acceptance of the status quo. Indeed, John Rawls, commonly regarded as the most important contemporary political thinker, constructed his elaborate defence of the principles of political liberalism on the assumption that a certain degree of social-economic inequality is both inevitable and necessary. Some theorists, however, have begun from a far more radical challenge to both the socio-economic status quo and the very framework of the state.

Challenging the state

What all the theorists referred to above, from Mill to Tooley, have in common is that they assume the existence of the state as more or less inevitable. Even Tooley, often referred to as 'radical', in his concern to 'reclaim education from the state' does not question the underlying values of the liberal state, nor does he see the state framework itself as problematic; he simply does not believe that it is not the most efficient way to deliver education. In fact, most contemporary political theorists assume that the nation state, in some form or another, is here to stay. Some, notably Robert Nozick, have offered a theoretical defence of the argument that the state is, at the very least, a necessary evil.

However, there is a long tradition of radical critics of state education who are motivated by a vision of a society without the state. As early as the eighteenth century, before state education was established, anarchist thinkers were arguing against its very idea: 'The project of national education,' wrote William Godwin, in 1793,

> ought uniformly to be discouraged on account of its obvious alliance with national government. [. . .] Before we put so powerful a machine under the direction of so ambiguous an agent, it behoves us to consider well what it is that we do. Government will not fail to employ it, to strengthen its hands, and perpetuate its institutions . . .

Although Godwin's position is fairly close to Mill's position on individual liberty, it was later developed by nineteenth century social anarchist thinkers. Although it is problematic to offer an exhaustive definition of anarchism as a political ideology, people who, throughout history, have called themselves anarchists, ranging from individualist to socialist ends of the political spectrum, share a few key commitments. Crucially, they object to the state as a model of political organization, and are suspicious of all hierarchies, promoting instead a model of a decentralized, self-governing society. While anarchist thinkers shared Mill's objection to imposing a single model of education on children, unlike Mill, they did not believe that autonomous individuals could flourish within the framework of the liberal state, as they saw the very structure and institutions of the state as inimical to authentic human freedom. Their critique centred on the capitalist, free-market state system, which they regarded as perpetuating structural inequalities and hierarchical relationships between people. In defending their alternative vision of a stateless community, they saw constructing educational projects free from state control as a means to both undermine the power of the state and promote alternative experiments in human living.

On the anarchist view, the school should be a microcosm of alternative society, demonstrating non-hierarchical relationships based on mutual aid and individual freedom. While anarchist educators shared some of the pedagogical principles developed by libertarian thinkers, they were not motivated by a belief in individual freedom *per se* but by a vision of a free, just and equal society. Thus although they often advocated non-coercive pedagogy, they did not believe – as Neill did – that moral or political neutrality in education was either possible or desirable, and they promoted explicit moral and political values through their curriculum and school ethos.

The Escuela Moderna, 1904–1907

In 1904, Francisco Ferrer, a Spanish anarchist, set up an anarchist school in Barcelona. In an open challenge to the control of education by the Catholic Church, he declared in his prospectus: 'I will not ram a dogma into their heads. I will not conceal from them one iota of fact. I will teach them not what to think but how to think' (Avrich, 1980, p. 20). The school was coeducational, open to children from all socio-economic backgrounds, and there was no system of examinations, rewards or punishments. There was no set timetable, and children were allowed to come and go as they pleased. The classes on offer combined practical training and field-trips with theoretical learning, thus reflecting the central anarchist idea, developed by Kropotkin, of 'integral education'. Ferrer saw his school as a vanguard of the future anarchist society where hierarchical divisions between classes would be broken down and where, in the words of Proudhon, 'the industrial worker, the man of action and the intellectual will all be rolled into one'. Although Ferrer was executed by the Spanish authorities in 1909 and the school closed down, his ideas were taken up by anarchist educators at the beginning of the twentieth century who established similar schools in many countries across the world, including Britain and the United States.

Many anarchist activists set up anarchist schools that were often part of self-governing experimental communities. Such schools taught children about internationalism and pacifism, promoted the values of solidarity and mutual aid, and rejected all nationalistic, militaristic and religious messages. Anarchist educators were not just rejecting state control of education and asserting the rights of the individual to make educational choices, but were actively promoting a positive model of an alternative kind of society without the state.

Marxist positions

Early Marxist thinkers shared many of the social anarchists' suspicions of state education. However, their objection was not to the state as such, but to the capitalist state that, they argued, would inevitably reproduce its own structural inequalities. This critique can be followed through to the work of contemporary Marxist critics of state education, who have developed sociological analyses of the effects of state education, drawing on Marxist reproduction theory. For Marx, the economy, defined as the mode and relations of production, is the base of society and the corresponding social and political arrangements (e.g. education) are the superstructure. The general conditions of social, political and intellectual life and consciousness are determined by the basic structure of society, so the only way to change human consciousness is to change this structure. On this view, education in capitalist society is oppressive because it reproduces the relations of domination – that is, class domination – of society and the values of the dominant class. There are various versions of 'reproduction theory' or 'correspondence theory'. Some have argued that state schooling is a mechanism by which the bourgeoisie ensure the production of future generations of workers by training children in the skills and attributes of the working class, thus preserving the economic status quo. Other theorists have developed the idea that the cultural background and aptitudes of middle class pupils are rewarded by the school and translated into 'cultural capital', which translates, in turn, into more powerful socio-economic positions, while the cultural capacities and attributes of working class children are not recognized as part of official school knowledge. Later Marxist theorists offered an important supplement to this rather depressing view that the school inevitably reproduces socio-economic inequalities, by developing theories of resistance, notably the idea and practice of Critical Pedagogy that could lead to critical consciousness and subvert the structures and knowledge of the oppressive system.

Another tradition that offers a radical challenge to the model of state schooling is that of 'deschooling.' This position was first articulated by Ivan Illich who, in *Deschooling Society* (1970), argued that it is not education *per se* which is problematic, but the institutionalization of education which, similar to the institutionalization of other social functions – healthcare, care for the elderly, childbirth – has created a dependency on institutions. The modern, industrialized state, in this view, has become a 'schooled society', obsessed with certification, selection, social control and the 'ritualisation of progress'. Illich, like other radical thinkers, draws our attention to the point that *schooling* and *education* are not the same thing, and argues that the monopoly of schools prevents other social institutions from becoming truly educational. The only way, Illich argues, to recover a genuinely educational alternative is through the establishment of 'learning networks' based on spontaneous, voluntary cooperation.

Conclusion

Taking a broad historical perspective on questions about state education forces us to ask not just: what are aims of education in the liberal state, and what are the rights and duties of the state, parents and children, but also to pose far more radical questions about the very framework of the state, its underlying values, and their justification.

This chapter does not purport to have answered these questions. It does suggest, however, that thinking about such issues demonstrates that questions about what our society should be like overlap so much with questions about what education should be like 'that the two cannot sensibly be kept apart' (White, 1982, p. 1).

There is an important tradition of schools and other educational experiments that have existed, and continue to exist, outside state control. Some of these, like Summerhill, focus on individual freedom; others, like anarchist schools, seek to challenge the very framework of the state as a form of political organization. Considering some radical alternatives can remind us that our thinking about education does not need to be constricted by the familiar frameworks of our existing political systems.

Further reading

For work by contemporary philosophers of education on the aims of education in a liberal state, see: Callan, 1997; Feinberg and McDonough, 2002; Gutmann, 1987; White, 1996 and, particularly on the central role of autonomy, Levinson, 1999 (especially Chapters 1–2). For a fascinating history of the anarchist school movement, see Avrich, 1980. A more general discussion of libertarian educational ideas can be found in Smith, 1983. For a philosophical analysis of the anarchist educational position, see Suissa, 2006. A classic Marxist study of the effects of state schooling is Bowles and Gintis, 1976. A central work in the area of Critical Pedagogy is Freire, 1972.

Note

1. For a fuller discussion of the idea of autonomy and compulsory education, see Gereluk, in this volume.

Educational Opportunities – Who Shall We Leave Out?

9

Carrie Winstanley

Introduction

Education is not funded very generously in comparison with many other social services and as a result there is fierce competition for scarce resources. With competing needs from myriad deserving causes, the policy-maker is hard pressed to meet the requirements of children in education and to appease their advocates. This chapter considers the very real issues faced by those who decide how best to support children and young people who have need of resources and/or services beyond those provided through mainstream education. These children and young people do not constitute a homogenous group; they comprise an enormous range of different people and even those who are dedicated to enhancing their educational experience cannot always agree on what they need, or even how best to characterize their needs, abilities, wants and desires.

Some of the other questions tackled in this section have a direct bearing on how we answer the question of providing educational opportunities. For example, if philosophers, policy-makers and educators cannot agree upon what education is for or what should be taught in schools, wondering about how to ensure access to education seems rather pointless. In answer to the question about whether or not children have rights, it would seem inappropriate to assign fewer rights to those who have educational difficulties.

In answer to the question 'Who shall we leave out?' this chapter will cover a range of issues, largely concerning equality and the fair distribution of educational resources. The particular case studies concerning who should be prioritized in terms of receipt of educational goods will relate mainly to children with special educational needs, as this is where the most emotive and vociferous arguments tend to rage. A section on educational opportunity will be followed by discussion of various types of equality and the notions of what children and young people merit and what they deserve in terms of education (known as 'desert'). Ideas of inegalitarianism and elitism are then examined and the chapter finishes with the application of these ideas to practical cases of pupils and their needs and a conclusion. Further readings will be highlighted as appropriate.

Educational opportunity

An understandable instant reaction to the issue of educational opportunity would be to assert that all should have equal opportunities. This seems uncontentious. On closer examination, however, it is not clear exactly what is meant by equality of opportunity, or even what opportunities are in question. If we are thinking about educational achievement, we could quite simply lower the expectations and requirements of education, giving all the equal opportunity to achieve the basic minimum, such as fundamental literacy and numeracy and little more. This would be cheaper than the system we currently employ, would be simpler to apply (in some senses) and could deliver absolute equality. It implies, of course, that where possibilities exist for only some pupils to train for national level sports, or learn the violin, all should be denied these chances in the name of equality. This of course is ultimately unfair and is an impoverished understanding of education.

Although most teachers would subscribe to an ideal of educational equality, this is surely not what they have in mind; a more careful account is needed, and breaking down some of the concepts in the equality debate should help deal with this issue. In order to comprehend the arguments in this field of education, largely to do with political philosophy and social justice, it is important to be clear about definitions of key words being used. We need to think carefully about what we understand by equality, egalitarianism and fairness. Despite first appearances and rather counter-intuitively, there is no real reason why everything should be equalized. It may well be that the unequal distribution of resources and provision for pupils ultimately allows for greater fairness. Think of the children with a visual impairment who need a specific kind of Braille text to complete their work. They should get this, but not everyone needs such resources and so we have unequal use and distribution of specialist materials to make education more fair for all pupils concerned.

Of course there are broader and narrower ways to look at this issue; at the level of school policy there may be differences that relate to the distribution of goods than at the wider level of social policy. How people feel about these issues reflects the extent to which they consider the role of the school as levelling the social playing field. If the school must put right the societal equality that exists, those schools in difficult areas, with less supportive communities should be funded more generously in order to compensate the children for a lack of family support (financial and otherwise). In such cases, it is perfectly acceptable to pursue a non-egalitarian distribution of goods in order to achieve fairness. It might be that you think the state ought to give everyone the same; after all, middle class parents pay significant taxes and any extra funds they might choose to use for education outside of school is their own choice. They should still, therefore, be entitled to schooling with maintenance of proper funds. The difficulty here is that funding would likely be directed towards both predominantly middle class schools as well as those in less privileged areas which would probably entrench some of the existing inequalities. This may not be a concern if you believe education to be about making the most of what you have, rather than as a tool for social change.

Responses to the vexed questions of who gets what in education will depend on what you think are its aims and purposes.

May be, against most teachers' instincts, there is more reason to be inegalitarian than to be egalitarian in terms of distributing resources. Both egalitarianism and inegalitarianism are imprecise terms (Winch, 1996, p. 128) and although at first it seems obvious to side with equality, on closer inspection it may be that in order to demonstrate 'a genuine commitment to meeting everyone's educational needs' (White, 1994, p. 180), an anti-egalitarian stance should be adopted.

Think again about what follows from the principle of equality of treatment. If we apply this notion of equality, it: '. . . requires that goods and outcomes be allocated equally to all, regardless of factors of entitlement, need or desert' (Winch, 1996, p. 115).

Few teachers would want to ignore the important nuances of entitlement, need and desert when deciding how to allocate resources. If you know the pupils with whom you work, you want to be sure that they are fairly provided with what they require to maximize their capabilities, even if this differs from pupil to pupil. As Swift (2001, p. 92) summarizes:

> What matters is not that people have equal shares of good things. Nor is it even that people have equal opportunity (or access to) good things. What matters, if we think about it, is that everybody has enough, or that those who have least have as much as possible, or that people who most need things take priority.

Differentiating again between social and school policy, while most teachers would agree with Swift about what matters, they would also want to take into account the principle that 'members of a political community should be treated as equals, that the state should treat its citizens with equal concern and respect' (cited in Swift, 2001, p. 93). This notion is described by Kymlicka as an 'egalitarian plateau':

> Considering these ideas in more detail leads us to the different aspects of equality tackled through the literature: equality of resources; equality of outcome; and equality of opportunity.

Equality of resources

Concerning the distribution of resources, some training and learning is simply more expensive than others and it would be both unnecessary and prohibitive to allow for fund-matching for all potential pupils and also for all adult students. At first sight, Wilson's suggestion seems logical; he suggests that resources should be awarded to those who can 'profit from them most'. What is meant though from 'profit most' and how could this be predicted? It could be to do with giving education to pupils who can attain the highest examination grades, but that would mean giving the most to highly able pupils from advantageous backgrounds which is definitely not what most teachers would choose. However, if 'profit' is considered to be 'adding value', disadvantaged, disabled or weaker students should be key beneficiaries; if 'profit' is measured by enjoyment, children with an enthusiastic disposition would be rewarded by resources, and so on. How would we measure how profitable the investment has been and what would happen if it failed to reap the predicted benefits?

There is a difference also in terms of the age of the students and the phase of education. In the early years, pupils have little say over what kind of education they receive and it may be more important here to ensure that fair resource distribution is guaranteed. Adults, however, are generally freer to make their own choices, although access to Higher Education is often decided around the early teen years, with some groups of (less privileged) people ruled out and others all but guaranteed participation. It would seem fair to ensure that as many people as possible have choice about their educational provision and this would imply an inegalitarian distribution of resources, compensating people from impoverished backgrounds when necessary. Resources should thus be distributed according to need, favouring those from difficult backgrounds in order to increase the likelihood of their success.

Equality of outcome

Equality of outcome is another seemingly simple concept that is, in fact, open to a range of interpretations. It is unclear at which point the outcome should be measured. The obvious measure would be pupil achievement (such as, having five top grades in the school-leaving certificate, or being functionally literate). But just because these are common goals, they are not the only possibilities. Outcomes can concern attitudes, values or even just experiences (although these are more difficult to measure). Imagine a school system where the overall aim is for all pupils to leave as 'useful citizens' or where the outcome is measured merely as 'participation in x years of education'. Winch (1996, p. 115) defines the idea:

> Equality of outcome is a principle of equality that asserts that the endpoint of a process ought to be the same for everyone who goes through it.

However, it can be difficult to define the 'endpoint' and the 'process' – do we mean the end of each phase of education, or the very end of all education? Winch's definition could be interpreted along a spectrum from a weak to a strong conception. A weak notion would require something like the National Curriculum which is a fairly rich minimum of educational experience, covering a reasonable range of subjects and considering that children should emerge from school with roughly the same set of life skills. A much stronger interpretation would require specificity about the school experience, or process, perhaps implying less diversity in schooling. In order to allow everyone to achieve the same endpoint, teaching would have to be in far smaller groups, or minimum levels would need to be set at a fairly low level. In some countries where a more egalitarian stance is adopted (e.g. in Sweden and some Australian states) this kind of equality is more commonly found, with able children prevented from joining enrichment programmes to stop them outstripping peers and upsetting the equality of outcome.

Equality of opportunity

For the purposes of this chapter, the most useful discussion of equality of opportunity can be found in the work of Swift, where three understandings of the concept are identified: 'minimal'; 'conventional'; and 'radical' (p. 91). The 'minimal' view considers that people's gender, religion or race must not prevent them from opportunities in areas such as education and employment. This is uncontroversial and a fairly basic understanding of fairness and equality. The 'conventional' view goes further, suggesting people's competencies should be considered above their gender, religion or race. More significantly, the conventional view requires that people should have had an equal chance to acquire the competencies in the first place, which implies a compensatory role for education in the case of pupils with impoverished backgrounds. Since this cannot be guaranteed, the conventional view might lead instead to restrictions or demands on certain practices in the home, such as supporting children with homework. Without equalizing parental support, 'conventional' equality of opportunity cannot be assured, but most would baulk at some of the measures that might have to be taken.

The third conception of equality of opportunity is labelled 'radical' and 'requires that untalented children – whether rich or poor – should have the same opportunities as talented children' (p. 102). This is radical in the sense that we normally apply some kind of notion of desert or merit to the allocation of resources. If we ignored this and gave all people the same opportunities, we would have to revise policy-makers' structures and values, including meritocratic aims where children are provided with what they deserve, rather than all being treated the same.

What is meritocracy?

Consider this definition of the principle of meritocracy:

> . . . each person's chance to acquire positions of advantage and the rewards that go with them will depend entirely on his or her talent and effort. In such a society inequalities in different people's life chances will remain, but social institutions will be designed to ensure that favoured positions are assigned on the basis of individual merit (talent times effort) and not allocated randomly, or by ascriptive characteristics such as race or gender, or by the machinations of the already powerful. (Miller, cited in Brighouse, 2002, p. 177)

To which of Swift's conceptions of equality of opportunity do you think Miller would subscribe, 'minimal', 'conventional', or 'radical'? How have you reached your conclusion?
  Miller holds a notion of merit being 'talent times effort'. What do you think of this idea? Does it match the way that resources were allocated when you were at school? Is it more / less fair than your own experience?

Desert and merit – who deserves provision?

Is merit something that is earned, or is it a question of being born in the right place at the right time? Generally in education we rarely talk about 'deserving' provision; we speak, rather, of being 'entitled to' resources, opportunities and experiences. No one would want to deny a child with a disability the chance to participate in the same activities as their peers wherever this can be practically realized. In considering 'desert', it is more controversial and challenging to think about one area of inclusive and special education that does not always get an airing; that of provision for more able children. Such pupils may well need additional or different activities, resources or experiences if they are to make the most of their talents, but since they may have been endowed with these abilities through their genes, or the fortuitous family into which they were born, do they deserve extra or particular provision?

Rawls (1971) considers that people cannot be held accountable for their degree of talent and that luck plays a vital role. Brighouse agrees, arguing against 'desert' as a principle for distribution of educational resources. Both prefer a system that favours the underprivileged and less talented:

> . . . natural ability, like social class background is something we cannot reasonably be held responsible for, [. . . this] suggests a strongly compensatory principle, that significantly more educational resources should be spent on the less able than the more able. (Brighouse, 2000, p. 40)

The aim is to achieve social justice and most people would, at first sight, agree with this notion. However, popular opinion departs from this when it comes to how much adults are entitled to earn, as they are generally happy to support a society where some earn more than others, even when this difference is for reasons beyond the control of the participants.

Again, Swift usefully provides us with summaries, showing contrasting views of 'desert' which he labels as 'conventional', 'extreme' and 'mixed' views. The 'conventional' view is the one already noted that allows for inequality in earnings and supported by popular understanding. The 'extreme' view disallows reward for effort as well as talent because it is considered that how hard someone works is out of their control. In this view, it is irrelevant whether a strong work ethic is in-born or instilled at an early age, but it is clear that this should not be an incentive for higher pay. The 'mixed' view allows for rewarding aspects that people can control and choices they have made, but not rewarding people for their existing good luck. Rawls rejects this mixed view as he considers it impossible to discern which aspects of someone's performance can be derived from their own efforts and which come from luck.

Teachers in the West tend to hold the mixed view when it comes to deciding which children should receive rewards (such as being in a top stream or participating in enrichment activities). Children are expected to demonstrate both parts of the merit equation (using their 'given' talent with maximum personal effort). As a result, children can be disqualified from rewards if they are considered to be lazy and this sometimes happens even when there are extenuating reasons for underachievement, such as learning problems. The Western attitude is that a work ethic is well within an individual's control and any given talent should be properly utilized; children not living up to these requirements can comfortably be left out of provision as they have not earned participation, in this view. (This notion contrasts with Asian and Pacific Rim cultures in which talent is viewed exclusively as the reward of effort. University places and other such educational privileges are distributed entirely on the basis of a conception of talent as success earned through endeavour.)

Who would you reward?

As class teacher to a group of 9-year-old pupils, you have access to one place on an off-site enrichment course at a local university. Whoever you send along will spend the day with lecturers in the media lab, building website pages together with other Year Four pupils from all over the borough. Look at these pupil profiles. All fall under the school definition of 'able' yet none have participated in any enrichment so far this year. Who will you leave out?

Jay lacks confidence in his own abilities, but teachers suspect that he is more able than he appears at a first glance. He is shy and tends to keep quiet in class. He has shown particular interest in computing, mathematics and reading.

Daisy has problems with the basic mechanics of reading and writing, but is confident orally and is clearly very able, often producing the most original and interesting responses to set tasks. Her favourite subjects are music and drama.   ⇨

> Tom is able and a high achiever; he works very conscientiously and is better than average at most school subjects. He is well liked and enjoys sports as well as his more 'academic' schoolwork.
> Jordan has a hearing impairment and needs a signer with her for all lessons, although she prefers to play without an adult nearby at playtime and she manages to communicate effectively. She is adept at using the computer and is interested in most subjects at school.

Is it acceptable to be inegalitarian?

The first response to this question would more than likely be 'no'. Considering egalitarian policies as vital should help to stamp out elitism and unfairness. Most educationists reject the idea of elitism; it seems counter-intuitive to disallow access to services for anyone. Of course, elites can be simply those who are the best at something, such as Olympic athletes or international orchestra members. Refusing access to the Olympic team to someone with no athletic prowess who has not undertaken any training would be perfectly reasonable. However, in general, and certainly in school, we want all pupils to have opportunities to explore their abilities and have as many interesting experiences as possible. So far we have seen that this may not be as straightforward as it may first seem. In order to allow for this, within the realism of school budgets, there will be some inequity in resource allocation.

Are you elitist?

The UK organization for the country's most distinguished scientists struggled with this notion fairly recently. See here an extract from the discussion about its funding and membership policies:

> The Royal Society, by its very nature, is an elitist organisation. What else can a national academy of science be? Its whole raison d'être is to represent the best of science in this country. [. . .] The word elitist means different things to different people [. . .] elitism has (also) become an all-purpose boo word for condemning any kind of exclusivity, justifiable or not. One doesn't want to be elitist in the sense of saying 'we're only going to have white men' or 'we're only going to have people who went to Oxford', [. . .] the society has an historic problem. (Watts, 2002, p. 18)

Thinking about elitism, consider these questions and think of reasons for your answers in relation to your understanding of elitism and how it fits into your ideas about the purpose of education:

1. Would you characterize the Royal Society as an elitist institution? Does it have a place in contemporary society?
2. Is it possible to have a non-elitist society that is a monarchy?
3. Should parents always be allowed to pass their wealth to their children?

4. Should people from difficult backgrounds be allowed lower grades as passes for entrance exams when applying for organizations such as orchestras, the police force, fee-paying schools and the army that are usually dominated by the wealthier members of society who can afford more thorough preparation?
5. Have you ever been a member of a group that was not open to all? If so, how do you consider this relates to the notion of elitism?

One educational philosopher has noted that rejecting both egalitarianism and equality, does not imply embracing unfairness. He says that meeting children's needs should be separated from valuing equality, and emphasizes that equal access to leading a flourishing life need not mean equal distribution of goods (White, 1994, p. 174). He cites Raz, emphasizing that the real concern is for the suffering or need of the individual in question, not merely to create equality. The redistribution of goods is in order to relieve hardship (ibid., p. 175). According to White, this supports the notion that '. . . one has good reason to attend more to the needs of those more lacking' (ibid., p. 180).

Brighouse also modifies his support for the notion of equality of opportunity, finding it only to be a desirable ideal if qualified by other principles to stop it undermining more important values. Swift also highlights the complexity of the notion:

> It is perfectly coherent to reject equality at the philosophical level, as a fundamental ideal, while arguing that, for other reasons, resources should be more equally distributed – perhaps much more equally distributed – than they are at present. (2001, p. 92)

Let us bring this back to children in schools who have particular needs that lie beyond the normal curriculum offer. It would be inegalitarian in some senses to match provision to children's needs as meeting some will cost more than meeting others. It seems unlikely that anyone would defend the removal of support for children with disabilities on the grounds of it costing more for children than for those who do not need specialist equipment. Here, Rawls' notion of ensuring the greatest benefit to the least advantaged trumps the underlying desire for equality.

Inclusion and the field of 'special education'

Part of this title is in inverted commas as the field itself continues to wrangle over how best to talk about children with additional educational needs. Some people continue to use the phrase 'special educational needs' while others object to the use of any label at all. Since the first schools for children with additional needs were established in the nineteenth century, there has been controversy about whether provision should be segregated or integrated and to what extent all children should be expected to meet the same standards as those in mainstream schools.

As the way society understands disability and difference has developed, there has been a shift away from seeing a difficulty as being within the person as a kind of defining characteristic. In its place we have a broader concept of trying to embrace difference and show where society should be more usefully adapted to ensure that all its members have an equal chance to participate at every level; the right not to be excluded. As a result of this gradual shift, in the field of education for pupils with learning difficulties, disabilities, sensory impairments and other problems, the debate about the nature of inclusion has dominated in recent years. The National Association of Head Teachers define this as follows:

> Inclusion is a process that maximises the entitlement of all pupils to a broad relevant and stimulating curriculum, which is delivered in the environment that will have the greatest impact on their learning. All schools, whether special, or mainstream, should reflect a culture in which the institution adapts to meet the needs of its pupils and is provided with the resources for this to happen. (Cited in Warnock, 2005, p. 41)

The notion of inclusion is to ensure that no-one is left out at all, but of course it is more complex than a simple assurance. There are wrangles about what is meant by the terms 'inclusion', 'integration' and there are vociferous voices that advocate opposite ideas as perfect solutions. Some people have found the experience of being educated in a segregated school to be damning, isolating and disastrous, while others attest to the freedom, confidence and support they have felt through being in a school that was only for people with problems similar to their own.

More recently there has been some use made of Sen and Nussbaum's capabilities approach to helping support people with additional needs. This notion cuts through the discussions about which support should be made policy, adopting a different angle. The issue is about the capability of the individual to participate fully in society. It is not about whether one has any kind of impairment, but the extent to which successful educational experience is prevented or facilitated.

The nature of difference

The great concern is the fairness of provision for those who have additional needs that are not met at all, or only partially met, through 'normal' mainstream school provision. Children who fall under this definition would include (but not be confined to) children coping with the following issues:

- mobility difficulties
- sensory impairments

- cognitive impairment
- learning difficulties
- autism/Asperger Syndrome
- mental health problems
- long-term medical conditions
- Attention Deficit/Hyperactivity Disorder (ADD/AD/HD)
- social/behavioural/emotional difficulties
- cultural disadvantage

Look at this non-exhaustive list and consider the issues in relation to the following points:

1. How differently do the issues present themselves when you consider them from the standpoint of being difficulties located within the child, rather than problems of participation caused by societal structures?
2. Thinking about the standard National Curriculum, consider what adjustments need to be made to accommodate pupils with the concerns listed?
3. Would it be possible and helpful to group these difficulties in any coherent way to support pupils better?

Conclusion

In order to make useful policy about sharing resources in education, there needs to be shared and agreed understanding of what counts as fair provision for children and young people. The principles used to distribute resources must be founded on reasonable argument and should not be based on the idea of equality being synonymous with uniformity. Individual and group needs must be taken into account and choices must be explained coherently.

This chapter reviewed the key issues concerning fair distribution of resources to young people and children. Through breaking down the idea of equality it is possible to see the complexities that underlie the decisions made by policy makers and teachers. Concepts such as merit and desert were discussed as these issues are often used as reasons for providing or holding back certain privileges or favours. The text boxes allowed for readers to consider their own values concerning how they would allocate assets to children and to reflect upon their own experiences of being favoured or denied. Notions of inegalitarianism were explored and the chapter then applied some of these ideas to the field of inclusive education and special educational needs.

Further reading

Useful sources that explore and extend some of the themes discussed in this chapter are included in Ruth Cigman's (2006) collection of chapters in her book on inclusion and exclusion.

Chris Smith (2003) asks the question 'Can inclusion work for more able learners?' Adam Swift's (2001) *Political Philosophy* is an excellent introduction to the subject. John White (1994) is an important contribution to the debate on egalitarianism in education.

Useful websites

TeacherNet has information and guidance on issues of educational equality:

http://www.teachernet.gov.uk/wholeschool/equality/

UNICEF has a global perspective on equality and education with a particular emphasis on gender equality:

http://www.unicef.org/girlseducation/index.php

The Human Development and Capability Association promotes research from many disciplines on problems related to impoverishment, justice, and well-being:

http://www.capabilityapproach.com/Home.php

EENET is a global information-sharing network on the issue of inclusive education, hosting debates about inclusion and rights in education:

http://www.eenet.org.uk/bibliog/scuk/schools_for_all.shtml

Should Parents Have a Say in Their Children's Schooling? 10

Dianne Gereluk

Introduction

The question of whether parents should have a say in their children's schooling is contentious. The pendulum can swing drastically with parents having little to no say in nationalized education systems to circumstances where parents have incredible discretion and decision making at the other end of the spectrum. Some believe that it is the parents' right to raise their children in a particular way, others argue that it is a privilege (Levinson, 1999; Reich, 2002a). Parents' ability to make decisions and influence their children's upbringing range in multiple ways, for example, the school their child attends, what is taught, the learning style that is used, the ethos or community of the school, the type of governance of the school, and the decision making input by staff, community, parents and children. These philosophical dilemmas have tangible policy implications including greater school accountability measures, voucher schemes and charter schools, greater parental and community involvement, home schooling initiatives, and greater or lesser communication lines between schools and parents. The extent to which parents have a 'right' in these matters greatly determines the type of schooling a child will experience.

It is rare that parents have a complete say in how their children are schooled, and conversely, it is rare that parents have little to no say in developed nations. Defining the acceptable parameters of how much of a claim parents have in raising their children in a particular way is incredibly complex and difficult. Before we turn to the arguments for and against, you may wish to reflect and consider what your initial thoughts and positions are regarding parental rights.

To what extent should a parent have a say in their child's schooling?

If you were a parent, would you want your child being challenged about the values and beliefs that are shared in your family?

What avenues are already in place for parents to have a say in their children's schooling at your local school?

Are there varying opportunities for parents to have a say depending on whether their children attend primary or secondary schooling? State or private schools?

Should there be more or less opportunities for parents to have a say?

Arguments in favour of parental rights

Three common arguments are given for increasing parental rights in their children's schooling:

- parents are the best people to protect their children's interests;
- parents have a natural right to raise their children in a particular way congruent with their norms and values;
- if the state believes in freedom of the individual, then it must not interfere with the rights of parents to pass on their values and beliefs on to their children.

Let us consider these arguments accordingly and consider their merits.

Argument 1: parents are the best people to protect their own children's interests

A strong case is usually made that parents will do the best job in fostering and protecting their children's interests. John Locke made this explicit when he wrote:

> God hath woven into the Principles of Human Nature such a tenderness for their Off-spring, that there is little fear that Parents should use their power with too much rigour; the excess is seldom on the severe side, the strong byass of Nature drawing the other way. (Locke, 1960, p. 355)

The correlation that a strong bond will lend itself to securing the best interests of the child commonly follows. Parents will have greater insight into their children's best interests, and because this bond is not easily broken, parents have extra incentive and reason to ensure that their child flourishes. John Kleinig states:

> There is some reason to think that the developmental needs of children are likely to be met most successfully in an environment in which primary responsibility, and the authority that is derivative of that, lies with the parents. There are grounds or believing that parents, more than anyone else, will have the kind of commitment to their offspring that will safeguard and promote their welfare interests, and encourage the formation of an identity and life-plans compatible with their individual character, abilities, and talents. Parents, therefore, are permitted a wide range of discretion so far as the treatment of their children is concerned. (1983, p. 145)

The strong attachments and commitments that parents naturally exude to their children is the primary justification for primary authority resting with parents. As such, defenders of this argument claim that parents are best placed to protect the interests of their child.

Argument 2: parents have a natural right to raise their children in a particular way that is congruent with their norms and values

This argument has two interesting interpretations and consequences for why parents may have a right to raise their children in a particular way. The first claim suggests that in attempting to give birth to a child, the parents must make certain sacrifices in their own life in order to have a baby. They may accrue financial stress in the extra costs associated with having a child. Emotional stress is commonly experienced by adults in trying to conceive a child along with the potential risk of miscarriages, and the continual stress of raising a child that accompanies the job description of all parents. Similarly, physical sacrifices may result, particularly by the mother, who may be impeded by being pregnant for nine months, and may go through a difficult labour.

In potentially understanding the risks and potential negative aspects of child rearing, parents may claim a right to raise their child in a particular way given the associated costs and risks of raising a child. The claim is that one of the major benefits of raising a child may be, in fact, to raise them in a particular way that is similar to your worldview and lifestyle. This is a less commonly used argument for increased parental say in children's schooling, but it is one that is nonetheless propagated as a legitimate right.

A more common argument is that parents have a right to raise their children in a particular way that is akin to their own particular beliefs and values. Bruce Ackerman (1980) argues that young children are dependent upon their parents, both physically and emotionally, and developing autonomy must be thought as a slow, gradual process. Attempting to inculcate in the child various moral and religious doctrines would be foolhardy; what is required is some form of stability, where the child receives some moral foundations from their parents and their immediate environment. Once the child has some solid understanding of the morals and values passed down from the parents, it is at that point that the child can become introduced to broader and contradicting moral doctrines. Ackerman writes:

> While an infant may learn English or Urdu or both, there are limits to the cultural diversity he can confront without losing a sense of the meanings that the noises and motions might ultimately signify. Exposing the child to an endless and changing Babel of talk and behaviour will only prevent the development of the abilities he requires if he is ever to take his place among the citizenry. (1980, p. 141)

Ackerman does not believe that subscribing to a 'primary culture' will necessarily indoctrinate the child; rather, conflicts between parent and child invariably arise as the child becomes older challenging established moral codes and pushing the set boundaries as defined by the parents.

Will Kymlicka suggests that a right to culture should be included as a primary right often neglected as a fundamental freedom. Kymlicka (1989) suggests that liberal states need to protect collective group rights because belonging to cultural membership may be a primary precondition for an individual's sense of identity. For a state not to protect the interests of a group would greatly hinder and impinge on one's identity if that community were to dissipate. He states:

> (1) that cultural membership has a more important status in liberal thought than is explicitly recognized – that is, that the individuals who are an unquestionable part of the liberal moral ontology are viewed as individual members of a particular cultural community, for whom cultural membership is an important good; and (2) that members of minority cultural communities may face particular kinds of disadvantages with respect to the good of cultural membership, disadvantages whose rectification requires and justifies the provision of minority rights. (1989, p. 162)

If individuals have a right to cultural membership, one may apply Kymlicka's principle to the notion that parents have a right to induct their children into their particular cultural membership. It is naïve to suggest that children can remain outside of the community of which their parents are a part.

Argument 3: the state should not interfere with the rights of parents to raise their children in a particular way

Whereas argument two suggests that parents have a right to raise their children in a particular way as part of their 'primary culture' (as Ackerman suggests) or as a right to their 'cultural membership' (as Kymlicka argues), this argument comes from a different angle. The claim here is that if we believe that a society should foster respect and diversity within a liberal ideal, then one may argue that within this ideal, allowing parents to raise their children within certain beliefs and values should be honoured within the principles of toleration and diversity.

This falls in line, largely, with a libertarian viewpoint that calls into question the involvement of the state in the private sphere of the family. Non-interference by the state is an essential criterion amongst Libertarian perspectives. The fear of intrusion by the state should not be underestimated. Judith Shklar (1989) argues that the intrusion of the state is akin to a form of tyranny of control over the lives of children.

Mainstream liberal thought raises similar concerns about the degree to which the state should become involved in the private lives of individuals. Rawls (1993) argues that because we do not have decisive ways in which to decide what counts as reasonable and unreasonable, we must have strong grounds to suggest that some doctrines are intolerable and unacceptable in society, 'otherwise our account runs the danger of being arbitrary and exclusive' (ibid., p. 59). So, despite our belief that some views are contrary to the principles of free and equal persons, we may still have to *tolerate* them within the boundaries of reasonable pluralism. The idea that the state should have an arm's length approach can be applied in the unnecessary interference in the ways that parents should raise their children.

While advocates of this position call into question the perceived increasing 'nanny state', a similar critique may simply be that states are less effective in attending to the protections of all children. Children require enduring relationships rather than a mere benevolence from a range of providers (Goldstein, Freud and Solnit, cited in Callan, 1997, p. 138). Orphanages are a good example. Despite the state's good intentions in fostering care to children who do not have a parent or guardian, the general perception is that states do a fairly poor job in providing a good quality of life for those children.

While the aim of the state may be to ensure that a minimum threshold of protections are secured for all individuals, this may not necessarily provide the most robust or vibrant upbringing for children.

Before moving on to contrary arguments for why parents should not have a say in their children's schooling, let's review the arguments and consider whether you are persuaded by the claims that are made.

In what ways might parents do a better job in looking out for the best interests of their children?

Can you think of any instances when a parent may (consciously or subconsciously) hinder the child's best interests?

What are the advantages and disadvantages of having parents pass on their values and beliefs to their children?

Is the state becoming too interfering in the lives of families?

Can you think of instances when it is appropriate for the state to become involved in the private lives of families?

Arguments against parental rights

Counter argument one: parents, although well intentioned, may not be the best equipped to know how to foster the best interests of their children

Although value is often placed on the parents' rights to raise their children in similar beliefs and values that are consistent with the family, one should not assume that parents will necessarily have the multitude of skills that will help to foster children in a well rounded way. While a parent's love is arguably the most intense, it does not necessarily follow that parents will have intellectual skills to foster rational deliberation and critical thought necessary for children to make critical judgements about how they wish to lead their life. Meira Levinson argues that 'even the most liberal or autonomy-loving family cannot escape the conceptual and emotional bounds of its own commitments; nor can it ensure the child's honest exposure to that which the family would find utterly foreign or repugnant' (1999, p. 61). Despite the care and trust that parents may exude, it is near impossible to detach one's familial values in order to develop a range of critical capacities essential for the development of children's future autonomy. In schools, children are exposed to many different individuals from different perspectives and levels of expertise that will foster the development of the child.

This argument is often used in circumstances where parents not only want a say in their child's schooling, but wish to facilitate much of their children's schooling. An obvious example of this is homeschooling, but it can apply to those families that are geographically segregated within a particular community with little to no exposure to alternative lifestyles. Rob Reich (2002a) considers the concerns that homeschooling poses for the development of children's autonomy. While Reich is not outright opposed to homeschooling, he calls for greater regulations and monitoring to ensure that children's minimum autonomy is protected. And one of the concerns is simply that parents may not be well enough equipped to provide an education that will meet the needs of a child. If homeschooling is to be permitted, Reich contends that 'parents must demonstrate to relevant education officials that their particular homeschooling arrangements are up to educational standard' (2002a, p. 169). It is not enough to trust parents; basic regulations and monitoring must be implemented to ensure that children are not compromised by parents' potential limited to areas of certain knowledge and understanding.

Counter argument two: children should be exposed to alternative ways of life that are counter to their upbringing

This argument focuses primarily on the concern that parents may not expose their children consciously or subconsciously to alternative ways of life counter to their upbringing. Allowing parents to have the primary say in a child's upbringing may significantly limit their exposure to alternative values, beliefs and experience. This includes challenging the assumed beliefs and values of one's own family, and deciding for oneself whether that is the way they wish to lead their life.

A primary aim of education is to provide a multitude of opportunities that both support and challenge one's assumptions. Harry Brighouse argues:

> Autonomy-facilitation requires a modicum of discontinuity between the child's home experience and her school experience, so that the opportunities provided by the home (and the public culture) are supplemented, rather than replicated, in the school. (2006, p. 22)

For Brighouse, the role for schools is not just supporting and extending the family's belief system, but providing opportunities to deliberate about different perspectives, particularly those that are incongruent with one's family values. Children's critical judgement and informed decisions rely on the ability to understand and have the opportunity to pursue various experiences that may not be afforded to them within the family unit. Levinson more boldly states that:

> . . . it is difficult for children to achieve autonomy solely within the bounds of their families and home communities – or even within the bounds of schools whose norms are constituted by those held by the child's home community. If we take the requirements of autonomy seriously, we see the need for a place separate from the environment in which children are raised, for a community that is defined not by the values and commitments of the child's home, whatever they happen to be, but by the norms of critical inquiry, reason and sympathetic reflection. (Levinson, 1999, p. 58)

It is not a mere preference that children should be exposed to different experiences in order to secure autonomy, but a necessity. This exposure must be located in a school that challenges the established values and norms of the community. Exposure to and participation in varied experiences and alternative ways of living help to secure individuals' capacities to lead a life of their own will as adults.

If we allow parents to have a primary control over their children's schooling, children may have limited exposure to alternative lifestyles in at least a couple of ways: (1) parents who may be economically disadvantaged may have fewer opportunities to provide their children with multiple experiences; and (2) parents who consciously choose not to expose their children to alternative lifestyles either as a way to shelter them from harm or to make them more complicit within the set value system of the family (Gereluk, 2006, pp. 122–9). Despite parents' inabilities or reservations about limiting their children's exposure to alternative lifestyles, schools have the ability to provide children with opportunities to be exposed to and participate in different meaningful experiences. Further, if left to parents, children will have differing levels of exposure and opportunities. And while schools will not level this out, providing a school system that attends to a number of different experiences will reduce such inequalities. If one agrees with the assumption that a primary aim of education is to promote autonomy in children, then arguably it is integral that a school system be developed that supports this aim. In order to secure children's abilities to make informed judgement and choices about how they wish to lead their life, both in the present and in the future, we cannot leave it to chance to hope that individual families will provide sufficient exposure to alternative lifestyles.

Counter argument three: the state has a particular role and right in developing a political education for children that is consistent with the rights and responsibilities of the political society from one generation to the next

The final argument builds on from argument two in that not only should schools serve the purpose of developing autonomy in children, they also have the duty to develop civic virtues that are necessary for the sustainability of a vibrant political society. The vitality of a democratic state depends on, 'an education adequate to participating in democratic politics, to choosing among (a limited range of) of good lives, and to sharing in the several sub-communities, such as families, that impart identity to the lives of its citizens (Gutmann, 1987, p. 42). Amy Gutmann argues that this development of civic virtues in children is not a mere ideal or preference, but is vital if we are to preserve and foster democratic sovereignty. Letting parents and families cultivate such virtues is problematic because human tendency is to have natural biases toward certain preferences and orientations creating certain prejudices in their children. Schools have the ability to provide a political education that could teach all children the civic virtues necessary to participate in and shape the political structure and stability of society as future adults and citizens.

Schools as institutions are integral to preserving the political culture necessary for a liberal democracy to thrive. Understanding and participating in a political culture is not something one just comes to know, it encompasses certain habits, skills and dispositions that each individual must be inducted into in a meaningful way. Eamonn Callan makes this point when he states that public institutions play a vital role in the way that we induct individuals into the larger political sphere:

> . . . it is a shared way of public life constituted by a constellation of attitudes, habits, and abilities that people acquire as they grow up. These include a lively interest in the question of what life is truly and not just seemingly good, as well as a willingness both to share one's own answer with others and to heed the many opposing answers they might give; and active commitment to the good of the polity, as well as confidence and competence in judgement regarding how that good should be advanced; a respect for fellow citizens and a sense of common fate with them that goes beyond the tribalisms of ethnicity and religion and is yet alive to the significance these will have in many people's lives. (1997, p. 3)

Taken together, this encompasses a demanding type of education, not left to chance by parents. It requires a logical and coherent political education, deliberately considered and developed in children – not through mere osmosis or exposure, but through active and deliberate thought processes and engagement about civic virtues.

In reading these three counter arguments, consider whether your viewpoint has changed significantly. Use the following questions to reflect and consider whether, and to what degree, your position may have changed.

> Do parents have a better sense of judgement in deciding what is best for their children?
> Do schools provide more opportunities to expose children to alternative lifestyles and experiences?
> Are there other ways in which to develop children's exposure to different experiences other than schools? Is this sufficient?
> Should schools develop certain civic virtues as part of sustaining and fostering the political culture of society?

A case study: Wisconsin v. Yoder

The balance between parental rights and state authority is continually being debated and challenged. In this final section, I wish to examine a landmark American court case and provide excerpts of the verdict given. *Wisconsin v. Yoder*, 406 U.S. 205 considered whether the Amish could exempt their children from attending state schools after the eighth grade (aged fourteen). The parents wished to challenge the state legislation that made schooling compulsory on the basis that state schooling would substantially compromise the cultural integrity of that faith community. In a 7-0 decision, the American Supreme Court ruled in favour of the Amish to exempt their children from compulsory schooling after the eighth grade. The following three excerpts are taken from the Supreme Court judge's opinions on the particular court ruling.

Excerpt 1

A related feature of Old Order Amish communities is their devotion to a life in harmony with nature and the soil, as exemplified by the simple life of the early Christian era that continued in America during much of our early national life. Amish beliefs require members of the community to make their living by farming or closely related activities. Broadly speaking, the Old Order Amish religion pervades and determines the entire mode of life of its adherents.

Excerpt 2

Formal high school education beyond the eighth grade is contrary to Amish beliefs, not only because it places Amish children in an environment hostile to Amish beliefs with increasing emphasis on competition in class work and sports and with pressure to conform to the styles, manners, and ways of the peer group, but also because it takes them away from their community, physically and emotionally, during the crucial and formative adolescent period of life. During this period, the children must acquire Amish attitudes favoring manual work and self-reliance and the specific skills needed to perform the adult role of an Amish farmer or housewife.

Excerpt 3

There is no doubt as to the power of a State, having a high responsibility for education of its citizens, to impose reasonable regulations for the control and duration of basic education. Providing public schools ranks at the very apex of the function of a State. Thus, a State's interest in universal education, however highly we rank it, is not totally free from a balancing process when it impinges on fundamental rights and interests, such as those specifically protected by the Free Exercise Clause of the First Amendment, and the traditional interest of parents with respect to the religious upbringing of their children so long as they 'prepare [them] for additional obligations.' It follows that in order for Wisconsin to compel school attendance beyond the eighth grade against a claim that such attendance interferes with the practice of a legitimate religious belief, it must appear either that the State does not deny the free exercise of religious belief by its requirement, or that there is a state interest of sufficient magnitude to override the interest claiming protection under the Free Exercise Clause. . . . The essence of all that has been said and written on the subject is that only those interests of the highest order and those not otherwise served can overbalance legitimate claims to the free exercise of religion. We can accept it as settled, therefore, that, however strong the State's interest in universal compulsory education, it is by no means absolute to the exclusion or subordination of all other interests. (Wisconsin v. Yoder, 406 U.S. 205)

Let us consider the factors related to this case. The Supreme Court decided that the Amish children who attended state schooling would substantially compromise the cultural integrity of that faith community. They further thought that it did not warrant state interference to force Amish children to go to state schooling. It should be noted that the verdict might have been considerably different if the Amish families challenged that their children not attend *any* state schools. The Amish provided a compelling case that the children would attend primary education until the eighth grade. Further, they guaranteed that the children would still receive education within the Amish community, reflecting the skills and training needed for their agricultural way of life. Finally, those skills developed in the Amish community could be transferable to skills outside of the Amish community, and in this way, should the teenagers wish to leave the Amish, they could find suitable alternative forms of work within the modern world.

Do you agree with the verdict reached regarding the *Yoder* case?
Why or why not?
Do you think the balance between parents' rights and the state's obligation to protect children was achieved?

Conclusion

It is clear that few would suggest that the education of children should rest solely with either parents or solely with the state. The concern that children should be influenced primarily through the values and beliefs of parents raises several concerns regarding limited or narrow levels of expertise, limited exposure to alternative ways of living, and a limited ability to foster the dispositions required for the larger political sphere in civil society.

Conversely, sole responsibility that rests with the state and educational authorities creates similar difficulties. A centralized education system which does not include parental views may fail to provide the flexibility to attend to differing needs of children. Completely disregarding the values and beliefs of families and communities seems to contradict the overarching liberal aims of education (and society) of fostering diversity and tolerance. Either extreme seems both untenable and undesirable to implement. The debate therefore hinges on striking a balance between these two competing positions.

Further reading

For a rigorous, yet accessible account of the pros and cons of the argument that parents are the best people to protect their own children's interests, read Meira Levinson's chapter on 'The development of autonomy' in *The Demands of a Liberal Education* (1999). Two articles are particularly helpful in understanding the parental rights argument based on one's norms and values. Terry McLaughlin's article entitled, 'Parental Rights and the Religious Upbringing of Children' is largely a response and counter argument to David Bridge's article on 'Non-paternalistic arguments in support of parents' rights over their children's education'. Judith Shklar's (1989) account of a relatively libertarian argument of an increasingly nanny state helps to understand this line of debate.

The debate between Perry Glanzer (2008) and Rob Reich (2002b) highlight the arguments of whether parents are the best individuals to judge what is best for their children. Brighouse's (2006) book *On Education*, is a succinct account of the key arguments found in liberal thought. Part One of his book is particularly useful for this discussion. Gereluk's (2006) chapter on 'Liberal Communities in Schools' provides a useful rationale for why schools are optimal for providing a range of varied activities. Callan's (1997) and Gutmann's (1987) books are of paramount importance to the argument towards civic education. Chapter one of Gutmann's book provides a lucid account of the different arguments made for parental authority, with a strong critique following thereafter. The introductory chapter of Callan sets the stage for justifications for why individuals require a robust civic education programme. A great article that highlights the main points of two landmark cases, Yoder and Mozert can be found in Rob Reich's (2002b) article, 'Yoder, Mozert, and the Autonomy of Children'.

11 What's Wrong with Indoctrination and Brainwashing?

Richard Bailey

Introduction

One of the peculiarities of philosophical writing on education is that as much space seems to be taken up exploring what education is *not* as examining what it is. Most texts on the subject include extended discussions of the differences between education and a host of similar but non-educational concepts that can take place in schools, such as training, preparation and, most commonly of all, indoctrination.

The term indoctrination has, generally speaking, strong pejorative associations. This has not always been the case: until the second half of the twentieth century indoctrination was understood as no more offensive than concepts like education or teaching. Even today, dictionaries generally define indoctrination in a neutral way, emphasizing the transmission of *doctrines* or beliefs. However, in educational and political debates indoctrination is usually used as a derogatory term. In fact, indoctrination is usually positioned as the antithesis of the sort of educational practices considered appropriate in a modern, liberal, democratic society.

A wide range of subjects and practices have been tarred with the brush of indoctrination: teaching left wing politics (Horowitz, 2007); teaching free market economics (Chomsky, 2003); citizenship education (Flew, 2000); and peace studies (Scruton et al., 1985). However, by far the most popular target for the charge of indoctrination is religious-based schooling.

Religious instruction seems to have been singled out because, its critics say, it contravenes two of the principal aims of education (at least in modern, liberal societies). The first aim is 'open-mindedness': 'to be open-minded about something is not to have made up one's mind or to have made it up firmly' (Gardner, 1993, p. 42). The second aim is autonomy, which leads people 'to make and act on well-informed and well-thought out judgements about how to live their own lives' (Brighouse, 2006, p. 14). For many philosophers religious teaching is a contradiction in terms because it necessarily involves the teaching of doctrines (e.g. Flew, 1972), which can amount to little more than unfalsifiable beliefs (i.e. beliefs that cannot, in any way, be shown to be wrong). This is the position of the British philosopher Antony Flew (1972, p. 114) who wrote 'the outstanding paradigm case of indoctrination [is] the enormous and generally effective effort made . . . to fix in the minds of children an unshakeable conviction of the truth of its specific distinctive doctrines'. So, the argument goes, they are inherently non-rational propositions which, rather than opening minds, act as 'stoppers' that control, limit and channel thought, disavow alternative beliefs, and frustrate critical thinking (Kazepides, 1994, p. 406).

A telling example of the religious-teaching-as-indoctrination argument is provided by Barrow and Woods (2006) in 'An Introduction to the Philosophy of Education'. They open their chapter on indoctrination with a description of a Catholic school, in which all the teachers are committed Catholics, where all children are from Catholic homes, and where the whole school is openly committed to nurturing children in the Catholic faith and an unshakeable commitment to the truth of Catholicism (p. 70). The authors close their account of the school with these words: 'It is difficult to conceive of anyone seriously doubting that these teachers are indoctrinating' (p. 66). This may be so, but it is necessary to enquire into the features of this model of schooling that lead it to being characterized as indoctrinating its students. Also, we might question whether this type of teaching is necessarily harmful or morally objectionable.

Consider these quotations:

> Indoctrination typically supplies authoritarian principles for the authoritarian personality to follow . . . Moral education is incompatible with imparting authoritarian beliefs because the content of authoritarian beliefs necessarily limits the moral autonomy of children by constraining them to think in prescribed ways. (Kupfer, 1994, p. 63)

> Indoctrination has a perfectly important role to play in education. [and] may be useful as the prelude to teaching . . . we need not offer reasons for every belief we think important for children and adults to hold. (Green, 1972, pp. 44–5)
>
> . . . one could argue that attempts to avoid facing up to the issue of sexism in both the hidden and planned curriculum may be akin to indoctrination by default. (Baines, 1984, p. 57)
>
> How is the word 'indoctrination' being employed in these statements?
> In particular, how do the three authors presume indoctrination takes place?
> What assumptions about education and / or indoctrination are made in the quotations?

The problem of indoctrination

Life would be intolerable if we did not follow at least some conventions and common practices. Of course, some practices such as those labelled as matters of etiquette are sometimes mocked at for being rather quaint and old-fashioned. How bad would it really be if the British no longer queued at every given opportunity? And what is wrong with breaking wind or picking one's nose in public? Conventions like these are hardly matters of life-and-death affairs, and since cultures seem to manage reasonably well without them. We might claim, as I would, that such instances of 'good manners' help keep the world moving on in a relatively civilized and bearable way. But I would not suggest, even after witnessing flagrant queue-jumping, that breaking these rules is especially heinous. Some practices, though, are more serious. That car drivers stay on one side of the road is a mere convention (in the sense that there is no logically correct side), but all of them need to follow the pre-established rules if many people are not to die.

Social life depends on and assumes the acceptance of a complex set of conventions. Without them, humans would have to resort to negotiating every new situation afresh, and would run the risk of social break-down. So, it seems reasonable to argue that young people need to learn the conventions of their social setting. In fact, it is almost inconceivable that they could grow up in the middle of a family, within a neighbourhood, within a culture without being influenced by their values, rules and beliefs.

After the family, the school is probably the primary context in which children are socialized. Students spend tens of thousands of hours at school during the period of development when most values and social behaviours become established. And, of course, without rules, regulations and routines, school itself would be chaotic. There are bound to be times when the values promoted by schools are questioned. There might be family practices that conflict with those of the school. Or young people might object that the values presented to them are out-of-date and irrelevant for their generation. Overall, though, there is no inherent reason to deny that children should be deliberately socialized into the expectations of the wider society, and that schools have a role to play in this process.

So, socialization is inevitable and it seems desirable in principle. Very few parents or teachers would question this, even if they would reject certain forms.

There are numerous ways of bringing people to accept others' views. The threat of death, for example, is a historically popular approach. Another widely used method of forcing compliance is the threat or use of torture. There is an especially vivid portrayal of torture and its rationale in the novel 1984 by George Orwell. If you've read the book, you will know that Winston Smith lives in a state ruled by an authoritative figure called Big Brother. Winston's personal rebellion against this state results in his arrest and torture. His captor O'Brien makes the goal of the interrogation clear:

> 'Shall I tell you why we have brought you here? To cure you! To make you sane! Will you understand, Winston, that no one whom we bring to this place ever leaves our hands uncured? We are not interested in those stupid crimes that you have committed. The Party is not interested in the overt act: the thought is all we care about.' (Orwell, 1954, p. 265)

O'Brien's aim of 'curing' Winston is revealing and it highlights a vitally important point in this discussion: perpetrators of extreme social control methods are not necessarily acting out of malice; they might be acting in what they think are the interests of their victim.

Stephen Law, in 'The War for Children's Minds' (2006), offers a useful list of teaching methods designed to bring individuals, especially the young, to conform to authority.

Punishment	e.g. physical punishment, detention, withdrawal of privileges
Rewards	e.g. stars and awards, promotion, special uniforms
Emotional Imagery and Manipulation	e.g. iconic images and posters emotion-laden films
Social pressure	e.g. shame and stigma
Repetition	e.g. reciting key phrases or tenets
Control and Censorship	e.g. removing inappropriate books from libraries, forbidding the expression of certain viewpoints
Isolation	e.g. discouraging socializing with non-believers
Uncertainty	e.g. warning of the complexity and meaninglessness of life outside of the community
Tribalism	e.g. distinguishing between 'us' and 'them', stereotyping other groups

Have you witnessed any of these methods (or versions of them) in schools?

Are any of them acceptable? If so, in what circumstances are they acceptable?

Are any of these methods instances of indoctrination?

Demarcating indoctrination

If it is accepted that education ought to involve only morally acceptable ways of teaching, then most people will conclude that indoctrination is not admissible. As we have seen, though, the term is used in numerous different ways and, so far, we have not identified a clear definition. This is not a merely academic matter: teachers and parents need to understand which approaches are morally admissible, and which are not. In other words, they need to identify some sort of criteria for demarcating indoctrination from education.

As we have already seen, at a very general level indoctrination involves leading people to hold certain beliefs in certain ways. However, it does not follow that we necessarily ought to denounce all teaching of beliefs. For example, if a child is taught that the earth rotates around the sun, or that animals need oxygen to breath and move, it would seem silly to say that the child has been indoctrinated. Philosophers would say that imparting beliefs is a *necessary* condition of indoctrination, but not a *sufficient* condition. Some other condition (or conditions) are needed to say that indoctrination has taken place.

The distinction between necessary and sufficient conditions is a vital one in philosophical thinking.

- A **necessary** condition for an event is something that is absolutely required to happen if the event is to occur.
- A **sufficient** condition for an event, on the other hand, does not have to exist for the event to occur, but if it exists, then the event will occur.

For example, oxygen is *necessary* for a baby to live, but it alone is not *sufficient*: the baby also needs food, sleep, maternal care and numerous other sources of nurture.

Turning to the matter at hand, we can say that teaching children to hold beliefs is a necessary condition for indoctrination to take place, but that is not sufficient. Before we discover what philosophers of education have written about this, spend some time thinking for yourself about what other conditions might be necessary for indoctrination.

Not surprisingly, philosophers have offered a range of interpretations of the conditions sufficient for indoctrination. The first we will consider focuses on the *content* of what is taught. Most writers assume that indoctrination is related to a specific type of belief, namely doctrines. For example, R. S. Peters (1966, p. 41) states that 'whatever else "indoctrination" means, it obviously has something to do with doctrines'. Even those philosophers who reject the claim that content is the sufficient condition for indoctrination still maintain that the teaching of doctrines often involves indoctrination (e.g. White, 1972). The problem with doctrines, it is argued, is that they are not provable (Barrow and Woods, 2006). However, there are a number of difficulties with this position. One problem is that the criticism seems to apply with equal force to almost the whole of the school curriculum. The factual aspects of literature, whilst important, hardly amount to a worthwhile subject (how might we 'prove' an interpretation of a sonnet?). Much the same could be said for physical education, drama and, indeed, philosophy. More telling is the charge that the distinction between fact and 'mere opinion' is much less clear-cut than it might appear. Philosophers of science commonly acknowledge that the popular image of science as proven and certain is naïve, that a more realistic account recognizes the interests and biases of scientists; what counts as knowledge changes over time as new information comes to hand that alters or kills earlier theories (Musgrave, 1993). It does not follow from this that it is impossible or undesirable to distinguish between matters of broad consensus and widely contested claims. Nevertheless, the distinction is not strong or easy to articulate which makes it difficult to accept as a convincing criterion for demarcating indoctrination.

Discussions of the content of indoctrination invariably raise questions about the *methods* used to teach: as we have seen, authoritarian methods have often been used to foster authoritarian beliefs. This is the point made by Cohen (1969, p. 180):

> The teacher of bias, the teacher who, whatever his protestations, is concerned to indoctrinate, can be identified whenever one of a number of points of view is presented as though it were the only one possible; whenever questions are suppressed rather than answered; whenever certain areas of questioning are taboo; and whenever the educator is psychologically unable to tolerate the expression of dissenting views.
>
> In other words, the indoctrinator must resort to educationally dubious methods because the doctrines being promoted do not provide an adequate basis for less authoritarian alternatives.

Clearly, some methods of inculcating belief are indefensible, such as brainwashing, drugging, sleep deprivation and subliminal messages (Taylor, 2004). But very few teachers would contemplate their use. So it may be the case that focusing on methods as the condition of indoctrination can lull us into a false sense of security as we end up overlooking other, more subtle approaches. As Cohen (1981, p. 50) puts it: 'the more free a society is from cruder indoctrinatory practices, the more important becomes recognition of the more subtle ways in which indoctrination can manifest itself'.

The third contender for the sufficient condition of indoctrination is the *intention* of the teacher. Terence McLaughlin (1984, p. 78) followed this line of argument when he defined indoctrination as the intentional inculcation of unshakeable beliefs, and writes that indoctrination 'constitutes an attempt to restrict in a substantial way the child's eventual ability to function autonomously'. In this regard, there is an important distinction to be drawn between the teacher's *avowed* intention (what they say they are trying to do) and the *real* intention (what they are, in fact, trying to do) (Barrow and Woods, 2006). However, this rather presumes that the teacher acknowledges or is aware of his or her intentions. If the teacher has been educated within an indoctrinatory system, then it is possible that he or she is no more aware of the actual aims of schooling than the students: the teacher is both a victim and a perpetrator of indoctrination. Leahy (1994) talks about 'unintended indoctrination', by which he means inculcating beliefs expressing ideological biases built into the organizational structure of the school but unrecognized by the teacher, such as sexism, racism or class discrimination. A tight association between indoctrination and intention would, therefore, seem to exclude precisely the types of teaching that the concept of indoctrination was designed to address.

Perhaps the difficulties with the other proposed criteria for indoctrination are addressed by the fourth criteria, neatly expressed by Scruton et al. (1985, p. 16):

> The most fundamental feature of indoctrination, and the one that most clearly demonstrates its anti-educational character, is its domination by conclusions that are foregone.

This position is different from the content criterion because it is not concerned with the status of the conclusions reached – whether they are justified or not – but with the style by which they have been reached. Another way of phrasing this position is in terms of the *consequences* of indoctrination. According to this perspective, the educational process can be characterized by teaching students how to arrive at conclusions and how to assess them when they are controversial. Implicit in this account is a prioritizing of the students' ability to judge for themselves the validity of the lessons they are taught. Of course, students learn countless things based on the authority of the teacher, especially during the early stages of schooling. But this does not undermine the argument as a non-indoctrinatory approach would prepare even very young learners to think and act autonomously by equipping them with the intellectual apparatus to deal with reasons and evidence when they are able to do so. Another way of phrasing this position is offered by Thomas Green (1972, p. 37):

> when, in teaching, we are concerned simply to lead another person to a correct answer, but are not correspondingly concerned that they arrive at that answer on the basis of good reasons, then we are indoctrinating; we are engaged in creating a non-evidential style of belief.

Non-evidential – or perhaps *non-critical* – beliefs are impervious to contradictory findings and are, therefore, incapable of amendment by the introduction of evidence or criticism.

The consequence of style condition is not vulnerable to the criticisms levelled at the other proposed criteria, but it is also not incompatible with them. As Harvey Siegel (1988, p. 81) makes clear, while content, methods and intentions are neither necessary nor sufficient for indoctrination, 'they all tend to promote non-evidential beliefs'. This is the heart of the problem with indoctrination: it fosters a non-evidential or non-critical style of belief that makes open-mindedness and autonomy unattainable.

As we have seen, Barrow and Woods (2006) offer as a 'paradigm case' (i.e. a clear and indisputable example) of indoctrination a form of schooling that aims at the production of Catholic young people.

> Is this indoctrination?
> Does your answer apply to all forms of faith-based schooling?
> Now consider two forms of religious upbringing that might generally be considered more extreme than most.

Case 1: Amish Education

Dianne Gereluk, in Chapter 10 of this book, discusses the landmark American legal case entitled 'Wisconsin v. Yoder', in which a group of Amish parents wished to challenge the state legislation that made schooling compulsory on the basis that state schooling would substantially compromise the cultural integrity of that faith community.

Case 2: Westboro Baptist Church

This is a highly controversial church which bases its work on the belief expressed by its best known slogan 'God hates fags', and expresses the opinion, based on its interpretation of the Bible, that nearly every problem in the world is due to homosexuality. Children as young as seven years old regularly join adults to protest against institutions the Church believes support homosexuality, which seem to be almost all of them. However, unlike the Amish, Westboro Church allows its children to attend mainstream schools and socialize with peers unconnected to their community.

We have considered four positions regarding possible criteria for indoctrination:

- Content;
- Methods;
- Intentions;
- Consequences or style.

How would you evaluate the two cases outlined above in terms of each of these four conditions?

The apparent inevitability of indoctrination

Philosophers of education have almost universally portrayed indoctrination as a non-educational practice. Indeed, they have gone to some lengths to demarcate education from indoctrination. It is surprising, then, that many of them also believe that it is inevitable. James Garrison (1986, p. 272) describes indoctrination as 'inevitable' and 'desirable' and even goes as far as to claim that the 'failure to indoctrinate would perhaps be analogous to murder, or at the very least, abortion'. A similar point is made by Green (1972, p. 44), albeit in a more restrained tone:

> Indoctrination has a perfectly good and important role to play in education . . . and may be useful as a prelude to teaching . . . We need not offer reasons for every belief we think important for children and adults to hold.

Green is arguing here that there are cases in which it is not necessary or possible to teach in an evidential or critical way, and in these instances indoctrination is taking place. In accepting indoctrination as inescapable, these writers seem to assume a position akin to that of Wagner (cited in Tan, 2004), which is that indoctrination involves 'causing a person to hold a belief that they are unable to justify on rational grounds'. This is most telling in the case of very young children since it is often assumed that they are not capable of deliberately choosing to follow the rational course of action or capable of being persuaded rationally. Therefore, non-rational, authoritative methods are called for. R. S. Peters calls this the 'the paradox of moral education':

> What then is the paradox of moral education as I conceive it? It is this: given that it is desirable to develop people who conduct themselves rationally, intelligently, and with a fair degree of spontaneity, the brute facts of child development reveal that at the most formative years of a child's development he is incapable of this form of life and impervious to the proper manner of passing it on. (1966, p. 271)

This argument only holds up if we accept that method is the sufficient criteria for indoctrination, and there is a persuasive argument against that viewpoint. According to the other proposed criteria of indoctrination – content, intention and consequence – it is entirely reasonable to suggest that young children are *temporarily* unable to comprehend a set of beliefs and practices but that the content / intention / consequence are fully compatible with educational principles like autonomy. Accepting that many beliefs are acquired before a student is capable of rationally comprehending them, it is useful to distinguish between two distinct contexts: those in which the lack of reasons or evidence are temporary; and those in which they are a permanent state of affairs (Siegel, 1988). The central issue is not whether or not the students are given reasons or evidence in favour of a belief, but whether or not such reasons or evidence exist.

Emmanuel College in the North East of England is a state school with a Christian mission. It has received a great deal of media attention in recent years when it was reported that many of the school's staff (including the Head teacher and Head of Science) oppose evolutionary theory in favour of creationism (the religious doctrine that the Bible offers the best account of life on earth).

Is there a danger of indoctrination in this and similar schools? If so, what conditions would have to be met for it to occur?

Is it possible to teach non-scientific theories like creationism without indoctrinating students?

Is it possible to indoctrinate students with evolution or other established scientific theories?

Conclusion: so, what's wrong with indoctrination?

If it is agreed that education should involve only morally defensible ways of teaching, then philosophical questions about educational content, methods, intentions and consequences have implications for practice. Some approaches may need to be rejected because they contravene what might reasonably be taken as appropriate for students.

It has been suggested in this chapter that indoctrination can be usefully characterized in terms of a certain style of teaching which results in this inculcation of non-evidential and non-critical beliefs. Indoctrination is inadmissible in schooling because its consequences are incompatible with the principles of open-mindedness and autonomy that are generally regarded as central to liberal democracies. A compelling way of representing these principles is in terms of what Joel Feinberg (1992, p. 82) called 'child's right to an open future'. Indoctrination is unacceptable because 'an education that renders a child fit for only one way of life, forecloses irrevocably his other options'. It is unacceptable, therefore, because it harms that child by compromising his or her autonomy, and is morally unacceptable.

Further reading

Snook's 1972 collection is still the most comprehensive philosophical treatment of indoctrination, and most subsequent discussions are framed within the arguments presented in that book. Brighouse (2006) offers a very useful introduction to philosophical thinking about education, and is especially good at articulating the case for the liberal, democratic version of education presumed in this chapter. Bailey (2000a) and Cohen (1981) discuss indoctrination in more general discussions of the politics of education. Thiessen (1993) offers a strong defence of religious education to the charge of indoctrination, and is also the most thorough recent overview of the topic.

Useful websites

A useful summary of the Wisconsin v. Yoder case is available from Wikipedia (http://en.wikipedia.org/wiki/Wisconsin_ v._Yoder). A philosophical critique of the judgement of this case that relates to indoctrination in education is available from the 1991 US Philosophy of Education Yearbook entitled 'A Friendly Critique of a Child's Right to an Open Future' by Bertram Bandman (http://www.ed.uiuc.edu/EPS/PES-yearbook/2001/2001toc.htm).

A fascinating BBC documentary on the Church, fronted by Louis Theroux, is available at various places on the web, including Google Video and YouTube. It is entitled 'The Most Hated Family in America'.

Read about case of Emmanuel College at: http://news.bbc.co.uk/1/hi/education/1872331.stm; and http://www.guardian.co.uk/education/2002/jun/19/schools.aslevels. And make sure to visit the School's own website, too: http://www.emmanuelctc.org.uk.

Reading the Philosophy of Education

John Gingell

Introduction

Reading all philosophy is difficult. Partly, this is because we are simply not used to paying the close attention to a text that philosophy demands. When every word, phrase, sentence or paragraph may be significant then the possibility of reading in our normal, rather relaxed, manner becomes impossible if we are really to do the text justice. Partly, it is because philosophers are usually trying to persuade the reader concerning some contentious issue, and because the issue is contentious – and if it wasn't there would be little point in writing about it – our own prejudices, or fully thought through ideas, may make us resistant to such persuasion. Thus, the typical philosophy text is asking us to engage with and *think* through what is being said, and, at the same time to re-examine our own thoughts on the matter in hand, and such thought is a difficult business.

When it comes to reading philosophy concerned with education the matter is made more difficult by the fact that we have all, at least some times in our lives, been engaged with processes of education. So, philosophy of education, like moral philosophy, attempts to talk to us about an area of life of which we have some experience and can pretend to some expertise, and where therefore, the possibilities of prejudice, or fixed ideas deriving from our own experiences, loom large. On the other hand the fact of such experience does provide us with a basis from which we can begin to assess what is being said. Here, as in moral philosophy, reading philosophy should help us make sense of our own experiences, which is a far cry from saying that it should validate them, for example, you *might* upon reading some philosopher's conception of education, and being persuaded by her arguments, decide that what you have been through, is either not a full-fledged version of education or, even worse, that it is a version of mis-education.

In what follows I am going to try to demonstrate that there is another difficulty with reading philosophy of education. I shall try to show that our natural expectations of what the subject may offer can be comprehensively frustrated by some philosophers' approach to the subject. That as well as the difficulties touched on above – which are essentially difficulties of engagement – there are also difficulties of scope with some treatments of the subject. That as well as asking ourselves, when we read this type of philosophical text whether we follow and agree with the arguments, we also have to ask ourselves, whether the account of education on offer can possibly offer answers to the type of questions we may want to ask.

The 'possibly' is important here. All philosophers, when they write, are concentrating on this or that problem and the particular problem which is the focus of their concentration may be, or may not be, of interest to the reader. But, as well as these particularities, all such writing exemplifies a type of approach – a methodology, if you like – which will dictate the range of problems that can be addressed by this type of approach. I want to persuade you – cards on the table – that a certain important conception of education offered by some philosophers is deeply flawed because of a narrowness of focus. That, at the most , it offers only a partial picture of the type of things that philosophers of education should be looking at and therefore it cannot even begin to address certain vital matters in contemporary British education. Whether I succeed or not partly depends on the cogency of my own arguments; but partly, upon the readers' willingness to think through their own experiences, attitudes and expectations.

Let me begin by citing two recent 'facts' about British education. The first concerns the West Dunbartonshire Literacy Initiative (MacKay, 2006) where it is claimed that, in an educationally deprived area of the country, a strategy has been designed that has drastically reduced illiteracy in schools and will, in the near future eradicate, it completely. The second concerns the recent publication (DES, 2008) of the years 'league tables' for secondary schools in England, where it is shown that, in terms of one measure of educational success, attainment at GCSE and 'A' level, the top state schools are approaching the achievements of the independent schools, but there is a yawning chasm between the achievement of pupils in these schools and the achievement of children attending schools in the bottom half of the tables.

The quotation marks around facts above indicate that both of these things may be matters of controversy. There may be some who will dispute whether the Research Report and/or the league tables are accurate. In what follows I will assume, in the absence of evidence to the contrary, that they are. But, as well of questions of accuracy, some may question the relevance of both, or either, to our knowledge and understanding of, British education. That they are relevant will be part of the burden of what follows. However, at least initially, it seems a plausible assumption that both indicate interesting and important aspects of our education system. The first seems to show that a persistent feature of our education system, that is, the problem that about *20 per cent* of our children do not learn to read at primary school can be successfully addressed. Such a matter should, surely, be of interest to us generally and must, again surely, be of interest to any parent with children of primary school age. The second shows that though some of our children do well in secondary school, in terms of a conventional measure of educational achievement, many of our children do very badly. Again, both as taxpayers and generally concerned citizens, this should concern us all, but it should be of special interest to those parents whose children are going through, or approaching, secondary education. And, if these things are of educational interest we would expect them to be of interest to philosophers of education. But, given a certain conception of education and therefore a certain conception of the scope of philosophy of education, this does not seem to be the case.

What I am going to do is use these 'facts' to test certain accounts of the nature of education. In fact, I am going to use them to suggest that these accounts *must be* inadequate. As such the examples act as counter examples to these accounts. This use of counter examples is one of the most common, but powerful techniques, of analytic philosophy. So, given any theory, one looks for examples – real or imagined – which would prove the theory wrong. Usually, the theory is given first and the counter examples follow. Here I've reversed that process partly, for dramatic reasons; and partly, because these very real examples seem to me so important.

It is a good exercise when beginning to read philosophy of education to ask yourself what educational problems you hope will be addressed in what you are reading.

In a recent paper, a leading proponent of the views I wish to consider, Professor David Carr (2003b, p. 253) argues thus:

[N]ot withstanding any and all pressure to regard teaching in institutional and professional contexts as a form of technical or managerial expertise directed to specific social ends, neither teaching nor the moral ends which it more widely serves seem reducible to practices in any such socially defined sense.

So, it would be a mistake to think, given a proper understanding of teaching, that it might have to do with the eradication of illiteracy or the attainment of five A – C passes at GCSE level. We need, Carr argues, to recognize:

[S]ome distinction between education and schooling. Schools are social institutions that occupy space and are appropriately organised and regulated but education is not in and of itself any such thing and does not need an institution to take place. It therefore makes perfect sense to speak . . . of schools in which little or no education goes on, or of persons as educated although they have never been to school. (ibid., p. 255)

The implication here is that our focus, certainly as philosophers of education, should not be on schools, which may or may not educate, but on those essential features of education itself. Before we go on to look at what Carr considers to be these essential features, it is worth noting an aspect of the above argument. The form of the argument seems to be:

- Some schools do not educate.
- People can be educated without going to school.
- Therefore: Schools have nothing to do with education.

But such an argument seems distinctly dubious. It is rather like arguing:

- Some people that have enough to eat are not happy.
- Some people are happy without having enough to eat.
- Therefore, having enough to eat has nothing to do with being happy.

But such an argument ignores the obvious fact that for many people getting enough to eat is a significant contribution to their happiness. And the schooling version of the argument seems to ignore, the equally obvious fact that for most people schools make a significant contribution to their education. To show that two things are not identical with one another is a far cry from showing that they have nothing to do with one another. Therefore if we are interested in the latter we ought to be interested in the former. Even a more charitable interpretation of his conclusion as: 'It is possible that schools have nothing to do with education,' would beg serious questions in that it is clearly the intended purpose of schools to educate and we would therefore need very strong reasons to suppose that the connection between schooling and education did not exist. All human institutions fail in fulfilling their purposes to some degree or another, but this does not mean that the failure entails that they have no such purposes, or that, they are so far removed from fulfilling their purposes that we can disregard such purposes.

The type of argument given above is all too common in philosophy. So, for example, some philosophers of art, dealing with painting argue:

- There are great works of art that do not have a significant content.
- There are works which have a significant content that are not great works.
- Therefore, a significant content has nothing to do with being a great work of art.

This simply ignores the fact that for many works of art the content of the work contributes to its greatness. The sleight of hand here involves presenting two true premises of an argument and a conclusion that seems related to these premises and hoping the reader does not notice that the conclusion is not actually guaranteed by the premises, that is, the premises may be true and the

⇨

conclusion false. In other words, the arguments are not valid. It is a great mistake to confuse truth and validity and it is possible to construct perfectly valid arguments whose premises are not true. Thus:

- All pigs fly
- Percy is a pig
- Therefore, Percy flies

is a valid argument even if at least the first premise is false. What this means is that *if you believe the premises* you *must*, in order to be rational, believe the conclusion!

And this is the key test, given any argument you have to ask yourself: if I believe the premises of this argument *must* I believe the conclusion. And, if your answer is, No, then the argument is not valid.

The distinction between the content and processes of education and its institutional context causes problems in other areas of education. So, for instance, in the latest statement of aims for the National Curriculum (DfEE, 1999) there seems to be no attempt to distinguish between what the Curriculum is designed to achieve and what the schools, independent of the Curriculum, are supposed to achieve. But, without such a distinction, we have no way of telling, if something is going wrong and these aims are not being achieved, where the fault is. We simply cannot tell whether it is the Curriculum and its design that has contributed to this failure, or the policies of the schools, or both.

If, as Carr seems to argue, education is not about schooling, what is it supposed to be about? For Carr, education and teaching are essentially moral matters. They are areas in which some of the moral virtues are practised, exemplified and passed on. In an important sense, for Carr all good education is moral education:

> Thus, good teachers need to have acquired some mettle or firmness of purpose, to exhibit self control in some degree of patience and control of temper, to weigh fairness to all against concern for the shortcomings of particular individuals, to be trustworthy and caring, to possess a fair measure of humility – tempered perhaps by a readiness not to take oneself too seriously – as well as, it goes without saying, the kind of knowledge of and passion and enthusiasm for what is taught that can trigger such interest in others . . . As a teacher I may recognise a need to be self controlled and fair, and also that my pupils are likely to become self controlled and fair by my good example – but as a good teacher, I will aspire to become self controlled and fair for its own sake irrespective of any possible benefits to others. (ibid., p. 261)

This is an excellent account of some of the qualities of good teaching. But the key question here is whether it is a fully adequate account. Given the two sets of facts that I mentioned above, that is, the literacy initiative and the league tables, how do such things fit in this conception of teaching and education? Certainly, on a superficial level they do not seem to fit at all. Such facts seem completely irrelevant to Carr's description. And, if teaching and education are about the exemplification and passing on of Carr's virtues, such things can obviously be achieved independently of addressing concerns either for literacy or for GCSE pass rates. Given that people can become fully moral individuals without being able to read or pass exams, one could, in Carr's terms, be a completely successful teacher if there were no such educational achievements. I am not envisaging a situation here where such achievements are beyond the grasp of these particular pupils but rather, one in which such achievements are not even addressed.

It might be the case that with a certain emphasis on the 'knowledge', 'passion' and 'enthusiasm' for what is taught that figures in Carr's account, that such concerns for achievement do become – even for Carr – the remit of the good teacher. However, given his reaction in the past to such suggestions, I suspect that this will not be the case. So, for instance, when Robin Alexander (1992) suggested that teachers needed to clarify their conception of 'good practice' and to work with a notion that included some reference to empirical evidence for effective teaching, Carr responded (1994) by accusing Alexander of having a technicist view of education which subordinated the value implicit within education to a quasi–scientific methodology. What seems to underpin Carr's position is the notion that if education is made to serve any values external to its own processes, or comply to any external norms, then this must mean the subversion of education itself.

What I have been suggesting so far is that Carr, in adopting his approach to education, presents us with a view of his subject matter which impoverishes our understanding of education and fails to address matters which many people see as of educational concern. But I think there are even deeper problems here. Carr argues for an understanding of teaching and education in terms of morality and, as far as his argument goes, he makes a compelling case. However, he does so only by neglecting some of the other moral aspects of education, for example, those aspects mentioned in the Foreword to the West Dunbartonshire Report. As the quotations I have used above seem to make clear, Carr's concerns seem to focus upon the interpersonal moral relationships present in teaching and learning. On how, in relating to a particular group of pupils, the teacher may be exemplifying some of the moral aspects of his or her character and therefore encouraging the growth of such characteristics within the pupils. And, in some ways this is all to the good. Carr is right to see such things as much more important than whether people training to be teachers pass courses in classroom management or behavioural objectives. But, as I said above, there are moral issues that are avoided in this account. Given the facts that I mentioned initially, let us suppose, as we know actually to be the case, that large numbers of children are failing to learn to read in our schools and, even larger numbers are failing to achieve satisfactory outcomes in terms of exam passes in their secondary education. In both cases, given the evidence of the Research Report and the evidence we have of successful state secondary schools, such failures seem likely to be due not to the inherent characteristics of the children who fail but rather, to what is done with them in schools. There is little doubt that some characteristics of children affect the task of schools.

But taken together The West Dunbartonshire report and the secondary school results suggest that it is a realizable aspiration that we could eliminate failure in schools. But this in turn suggests that schools are not, although they could, fulfilling their primary purpose. If this is true then the children in such failing schools are being harmed by their education (or, if you insist, their schooling). And, if this is the case, what we have here are profound cases of social injustice. But, social injustices which are obscured rather than highlighted by the Carr type of analysis of education.

This narrowness of focus concerning educational matters is not confined to Carr's writing. He is, in many ways, an exemplar of a certain type of contemporary practitioner of philosophy of education who, in reacting to attempts to present teaching and education as matters of technique, takes the emphasis too far in the other direction where few matters of fact, or empirical investigation, or questions of social policy have anything to do with education as 'properly' understood. But such narrowness of focus has, for rather different reasons, always been present in British philosophy of education.

If we look at the work of a figure who, for many, exemplified the beginnings of institution-alized philosophy of education in this country, R. S. Peters, we see the same narrowness of focus. It is at least arguable, and probably true, that modern philosophy of education is to be associated with the work of Professor R. S. Peters and that the key moment of such an association was the publication of his book *Ethics and Education* (1966). Although Peters later changed many of the views that he expressed within that book, his work there provides an important and influential example of thinking about education.

Peters was much concerned with questions of educational value and in *Ethics and Education* he wrote that the use of the word 'education' has 'normative implications'. What he means by this is that when we use this word:

> It implies that something worthwhile is being or has been intentionally transmitted in a morally acceptable manner. It would be a logical contradiction to say that a man had been educated but that he had in no way changed for the better, or that in educating his son a man was attempting nothing that was worthwhile. This is a purely conceptual point. Such a connection between 'education' a and what is valuable does not imply any particular commitment to content. It is a further question what particular standards are in virtue of which activities are thought to be of value and what grounds there might be for thinking these are the correct ones. All that is implied is a commitment to what is thought valuable. (ibid., p. 25)

In some ways this is clearly correct. We are concerned, both individually and collectively, that what goes on in education is of some value, for example, we worry that our children are getting a good education; we expect a large part of our taxes to be spent on education, and whilst we may wonder about whether enough or too much is being spent; or whether it is being spent on the right things; we, typically, do not wonder whether anything should be spent at all. Thus, we assume that something of value is going on in education and we are concerned that it should go on. However, note in the passage above, how tight is supposed to be the connection between education and value. Our worries and wondering may seem to be about whether the education of our children – individually and collectively – will fit them for life after education. Whether, for instance, it will contribute to them getting a job, how it will aid their social lives, what contribution it will make to their general well-being. Or, we might wonder, as people in commerce and industry seem to be continually doing, whether education contributes, or, contributes enough, to the economy. But such questions seem ruled out of court by the above passage. If it is literally the case that it would involve a 'logical contradiction' that a person had been educated but that they had in no way been changed for the better, for example, that in saying, as some people used to do, that education was a waste of time for girls, such people were literally contradicting themselves and therefore talking nonsense, then to ask such questions seems to involve us in a logical mistake. And to worry about whether the content of education contributes to our non-educational aims seems simply a waste of time.

In the pages that follow the above passage Peters elucidates the tightness of the supposed link between education and value. So, for instance, in his section on education and training (ibid., pp. 32–5) he seeks to distinguish between these two things by suggesting,

> [T]hat 'trained' suggests a development of competence in a limited skill or mode of thought whereas 'educated' suggests a linkage with a wider system of beliefs. (ibid., p. 32)

> If it is said that a person is 'trained' the questions 'To do what?', 'For what?', 'As what?', 'In what?' are appropriate for a person cannot be trained in a general sort of way. . . . With education, however, the matter is very different; for a person is never described as 'educated' in relation to any specific end, function or mode of thought. (ibid., p. 34)

Notice here that Peters is simply seeking to distinguish the difference between education and training. He is not suggesting, here or elsewhere, that training cannot be a part of education. I shall return to this point in a moment.

In his section on the aims of education (ibid., pp. 27–30) he argues, as Carr seems to do, against the notion that educational value has to do with the realization of values outside education itself. That education is simply a means to a valuable end that lies elsewhere. That we can meaningfully ask the question 'What is education for?' And he says:

> The natural way of asking for an extrinsic end is to ask what a man's purpose is in doing something or what his motive may be. These are strange questions to ask of education itself, for education implies the transmission of what is of *ultimate value*, it would be like asking about the purpose of a good life. (ibid., p. 29, my highlights)

So, presumably, as education is of *ultimate* value, we cannot even ask about whether being educated leads, or tends to lead, to a good life. For, to do so, would be to assume exactly what is being denied, that is, that education has intrinsic value. The strength of Peters' claim is worth noting. He seems to be denying that education could possibly have any instrumental value. But this certainly does not follow from what he says. Education might be of intrinsic value – even ultimate value – and still instrumentally valuable as well. It might be an end in itself, and at the same time, a means to other ends.

> That anything we recognize as education must involve values is a fairly uncontroversial claim. After all, we expect people being educated to be getting *better*, in some way, at something. However, when values are mentioned it is always pertinent to ask whether the values involved are extrinsic values, that is, valuable as a means to something else; or whether they are taken to be intrinsically valuable, that is, valuable in and for themselves. It seems reasonable to assume that if there are extrinsic values there must be some things that are intrinsically valuable. That a list of things that are good as means must end with something that is good in and for itself. But it is not to be thought that these two categories of value are mutually exclusive. Something may be both good as a means and good in and for itself. So, for instance, someone may play squash in order to keep fit, that is, as a means to fitness, but also because they simply enjoy the game i.e. the game is an end in itself.
>
> What things actually are of intrinsic value is a much-debated question within moral philosophy.

One thing that goes on in the above passages is a narrowing down of the conception of education and therefore a narrowing down of the type of questions we can meaningfully ask about education. The distinction between education and training is interesting in this context. As I said above, Peters never denies that training might play a part in education. His point seems to be that whilst it may be a part, this part is not to be confused with the whole. But it is certainly the case that some of those influenced by Peters took him to be saying that whilst education was a good thing – by definition – training almost certainly was not. Following the publication of *Ethics and Education* what were the Teacher Training Colleges rapidly became Colleges of Education and what had previously been taught in schools as physical training changed into physical education. To be involved in training programmes was thus to be involved in something that was necessarily inferior to education and the notion of, for instance, vocational education became a contradiction in terms. Again, if this is taken to be true, it further limits the scope of education and the type of meaningful questions that can be asked of education.

Some earlier commentators on Peters' work (Woods and Barrow, 1975) noted some of the problems of educational value, and in looking at the first passage by Peters quoted above, said:

> Peters is surely right in what he says. Vast sums of money are not spent on education simply because no other uses can be thought for it, or just for the fun of it, or in the hope that positive harm will result. In general, money is spent on education because people think that education is a good thing. (ibid., p. 10)

But what Woods and Barrow do not note is that, given what Peters says about education and value, what a strange thing it is that such money is willingly spent. Assume for a moment that

Peters is correct, that the values of education are intrinsic to education itself; that it simply misses the point to talk of education contributing to the economy, social and cultural life, or well-being generally. If this is so why should we be content that vast sums of our money are spent upon it? Simply to say that it is valuable in and for itself surely will not do. There are plenty of things that are valuable in and for themselves, for example, the taste of a good wine, the smell of a rose, the pleasures of convivial conversation; and no one thinks that the government should spend a large part of its budget setting up and running an enormous number of institutions dedicated to such values and ensuring, by force, that all our children attend such institutions so that they may realize such values. And Peters' notion quoted above that education is of *ultimate value* seems simple hyperbole, if this means that there are no other values which can be thought to judge educational values. Moral values may be such but educational values are not.

It is usually thought today that Peters was trying to do too much with too few resources. That linguistic analysis alone is not enough to either establish or defend our practices of education. But, as we saw with Carr's work, the same narrow focus upon parts of education at the expense of an understanding of the whole still goes on. What makes education interesting, and philosophy of education important, is that here we have an area of life where different concerns interact with one another in complex and important ways. And we would expect the philosophers dealing with the area to reflect these complexities. So, we would expect the formal rigour and linguistic acuity that is supposed to characterize philosophy generally; but also, a concern for ethics, epistemology, political thought, culture and economics, for all of these things interact in our practice of education. Philosophers of education not only have examined the basic processes of education such as teaching and learning, but also what is taught and learned and the ways in which these things go on. They have also examined the institutional and non-institutional places where such teaching and learning might go on: schools, universities, nursery schools, the places of vocational education, such as colleges and work places, and, of course, the home. Philosophers of education have thought and written not merely about the basic processes but also the most appropriate settings for such processes; whether for instance moral and religious matters are best taught at home or at school; whether vocational education, for example, for nurses or teachers, is best carried out in colleges or on the job. That is, they have examined not only what goes on, and what they think ought to go on, but also where these things should go on. They have also examined the mental underpinnings of education, for example, intelligence and its cognates, and the way our understanding of such things influences our understanding of education. They have also asked questions about the implications of education for the wider business of life, that is, the aims of education, and wondered whether education can, or should, contribute to the economy, politics, morality, culture and the general happiness of the population. My assumption, at least, is that in doing such things they are acting in a properly professional manner, that is, they are doing the type of thing that a philosopher of education ought to do.

If this is so, then any attempt to restrict their enquiries, as in the examples given above, must impoverish philosophy of education and thereby our understanding of education as such.

I have been trying to persuade you that there is a continuing tradition within philosophy of education which simply bypasses some of our very important educational problems. A simple look at the educational supplement in a decent newspaper should convince anyone that among the topics of interest concerning current British education – in our normal use of this word – are the cases of educational failure I introduced at the beginning of this chapter. Other topics of present concern are: the scope and limits of educational assessment, the raising of the age of compulsory education, the place of vocational education within schooling, faith schools in a liberal democracy and the divide between state and private schooling. Such issues seem to me to be important and, because they are important, I expect any philosophy of education worth its name to have something to say about them. If it *does not* then it is not addressing educational issues of public concern; but, if *it cannot,* then it seems to me that its status as a philosophy of education is seriously at risk.

Further reading

An obvious starting point for reading Philosophy of Education is R. S. Peters' *Ethics and Education* (1966), although many of it conclusions would be denied by many contemporary practitioners of the discipline. Good fun, and a very sensible attack on some of the wilder claims of educationalists, is R. S. Barrow's *Radical Education* (1978). Two more recent books by H. Siegel *Educating Reason: Rationality, Critical Thinking and Education* (1988) and *Rationality Redeemed? Further Dialogues on an Educational Ideal* (1997) deal with important issues concerning knowledge and education, and *Philosophy and Educational Policy* (2004) by C. Winch and J. Gingell, tries to show how educational issues are embedded within issues of social policy. For those who want a good, recent book on values – not necessarily educational – I recommend F. Feldman's *Pleasure and the Good Life* (2004) which is a spirited defence of the idea that pleasure is the essential value for a good life.

Useful website

The Philosophy of Education Society of Great Britain: www.philosophy-of-education.org/ also contains useful link to other sites.

13 Writing the Philosophy of Education

Richard Smith

By now the reader, even if he or she is new to the field but has gone though this book chapter by chapter, will have read enough philosophy of education to have given up the expectation, if she or he even had it in the first place, that any of this philosophy of education business is straightforward. And thus he or she will not expect, as the title of this particular chapter might have been taken in another context to imply, that simple guidance is on offer on how to write philosophy of education essays or other assignments. However I want to suggest here that the business of writing philosophy – and thus philosophy of education – is even odder than that.

It is easy to take for granted that philosophy of education naturally assumes the form in which we most commonly find it in our own time. It falls neatly into journal articles of around six thousand words or appears in books whose chapters are of roughly the same length. There is usually a respectable number of references to other publications, either foot- or end-noted, or set out in References at the end. The language is of a particular register: sober, decorous, grammatically orthodox, not much given to poetic flights of fancy (though the writer may, rather daringly, take examples from novels or – even more daringly – from film) – in short, the style is what we think of as *academic*. The writer is often confronting a problem in the practice of education caused by some kind of semantic or conceptual confusion, and his or her hope is to resolve that problem so that practitioners – teachers, administrators and others – can go about their business more smoothly and effectively.

This chapter questions some of these assumptions, and even questions the idea that *writing* is the form that philosophy of education should most naturally take. The chapter focuses on the distinction between philosophy as something we write, and something that we do – the latter as a matter of discussion, argument, or, to use a term that will be central to what follows, dialogue: a process in which two or more people toss ideas back and forward in a more focused version of ordinary conversation. Sometime they set out an idea in a few sentences; sometimes they seek clarification, either from each other or by interrogating what they have just said; they may offer or request examples; they may agree, object, complain of confusions, and so on. What they do not do in dialogue is to make long speeches. That, one might say, is what books do: and the whole virtue of dialogue is that it makes possible and to some extent more likely the kinds of conversational engagement of which I have just given examples.

It may seem odd to write of philosophy as something which should not, ideally, be written, and I shall indeed conclude that there are many oddities here, but oddities that are interesting, suggestive and enriching. First, however, we shall consider a few examples of the many philosophers who have claimed to value philosophical dialogue over philosophical text.

Plato and dialogue

At the beginning of what we now tend to think of as systematic, Western philosophy there was one influential thinker – the Greek philosopher Plato – who was prepared to question whether writing, that is, the written word rather than the spoken word, was the proper medium for philosophy at all. (Incidentally, since all of philosophy has been described as a matter of 'footnotes to Plato' (A. N. Whitehead, 1929) there can be no grounds for wondering if it is relevant to go back to the work of a philosopher who lived and taught in Athens in the fourth century BC.)

The early works of Plato (and perhaps some of his middle-period ones) are written in the form of dialogues, very much as if they were plays. Socrates, who was historically Plato's own teacher, is depicted in these dialogues in discussion and argument with distinctive individuals who, whether or not they represent his or Plato's real contemporaries (and whatever the historical accuracy of Plato's portrait of Socrates), have many of the characteristics of flesh-and-blood people who might be met with anywhere, at any time. Euthyphro, for instance, is only too sure that he knows what is the right and proper thing to do. When Socrates meets him, in the dialogue that bears his name, he is on his way to have his own father prosecuted for his involvement in the death of one of his slaves. Gorgias is a sophist, a travelling salesman who claims his wares – the skills of persuasion, or 'rhetoric' – will enable their purchaser to defeat his opponent in argument, especially in courts of law. Socrates shows that his confidence too is misplaced. Theaetetus is a promising young geometrician, but he is sometimes too quick with a pat response: his ideas run away with him, and he does not take time to consider the weight of the questions that Socrates puts to him. We meet people like this in our everyday lives in the twenty-first century. If these three interlocutors – Euthyphro, Gorgias and Theaetetus – give themselves over fully to the process of dialectic, the to-and-fro of question and answer, none of them will be quite the same by the end of the dialogue. Each will have been *educated* a little, or perhaps a lot, by the philosophy they have engaged in with Socrates. For this reason it seems fair to call these dialogues exercises in philosophy of education; and if all philosophy is indeed a series of footnotes to Plato, then all philosophy of education owes the same debt.

To return more directly to the topic of how and whether to commit philosophy of education to writing, it is necessary to examine in some detail the Platonic dialogue called *Phaedrus*. Socrates meets the young man after whom the dialogue is named while walking in the countryside outside Athens (this is unusual: Socrates is a city dweller, and that is where the dialogues usually take place). Phaedrus is a bright, lively and likeable young man who has been giving some thought to his future. Being a young man, and full of hormones, he knows that his relationships – we are talking here of friendship, love and sex (the Greek word *eros* which figures prominently in the dialogue captures some sense of both of the latter) – can make or mar his career. When the dialogue begins Phaedrus has been listening to, and much impressed by, the advice of the orator, or expert giver of advice (or, like Gorgias above, sophist), Lysias. This advice has been entirely instrumental. Phaedrus wants to get on in the world: so he should form a relationship with an older man who, without being 'in love' or emotionally over-involved with him in a way that might lead to loss of judgement on both their parts, will be in a position to smooth his path to success. He will help Phaedrus in his career: what Phaedrus will give him in return is not spelled out but we should note in passing that in ancient Athens sexual relationships between younger and older men were apparently entirely normal. Phaedrus has written down Lysias' speech and relates it enthusiastically to Socrates. It is nevertheless a flat, repetitive composition designed to persuade the listener that only the things that can be quantified and costed (no doubt by an experienced older man) are real or valuable.

We see in Lysias' speech that a particular kind of language – here the language of profit and loss, of what 'pays' and what doesn't, of cold calculation – can easily make itself at home and come to seem the natural language for grown-up people to use (very much, of course, as it has done in our own time too). Moreover when that language is written down (and in our time, when it is published in the right sorts of places and thus comes to seem doubly authoritative) it can be peculiarly hard to challenge. Later in the dialogue Socrates relates to Phaedrus a legend about the origins of writing:

> At the Egyptian city of Naucratis, there was a famous old god, whose name was Theuth; the bird which is called the Ibis is sacred to him, and he was the inventor of many arts, such as arithmetic and calculation and geometry and astronomy and draughts and dice, but his great discovery was the use of letters. Now in those days the god Thamus was the king of the whole country of Egypt; and he dwelt in that great city of Upper Egypt which the Hellenes call Egyptian Thebes, and the god himself is called by them Ammon. To him came Theuth and showed his inventions . . . This, said

Theuth, will make the Egyptians wiser and give them better memories; it is a specific both for the memory and for the wit. Thamus replied: O most ingenious Theuth, the parent or inventor of an art is not always the best judge of the utility or inutility of his own inventions to the users of them. And in this instance, you who are the father of letters, from a paternal love of your own children have been led to attribute to them a quality which they cannot have; for this discovery of yours will create forgetfulness in the learners' souls, because they will not use their memories; they will trust to the external written characters and not remember of themselves. The specific (i.e. recipe) which you have discovered is an aid not to memory, but to reminiscence, and you give your disciples not truth, but only the semblance of truth; they will be hearers of many things and will have learned nothing; they will appear to be omniscient and will generally know nothing; they will be tiresome company, having the show of wisdom without the reality.[1]

Then Socrates compares writing to painting: 'for the creations of the painter have the attitude of life, and yet if you ask them a question they preserve a solemn silence.' Long speeches too, like the speech of Lysias that so impressed Phaedrus, may seem intelligent; however they cannot respond to questions but always say the same thing. Then they fall into the hands of people who are liable to misunderstand and misrepresent them. There is 'another kind of word or speech far better than this, and having far greater power', Socrates says: 'an intelligent word graven in the soul of the learner, which can defend itself, and knows when to speak and when to be silent'. Phaedrus rightly interprets him to mean 'the living word of knowledge which has a soul, and of which the written word is properly no more than an image'. That is to say, philosophy that consists in lively argument and conversational exchange is much superior to philosophy that is written down, risks hardening into dogma, and becomes removed from any sense of what the occasions and persons were that prompted it in the first place.

It is of course an irony that Plato would hardly have been unaware of that these reservations about the written word occur in a dialogue that he himself *wrote*. To express the irony in terms of the many layers to be found in the *Phaedrus*, here Plato writes a text which takes the form of a dialogue, of speech: in which the young man Phaedrus is impressed by a particular mode of speech-making (as sold to him by the sophist, Lysias), so much so that he has committed it to writing. Socrates makes a better speech, but still of the Lysian sort; and then, after a discussion that is carefully crafted and has a distinctly literary flavour to the modern ear, Socrates tells a story, supposedly from Egypt, that represents writing as inferior to speech. To put it more briefly: Plato writes a book one of whose principal messages concerns the undesirability of writing. What are we to make of this? (And, of course, how would these ideas have come down to us if Plato had not written at all?).

Talking philosophy

Before we return to this question we should note, in case all the above sounds hopelessly paradoxical and perhaps part of a bygone age, that the ideal of philosophy as vibrant spoken dialectic still survives. For example, the author of this chapter was required as an undergraduate to *read* his essays aloud to his university philosophy tutor and then defend what he had written against criticism: there was no question of handing in an essay to be read, and getting it back with written comments and a mark. In a revealing essay called 'A school for philosophers' R. M. Hare, then Professor of Moral Philosophy at Oxford University, writes (of course) in praise of this approach to the subject, because his pupils are going to become politicians, schoolteachers, lawyers, journalists and so on, rather than (except in a very few cases) professional philosophers,

> . . . the Oxford tutor, if he can teach his pupils how to think more clearly and to the point, can have much more influence on the life of the country in this way than he is likely to achieve by writing books (p. 39) . . . We regard teaching, not writing, as our main job – what we are paid for (p. 40) . . . I can honestly say that I have learnt more from my pupils than I have from books (p. 41) . . . (Hare, 1972)

Here R. M. Hare is writing about undergraduates, but the general point he is making holds good for graduate study to an even greater degree:

> He (the graduate student) will go most days to seminars and discussions, and will spend as much time as he can arguing on philosophical questions with his contemporaries and with anyone else he can get hold of. When I say talking and arguing, I mean a co-operative activity. The budding philosopher whose idea of argument is to deliver long monologues, and who does not know how to listen to, and answer, the questions and objections that are put to him . . . will find that his company is avoided. (ibid., p. 43)

'On the whole', Hare concludes, 'we share Plato's attitude towards the written word; it is a *pis aller* (second-best course), and the best thing to do is to be as brief and clear as possible and answer the objections verbally as they arise in the course of the inevitable discussion' (p. 45).

To give one further example, in case Hare's reflections are thought to be peculiar to his own university and style of philosophizing, I have on my shelves a book called *Philosophy in the Open*, edited by Godfrey Vesey (1974). The title is significant partly in that the book was a prescribed text for Open University students, whose manner of study (roughly, by 'distance learning' with relatively few opportunities for face-to-face contact with tutors) is about as different from that of Hare's pupils as could be imagined. Nevertheless – or perhaps precisely because of this – the book is anxious to downplay its status as text. The Foreword tells us (p. 5) that 'What philosophers do is argue. They argue with anyone who is prepared to argue with them'. The front cover duly shows two men supposedly in philosophical debate, one apparently straddling a chair, hand held parallel to his face with first finger raised, and leaning towards his more conventionally seated interlocutor who has his back to the reader. The challenge of the book, the back cover declares, is contained not in chapters, those traditional divisions of written text, but in 'dialogues, discussions, and talks'.

It is an interesting question, which I shall not go far into here, whether there is something aggressive, and perhaps gendered too, about this conception of philosophical discussion and argument. When I entered academic life thirty years ago philosophy conferences generally took the following form. The speaker summarized his (the speaker was usually a man) paper, which would usually have been circulated beforehand, for roughly twenty minutes. There would be a reply offering a critique of the paper which would take perhaps ten minutes or longer. Then debate was open to all participants, with the majority usually making further criticisms of the first speaker and his paper. Often in the bar later there would be talk about people having been 'shot down in flames' or having had their argument 'blown to pieces'. As women came more and more into academic posts in the late 1970s and 1980s some of them were heard to suggest that there was something of the flavour of boys' games about all this. One caused uproar by beginning her own paper with words along the lines of 'I'm going to discuss some things I'm not quite clear or certain about and I hope you will join me in trying to sort them out'. She was told it was her job to present her argument and defend it before the tribunal of reasoned debate. She stuck to her own way of doing it, and continues, very successfully, to do so. Of course rational debate is a splendid thing; but perhaps it is not always what it pretends to be.

Philosophy and literature

One reason why speech might seem preferable to writing is that writing lends itself more to stylistic devices, to literary techniques that might be thought of as getting in the way of meaning and argument. The eighteenth-century philosopher John Locke puts the case forcefully:

> . . . all the art of rhetoric, besides order and clearness; all the artificial and figurative application of words eloquence hath invented, are for nothing else but to insinuate wrong ideas, move the passions, and thereby mislead the judgment; and so indeed are perfect cheats. (An Essay Concerning Human Understanding, III. 10. 34)

Speech, by contrast, can appear to have a hot-line to thought, proceeding directly and without intermediary from the mind of its originator. The scepticism against writing in general proceeds from much the same motive as a widespread, but not universal, tendency in philosophy to value a particular style of writing: prosaic, plain and unadorned. Such a style makes for clarity and rigour, the hallmarks of good philosophy, as opposed to the appeals to the imagination and emotions characteristic of more poetic and flowery uses of language.

This line of thought is set out at some length by the philosopher R. G. Collingwood in his book *Philosophical Method* (1933):

> [W]hat he (i.e., the philosopher) writes is not poetry but prose. From the point of view of literary form, this means that whereas the poet yields himself to every suggestion that his language makes,

> and so produces word-patterns whose beauty is a sufficient reason for their existence, the philosopher's word-patterns are constructed only to reveal the thought which they express, and are valuable not in themselves but as a means to that end . . . He must never use metaphors or imagery in such a way that they attract to themselves the attention due to his thought; if he does that he is writing not prose, but, whether well or ill, poetry . . . (pp. 214–15)

The case seems straightforward enough, and elsewhere Collingwood writes in favour of the dialogue form, and of the 'plain and modest style' proper to the philosophical 'confession' that takes the form of 'a search by the mind for its own failings and an attempt to remedy them by recognising them' (p. 210). But in the long indented quotation above I have omitted parts. The passage begins, '*The principles on which the philosopher uses language are those of poetry; but* what he writes is not poetry but prose'. In the last third part of the passage, before 'He must never use metaphors', the full text reads:

> The prose-writer's art is an art that must conceal itself, and produce not a jewel that is looked at for its own beauty but a crystal in whose depths the thought can be seen without distortion or confusion; and the philosophical writer in especial follows the trade not of a jeweller but of a lens-grinder.

Just as Plato has Socrates disparage writing, in a written text of great artistic sophistication, so Collingwood tells us that the philosopher must not use metaphors or imagery that call attention to themselves, and he does so with the wonderful – and entirely attention-worthy – extended image of the philosopher as jeweller or lens-grinder. It is tempting to say either that the writer, as opposed to the philosopher, in Collingwood has refused to be suppressed; or that the separation between philosophy and writing cannot be established so easily, or perhaps cannot be established at all.

One variation on the suspicion of the literary trickiness that philosophy may fall into can be found in the kind of philosophical writing that makes use of mathematical or algebraic tropes. This is worth illustrating at some length since it was particularly common in philosophy of education in what some think of as its heyday (i.e. the 1960s and 1970s). The two examples I take are from two philosophers (I nearly wrote 'writers') who demand especial respect. The first comes from Paul Hirst's *Knowledge and the Curriculum* (1974):

> Any notion of learning which is not the learning of some particular X, is as vague as the notion of going somewhere but nowhere in particular. Equally some particular person B is necessarily learning this X. Following the logical chain, it is therefore only in a context where both what is to be learnt and who is learning it are clear, that we can begin to be clear about teaching B, X. (p. 109)

I am not concerned to evaluate the argument here, which seems perfectly sound: rather to ask what we are to make of the mathematical notation and the associated talk of the 'particular' (three times), of what is 'clear' (twice) and of the 'logical' (once). The second example comes from Nel Noddings' *Caring: A Feminine Approach to Ethics and Moral Education* (2003):

> I want to provide a logical analysis of the caring relation. I have claimed that the perception by the cared-for of an attitude of caring on the part of the one-caring is partially constitutive of caring . . . Logically, we have the following situation: (W, X) is a caring relation if and only if:
>
> i) W cares for X (as described in the one-caring), and
> ii) X recognises that W cares for X. (pp. 68–9)

Again we see the mathematical notation (including the semi-technical 'if and only if'), the emphasis on 'logical' and 'logically', and the device of tabulation for clauses (i) and (ii).

There seem to be two oddities in these two passages. The first oddity is the assumption that good philosophy – here thought of as 'clear' and 'logical' – is best brought about by adopting mathematical notation, as if that guaranteed the elimination of metaphor and figurative language. But this notation is itself metaphorical. Its primary or original usage is in mathematics; here it is brought across (this is the etymology of the word 'metaphor') into discussion of education presumably for the sake of its effect in suggesting that the writer is being unusually rigorous. As in the case of R.G. Collingwood above, so too Hirst and Noddings succeed in being highly figurative at the very point where their implicit claim is to avoid figurative language altogether.

The second oddity concerns the notion of clarity. Now of course clarity is a good thing, if lack of clarity means muddled and confused thinking. But clarity itself contains a concealed metaphor, or at least one that generally goes unnoticed. 'Clear' writing is like water: you can see straight through it to the realities that lie beneath. I am writing this on the 13:17 from Peterborough: the truth of this claim consists in the fact, which the words mirror, that there is a real 13:17 from Peterborough and the real me is sitting on it typing on my laptop. But of course we often use language without the existence of any reality to underpin it in this way. There is a train behind the word 'train', but there is no tomorrow, no real tomorrow which we can inspect, behind 'tomorrow', and the reader will search in vain for real *ands*. The whole of poetry is like this. Its meaning does not come from referring to realities that we can see behind or beneath its words: which is why it is called 'poetry', from the Greek word *poiesis*, which means 'making'. Poetry is a making of meaning, not an attempt to mirror realities that are 'out there'.[2]

Once we have felt the full force of this argument — once the pretensions of mathematical tropes and the demands for clarity and the rigour that supposedly comes with those demands have lost their hegemonic status — it becomes easier for us to imagine other ways of writing the philosophy of education. We might draw on literature and film. For some splendid examples of writers doing so, the reader might turn to Jim Mackenzie's '*Stalky & Co.*: the adversarial curriculum' (see below for details of all the following articles): Mackenzie explores the benefits of 'pupil subversion of the school', drawing on Rudyard Kipling's stories of nineteenth century boarding-school life in *Stalky & Co.*, or to Duke Maskell's 'Education, Education, Education: or, What has Jane Austen to teach Tony Blunkett?'. Maskell draws on Jane Austen's *Pride and Prejudice* to analyse some of the differences between education and training.[3] We might draw on myth and legend, wondering, for example, if the story of Oedipus still has something to tell us about our human capacity for being very clever and extremely stupid at the same time (see Smith, 2006), or if the story of the Snow Queen contains important truths about (among other things) the way we can become intellectually obsessed at the cost of stunting our capacities for warmth and love, as Kay abandons his friend Gerda to go off with the Snow Queen, to her palace in the north where he must re-arrange blocks of ice on a frozen lake until they spell out the word 'eternity' (Smith, forthcoming 2008, where I also draw on a poem by Wordsworth).

Philosophy of education that takes the form of text promises a gentler conversation with the reader than many a philosophical argument or conversation. And if it draws on a wide range of textual sources, full of the figurative and the metaphorical as they are, it may help us to imagine human life, and the learning and education that go on in it, more fully and more richly. There is no more important task for philosophy of any kind, as Plato knew, than that.

Further reading

Philosophy of education has had little to say about the topic of this chapter. The interested reader should certainly include Plato's *Phaedrus* in his or her reading, and follow this up with a discussion such as Martha Nussbaum's (2000). Jonathan Rée (1987) offers a relatively short and very clear discussion problematizing what is distinctively 'philosophical', as opposed to literary, about a number of major figures in the philosophical canon, including Descartes. Mackenzie, J. (2002) and Maskell, D. (1999) are two lively examples of how literature can illuminate philosophical writing. Smith (2006) draws on both myth and literature, and offers a justification for doing so.

Notes

1. Plato's dialogues are usually referenced via the 'Stephanus pagination', first used in Henricus Stephanus's translation of 1578, that is common to all editions and translations. The extracts from the *Phaedrus* quoted here come from Stephanus pages 274–6. I have used the nineteenth-century translation by Benjamin Jowett, conveniently available at http:// ccat.sas.upenn.edu/jod/texts/phaedrus.html.

2. Elements of the above part of this section are adapted from my article 'To school with the poets: philosophy, method and clarity', *Paedagogica Historica*, 44.6, 2008, 635–45.

3. Tony Blunkett is a composite of Tony Blair and David Blunkett, who were respectively Prime Minister and Secretary of State for Education at the time of publication.

References

Ackerman, B. (1980) *Social Justice in the Liberal State*. New Haven, CT: Yale University Press.

Alexander, R. (1992) *Policy and Practice in the Primary School*. London: Routledge.

Archard, D. (1993) *Children: Rights and Childhood*. London: Routledge.

Archard, D. and Macleod, C. (eds) (2002) *The Moral and Political Status of Children: New Essays*. Oxford: Oxford University Press.

Arcilla, R. (2002) Why aren't philosophers and educators speaking to each other? *Educational Theory*, 52(1), pp. 1–11.

Arendt, H. (1992) *Eichmann in Jerusalem: A Report on the Banality of Evil*. Harmondsworth: Penguin.

Arnot, M. and Dillabough, J.-A. (eds) (2000) *Challenging Democracy: International Perspectives on Gender, Education and Citizenship*. London: RoutledgeFalmer.

Avrich, P. (1980) *The Modern School Movement: Anarchism and Education in the United States*. Princeton, NJ: Princeton University Press.

Bailey, C. (1984) *Beyond the Present and Particular: A Theory of Liberal Education*. London: Routledge & Kegan Paul.

Bailey, R. P. (2000a) *Education in the Open Society*. Aldershot: Ashgate.

—(ed.) (2000b) *Teaching Values and Citizenship across the Curriculum*. London: Kogan Page.

Baines, B. (1984) Sexism and the Curriculum. In R. Stradling, M. Noctor, M. and B. Baines (eds), *Teaching Controversial Issues*. London: Arnold.

Barber, B. (1984) *Strong Democracy: Participatory Politics for a New Age*. Los Angeles, CA: University of California Press.

Barr, N. (1993) *The Economics of the Welfare State*. London: Weidenfeld and Nicholson.

Barrow, R. S. (1978) *Radical Education*. Oxford: Martin Robertson.

Barrow, R. and Woods, R. (1988) *An Introduction to Philosophy of Education* (Third Edition). London: Routledge.

—(2006) *An Introduction to the Philosophy of Education* (Fourth Edition). London: Routledge.

Beck, L. W. (1969) *Immanuel Kant, Foundations of the Metaphysics of Morals* (with critical essays edited by R. P. Wolff). Indianapolis, IN: Bobbs-Merrill Publishing.

Bowles, S. and Gintis, H. (1976) *Schooling in Capitalist America*. New York: Basic Books.

Brennan, S. and Noggle, R. (1997) The moral status of children: children's rights, parents' rights, and family justice, *Social Theory and Practice*, 23, pp. 1–26.

Bridges, D. (1984) Non-paternalistic arguments in support of parents' rights over their children's education, *Journal of Philosophy of Education,* 18(1), pp. 55–61.

—(ed.) (1997) *Education, autonomy and democratic citizenship: philosophy in a changing world*. London: Routledge.

Bridges, D. and Jonathan, R. (2003) Education and the Market. In Blake, Smeyers, P., Smith, R. and Standish, P. (eds) *The Blackwell Guide to the Philosophy of Education*. Oxford: Blackwell.

Brighouse, H. (1998) Civic education and liberal legitimacy, *Ethics*, 108(4), pp. 719–45.

—(2000) *School Choice and Social Justice*. Oxford: Oxford University Press.

—(2002) Meritocracy and Educational Equality, from Seminar on Social Mobility and Meritocracy: Interdisciplinary perspectives on current issues, Nuffield College, Oxford University, 16 February.

—(2004) What's wrong with privatising schools? *Journal of Philosophy of Education*, 38, pp. 629–30.

—(2006) *On Education*. London: Routledge.

Brighouse, H. and Swift, A. (2006) Parents' rights and the value of the family, *Ethics*, 117(1), pp. 80–108.

Callan, E. (1997) *Creating Citizens: Political Education and Liberal Democracy.* Oxford: Clarendon Press.

Carr, D. (1991) *Educating the Virtues: An Essay on the Philosophical Psychology of Moral Development and Education.* London: Routledge.

—(1994) Wise men and clever tricks, *Cambridge Journal of Education,* 24(1), pp. 89–106.

—(2003a) *Making Sense of Education: An Introduction to the Philosophy and Theory of Education and Teaching.* London: Routledgefalmer.

—(2003b) Rival conceptions of practice in education and teaching, *Journal of Philosophy of Education,* 37(2), pp. 241–53.

Chomsky, N. (2003) *Chomsky on Democracy & Education.* London: Routledge.

Cigman, R. (ed.) (2006) *Included or Excluded: The Challenge of the Mainstream for Some Sen Children.* London: Routledge.

Cigman, R. and Davis, A. (2009) *New Philosophies of Learning.* Oxford: Blackwell.

Cohen, B. (1969) Bias and Indoctrination. In D. Heater (ed.), *The Teaching of Politics.* London: Methuen.

Cohen, B. (1981) *Education and the Individual.* London: Unwin.

Cohen, H. (1980) *Equal Rights for Children.* Totowa, NJ: Littlefield, Adams and Co.

Collingwood, R. G. (1933) *Philosophical Method.* Oxford: Clarendon Press.

Comte-Sponville, A. (2000) *Présentations de la philosophie.* Paris: Albin Michel.

Crick, B. (1999) The presuppositions of citizenship education, *Journal of Philosophy of Education,* 33, pp. 337–52.

Crick, B. and Porter, A. (eds) (1978) *Political Education and Political Literacy.* London: Hansard Society for Parliamentary Government.

Darling, J. (1982) Education as horticulture: some growth theorists and their critics, *Journal of Philosophy of Education,* 16(2), pp. 173–85.

—(1994) *Child-centered Education and Its Critics.* London: Paul Chapman Publishers.

Delanty, G. (2000) *Citizenship in a Global Age: Society, Culture and Politics.* Buckingham: Open University Press.

Department for Education and Skills (2001) *Schools – Achieving Success – White Paper.* London: HMSO.

—(2006) *Government's Response to the House of Commons Education and Schools Committee Report: The Schools White Paper: Higher Standards, Better Schools for All.* London: HMSO.

DES (2008) *School Achievement and Attainment Tables.* London: HMSO.

Dewey, J. (1916) *Democracy and Education.* New York: Free Press.

DfEE (1999) *The National Curriculum.* London: HMSO.

DfEE/QCA (1999) *The National Curriculum Handbook for Primary/Secondary Teachers in England.* London: DfEE.

Dudley-Marling, C. (2004) The social construction of learning disabilities, *Journal of Learning Disabilities,* 37(6), pp. 482–89.

Enslin, P., Pendlebury, S., and Tjiattas, M. (2001) Deliberative democracy, diversity and the challenges of citizenship education, *Journal of Philosophy of Education,* 35(1), pp. 115–30.

Feinberg, J. (1992) A Child's Right To An Open Future. In J. Feinberg, *Freedom and Fulfillment: Philosophical Essays.* Princeton, NJ: Princeton University Press.

—(2006) The Child's Right to an Open Future. In R. Curren (ed.), *The Philosophy of Education: An Anthology.* Oxford: Blackwell.

Feinberg, W. and McDonough, K. (eds) (2002) *Citizenship and Education in Liberal-Democratic Societies.* Oxford: Oxford University Press.

Feldman, F. (2004) *Pleasure and the Good Life.* Oxford: Clarendon Press.

Flew, A. (1972) Indoctrination and Doctrines. In I. Snook (ed.), *Concepts of Indoctrination: Philosophical Essays.* London: Routledge & Kegan Paul.

—(2000) *Education for Citizenship*. London: Institute of Economic Affairs.

Freire, P. (1972) *Pedagogy for the Oppressed*. London: Penguin.

Galston, W. (1989) Civic Education in the Liberal State. In N. L. Rosenblum (ed.), *Liberalism and the Moral Life*. Cambridge, MA: Harvard University Press.

Gamarnikow, E. and Green, A. (1999) Social capital and the educated citizen, *The School Field*, 3/4, pp. 103–26.

Gardner, P. (1993) Should we teach children to be open-minded? Or, is the *Pope* open-minded about the existence of God? *Journal of Philosophy of Education*, 27, pp. 39–43.

Garforth, F. W. (1966) *J. Dewey: Selected Writings*. London: Heinemann.

Garrison, W. J. (1986) The paradox of indoctrination: a solution, *Synthese*, 68, pp. 261–73.

Gereluk, D. (2006) *Education and Community*. London: Continuum.

Gillborn, D. (2006) Citizenship education as placebo. 'Standards', institutional racism and education policy. *Education, Citizenship and Social Justice*, 1(1), pp. 83–104.

Giroux, H. and McLaren, P. (1986) Teacher education and the politics of engagement: the case for democratic schooling, *Harvard Educational Review*, 56(3), pp. 213–40.

—(eds) (1989) *Critical Pedagogy, the State and Cultural Struggle*. Albany, NY: State University of New York Press.

Glanzer, P. (2008) Rethinking the boundaries and burdens of parental authority over education: a response to Rob Reich's case study of homeschooling, *Educational Theory*, 58(1), 1–16.

Godwin, W. (1793) *Enquiry Concerning Political Justice* (1971 edn. Edited by K. Codell Carter), Oxford: Oxford University Press.

—(1986) The Evils of National Education. In P. Marshall (ed.), *The Anarchist Writings of William Godwin*, London, Freedom Press.

Goodin, R. and Gibson, D. (1997) Rights: young and old, *Oxford Journal of Legal Studies*, 17(2), pp. 185–203.

Green, A. (1990) *Education and State Formation: The Rise of Education Systems in England, France and the USA*. London: Macmillan.

Green, F. T. (1972) Indoctrination and Belief. In I. A. Snook (ed.), *Concepts of Indoctrination: Philosophical Essays*. London: Routledge & Kegan Paul.

Gutmann, A. (1987) *Democratic Education*. Princeton NJ: Princeton University Press.

Halsey, A. L. (1978) *Change in British Society*. Oxford: Oxford University Press.

Halstead, J. M. and Pike, M. A. (2006) *Citizenship and Moral Education: Values in Action*. London: Routledge.

Hamlyn, D. W. (1973) Human Learning. In R. S. Peters (ed.), *The Philosophy of Education*. Oxford: Oxford University Press.

Hare, R. M. (1972) *Essays on Philosophical Method*. London: Macmillan.

Hare, W. and Portelli, J. (2007) *Key Questions for Educators*. San Francisco, CA: Caddo Gap Press.

Hart, H. L. A. (1955) Are there any natural rights? *Philosophical Review*, 64(2), pp. 175–91.

Haydon, G. (1997) *Teaching about Values: A New Approach*. London: Cassell.

Heater, D. (1999) *What is Citizenship?* Cambridge: Polity Press.

Heller, K. A., Monks, F. J., Sternberg, R. J. and Subotnik, R. F. (eds) (2000) *International Handbook of Research and Development of Giftedness and Talent*. Oxford: Elsevier Science.

Hirst, P. (1974) *Knowledge and the Curriculum*. London: Routledge & Kegan Paul.

Hirst, P. H. (1965) Liberal Education and the Nature of Knowledge. In R. D. Archambault (ed.), *Philosophical Analysis and Education*. London: Routledge & Kegan Paul.

—(1974) *Knowledge and the Curriculum*. London: Routledge & Kegan Paul.

Hobbes, T. (1996) *Leviathan*. Oxford: Oxford University Press.

Hollingdale, R. J. (trans. and ed.) (1968) *Friedrich Nietzsche's* Twilight of the Idols *and* The Anti-Christ. Harmondsworth: Penguin.

Horowitz, D. (2007) *Indoctrination U: The Left's War against Academic Freedom*. New York: Encounter.

Illich, I. (1971) *Deschooling Society*. London, Penguin.

Johnson, R. (1979) Really Useful Knowledge. In J. Clarke, C. Critcher and R. Johnson (eds), *Working Class Culture*. London, Hutchinson.

Kazepides, T. (1994) *Indoctrination*, Doctrines and the Foundations of Rationality. In J. Astley and L. Francis (eds), *Critical Perspectives on Christian Education*. Leominster: Gracewing.

Kleinig, J. (1983) *Paternalism*. Manchester: Manchester University Press.

—(1982) *Philosophical Issues in Education*, London: Routledge.

Kohlberg, L. (1984) *The Psychology of Moral Development*. San Francisco, CA: Harper and Row.

Kupfer, J. (1994) Education, Indoctrination, and Moral Character. In T. Magnell (ed.), *Values and Education*. Amsterdam: Rodopi.

Kymlicka, W. (1989) *Liberalism, Community and Culture*. Oxford: Oxford University Press.

—(1999) Education for Citizenship. In J. M. Halstead and T. H. McLaughlin (Eds), *Education in Morality*. London: Routledge.

—(2002) *Contemporary Political Philosophy: An Introduction (Second edition)*. Oxford: Clarendon Press.

Law, S. (2006) *The War For Children's Minds*. London: Routledge.

Leahy, M. (1994) Indoctrination, Evangelisation, Catechesis and Religious Education. In J. Astley and L. Francis (eds), *Critical Perspectives on Christian Education*. Leominster: Gracewing.

Levinson, M. (1999) *The Demands of Liberal Education*. Oxford: Oxford University Press.

Liao, M. (2006) The right of children to be loved, *Journal of Political Philosophy*, 14(4), pp. 495–6.

Locke, J. (1924) *Two Treatises of Civil Government*. London: Dent and Sons.

—(1960) The Second Treatise of Government. In *Two Treatises of Government*. (Introduction by Peter Laslet.) New York: Cambridge University Press.

—(1989) *An Essay Concerning Human Understanding*. London: William Tegg.

—(1997) *An Essay Concerning Human Understanding*. London: Penguin.

Lockyer, A., Crick, B. and Annette, J. (eds) (2003) *Education for Democratic Citizenship: Issues of Theory and Practice*. Aldershot: Ashgate.

MacCormick, N. (1982) Children's Rights: A Test-Case. In *Legal Right and Social Democracy*. Oxford: Clarendon Press.

Macedo, S. (2000) *Diversity and Distrust*. Cambridge, MA: Harvard University Press.

MacKay, T. (2006) *The West Dunbartonshire Literacy Initiative: The Design, Implementation and Evaluation of an Intervention Strategy to Raise Achievement and Eradicate Illiteracy, Phase One, Research Report*, Dunbarton: West Dunbartonshire Council.

Mackenzie, J. (2002) *Stalky & Co.*: the adversarial curriculum, *Journal of Philosophy of Education*, 36(4), pp. 609–20.

MacLeod, C. (2010) Primary Goods, Capabilities, and Children. In I. Robeyns, and H. Brighouse (eds.), *Measuring Justice*. Cambridge: Cambridge University Press.

Marples, R. (1999) (ed.) *The Aims of Education*. London, Routledge.

Marshall, T. H. (1950) *Citizenship and Social Class and Other Essays*. Cambridge: CUP.

Martin, J. R. (1981) The ideal of the educated person, *Educational Theory*, 31(2), pp. 97–109.

Maskell, D. (1999) Education, education, education: or, what has Jane Austen to teach Tony Blunkett? *Journal of Philosophy of Education* 33(2), pp. 157–74.

McCowan, T. (2006) The foundations of critical questioning in citizenship education. *Currículo Sem Fronteiras (Curriculum Without Borders)*, 6(2). Available at: http://www.curriculosemfronteiras.org/vol6iss2articles/mccowanen.htm

—(2009) Towards an understanding of the means-ends relationship in citizenship education, *Journal of Curriculum Studies*, 41(3), pp. 321–42.

McLaughlin, T. (1984) Parental rights and the religious upbringing of children, *Journal of Philosophy of Education*, 18(1), pp. 75–83.

—(1992) Citizenship, diversity and education: a philosophical perspective. *Journal of Moral Education*, 21(3), pp. 235–50.

—(2005) The educative importance of ethos. *British Journal of Educational Studies*, 53(3), pp. 306–25.

McLaughlin, T. H. (1984) Parental rights and the religious upbringing of children, *Journal of Philosophy of Education*, 18, pp. 75–83.

Mill, J. S. (1974) *On Liberty*. London: Penguin.

—(1863) *Utilitarianism* (available at: http://www.archive.org/details/a592840000milluoft)

—(1991) *On Liberty and Other Essays*. Oxford: Oxford University Press.

Miller, P. (1989) The historiography of compulsory schooling, *History of Education*, 18(2), pp. 123–44.

Mills, C. (2003) The child's right to an open future? *Journal of Social Philosophy*, 34(4), pp. 499–509.

Musgrave, A. (1993) *Common Sense, Science and Scepticism: A Historical Introduction to the Theory Of Knowledge*. Cambridge: Cambridge University Press.

Neill, A. S. (1962) *Summerhill: A Radical Approach to Education*. London: Gollancz.

Noddings, N. (2003) *Caring: A Feminine Approach to Ethics and Moral Education*. Berkeley, CA: University of California Press.

Norman, R. (1983) *The Moral Philosophers*. Oxford: Oxford University Press.

Nozick, R. (1974) *Anarchy, State and Utopia*. Oxford: Basil Blackwell.

Nussbaum, M. (1986) *The Fragility of Goodness: Luck and Ethics in Greek Tragedy and Philosophy*. Cambridge: Cambridge University Press.

—(2000) *Women and Human Development: The Capabilities Approach*. Cambridge: Cambridge University Press.

O'Hear, A. (1981) *Education, Society and Human Nature*. London: Routledge & Kegan Paul.

O'Neill, O. (1988) Children's rights and children's lives, *Ethics*, 98(3), pp. 445–63.

Oakeshott, M. (1962) The Voice of Poetry in the Conversation of Mankind. In *Rationalism in Politics*. London: Methuen.

—(1989) Learning and Teaching. In T. Fuller (ed.), *The Voice of Liberal Learning: Michael Oakeshott and Education*. New Haven, CT: Yale University Press.

Ofsted (2005) *New Ofsted evidence shows citizenship is worst taught subject at secondary level*. Available at: http://www.ofsted.gov.uk/portal/site/Internet/menuitem.e11147abaed5f711828a0d8308c08a0c/?vgnextoid=bb5bcc0eaaf3c010VgnVCM2000003607640aRCRD.

Orwell, G. (1954) *1984*. Harmondsworth: Penguin.

Pateman, C. (1970) *Participation and Democratic Theory*. Cambridge: Cambridge University Press.

Peters, R. S. (1966) *Ethics and Education*. London, Allen and Unwin.

—(1977a) *Education and the Education of Teachers*. London: Routledge & Kegan Paul.

—(1977b) Education and justification: a reply to R. K. Elliott, *Journal of Philosophy of Education*, 11(1), pp. 28–38.

Piaget, J. (1965) *The Moral Judgment of the Child*. New York: Free Press.

Plato. (2005) *The Republic* (trans. T. Griffith) Ferrari, G. R. F. (ed.). Cambridge: Cambridge University Press.

Pojman, L. (1999) *The Moral Life: An Introductory Reader in Ethics and Literature*. Oxford: Oxford University Press.

Popper, K. R. (1972) *Objective Knowledge: An Evolutionary Approach*. Oxford: Oxford University Press.

Postman, N. (1982) *The Disappearance of Childhood*. New York: Delacorte.

Pring, R. (1995) *Closing the Gap: Liberal Education and Vocational Preparation*. London: Hodder & Stoughton.

—(2004) *Philosophy of Education: Aims, Theory, Common Sense and Research.* London: Continuum.

—(2007) *John Dewey: The Philosopher of Education for the 21ˢᵗ Century?* London: Continuum.

Purdy, L. (1992) *In Their Best Interest? The Case against Equal Rights for Children.* Ithaca, NY: Cornell University Press.

QCA (1998) *Education for Citizenship and the Teaching of Democracy in Schools. Final Report of the Advisory Group on Citizenship.* London: QCA.

Rawls, J. (1971) *A Theory of Justice.* Cambridge: Harvard University Press.

—(1993) *Political Liberalism.* New York: Columbia University Press.

Raz, J. (1984) On the nature of rights, *Mind*, 93, pp. 194–214.

—(1986) *The Morality of Freedom.* Oxford: Oxford University Press.

Rée, J. (1987) *Philosophical Tales: An Essay on Philosophy and Literature.* London: Methuen.

Reich, R. (2002a) *Bridging Liberalism and Multiculturalism in American Education.* Chicago, IL: University of Chicago Press.

—(2002b) *Yoder, Mozert,* and the autonomy of children, *Educational Theory*, 52(4), pp. 445–62.

—(2008) On Regulating Homeschooling: A Reply to Glanzer, *Educational Theory*, 58(1), pp. 17–23.

Rooney, K. (2004) Citizenship Education: Reflecting a Political Malaise. In D. Hayes, (ed.) *The RoutledgeFalmer Guide to Key Debates in Education.* London: Routledge.

Russell, B. (1959) *The Problems of Philosophy.* Oxford: Oxford University Press.

Schapiro, T. (1999) What is a child? *Ethics*, 109(4), pp. 715–38.

Scruton, R., Ellis-Jones, A. and O'Keefe, D. (1985) *Education and Indoctrination: An Attempt at Definition and a Review of Social and Political Implications.* Harrow: Education Research Centre.

Sen, A. (1992) *Inequality Re-examined.* Oxford: Clarendon Press.

Shklar, J. (1989) The Liberalism of Fear. In N. Rosemblum (ed.), *Liberalism and the Moral Life.* Cambridge, MA: Harvard University Press.

Siegel, H. (1988) *Educating Reason: Rationality, Critical Thinking and Education.* London: Routledge.

—(1988) *Educating Reason.* New York: Routledge.

—(1997) *Rationality Redeemed? Further Dialogues on an Educational Ideal.* London: Routledge.

Smith, C. M. M. (2003) Can inclusion work for more able learners? *Gifted Education International*, 18(2), pp. 201–8.

Smith, M. (1983) *The Libertarians and Education.* London: George Allen and Unwin.

Smith, R. (2006) Abstraction and finitude: education, chance and democracy, *Studies in Philosophy and Education*, 25(1–2), pp. 19–35.

—(2008) Proteus rising: re-imagining educational research, *Journal of Philosophy of Education*. 42.1 2008, pp. 179–94.

—(2008) To school with the poets: philosophy, method and clarity, *Paedagogica Historica*, 44(6), pp. 635–45.

Snook, I. (ed.) (1972a) *Concepts of Indoctrination: Philosophical Essays.* London: Routledge and Kegan Paul.

Standish, P. (2006) The Nature and Purpose of Education. In R. Curren (ed.), *A Companion to the Philosophy of Education.* Oxford: Blackwell.

—(2007) Rival versions of the philosophy of education. *Ethics and Education*, 2, pp. 159–71.

Strike, K. (1999) Liberalism, Citizenship and the Private Interest in Schooling. In R. Marples (ed.), *The Aims of Education.* London: Routledge.

Suissa, J. (2006) *Anarchism and Education.* London: Routledge.

Swift, A (2001) *Political Philosophy: A Guide for Students and Politicians.* Cambridge: Polity Press.

Tan, C. (2004) Michael Hand, indoctrination and the inculcation of belief, *Journal of Philosophy of Education*, 38, pp. 257–67.

Taylor, K. (2004) *Brainwashing: The Science of Thought Control.* Oxford: Oxford University Press.

Terzi, L. (2005) A capability perspective on impairment, disability and special needs: towards social justice in education, *Theory and Research in Education*, 3(2), pp. 197–223.

Thiessen, E. J. (1993) *Teaching for Commitment*. Montreal/Kingston: McGill/Kingston University Press.

Tomasi, J. (1991) Individual rights and community virtues, *Ethics*, 101(3), pp. 521–36.

Tooley J. (2003) Why Harry Brighouse is nearly right about the privatisation of education, *Journal of Philosophy of Education*, 37(3), pp. 427–47.

—(2000) *Reclaiming Education*. London: Continuum.

Unterhalter, E. (1999) Citizenship, Difference and Education: Reflections Inspired by the South African Transition. In P. Werbner and N. Yuval-Davis (eds), *Women, Citizenship and Difference*. London: Zed.

Vesey, G. (1974) *Philosophy in the Open*. Milton Keynes: The Open University Press.

Waldron, J. (ed.) (1984) *Theories of Rights*. Oxford: Oxford University Press.

Warnock, M. (2005) *Special Educational Needs: A New Look*. London: Philosophy of Education Society of Great Britain.

—(ed.) (1972) *Utilitarianism*. London: Collins.

Watts, G. (2002) A bunch of jolly good fellows or old cronies who don't deserve £25m a year? *Times Higher Education* magazine, 5 April.

Wellman, C. (1985) *A Theory of Rights*. Totowa, NJ: Rowman & Allanheld.

White, J. (1994) The dishwasher's child: the end of education and the end of egalitarianism, *Journal of Philosophy of Education*, 28(2), pp. 180–92.

—(1982) *The Aims of Education Restated*. London: Routledge & Kegan Paul.

—(1990) *Education and the Good Life: Beyond the National Curriculum*. London: Kogan Page.

—(1997) *Education and the End of Work: A New Philosophy of Work and Learning*. London: Cassell.

—(2004) *Rethinking the School Curriculum*. London: RoutledgeFalmer.

—(2005) *The Curriculum and the Child: The Selected Works of John White*. London: RoutledgeFalmer.

—(2006) *What Schools Are for and Why*. London: Philosophy of Education Society of Great Britain.

—(ed.) (2004) *Rethinking the School Curriculum: Values, Aims and Purposes*. London: RoutledgeFalmer.

White, J. P. (1972) Indoctrination and Intentions. In I.A. Snook (ed.), *Concepts of Indoctrination: Philosophical Essays*. London: Routledge and Kegan Paul.

White, P. (1996) *Civic Virtues and Public Schooling: Educating Citizens for a Democratic Society*. New York: Teachers College Press.

Whitehead, A. N. (1929) *Process and Reality*. New York: Free Press.

Wilson, J. (1977) *Philosophy and Practical Education*. London: Routledge & Kegan Paul.

—(1979) *Preface to the Philosophy of Education*. London: Routledge & Kegan Paul.

Wilson, J., Williams, N., and Sugarman, B. (1967) *Introduction to Moral Education*. Harmondsworth: Penguin.

Winch, C. (1996) Equality, quality and diversity, *Journal of Philosophy of Education*, 30(1), pp. 113–28.

—(2000) *Education, Work and Social Capital: Towards a New Conception of Vocational Education*. London: Routledge.

Winch, C. And Gingell, J. (2004) *Philosophy and Educational Policy*. London, RoutledgeFalmer.

Winstanley, C. (2004) *Too Clever by Half: A Fair Deal for Gifted Children*. Stoke-on-Trent: Trentham Books.

Wittgenstein, L. (1958) *Philosophical Investigations* (Second edition). London: Basil Blackwell.

Woods, R. and Barrow R. S. (1975) *An Introduction to Philosophy of Education*. London: Methuen.

Wringe, C. (1981) *Children's Rights*. London: Routledge & Kegan Paul.

—(1988) *Understanding Educational Aims*. London: Allen & Unwin.

Yuval-Davis, N. and P. Werbner (eds) (1999) *Women, Citizenship and Difference*. London: Zed.

Useful Websites

Although there are very few websites specifically addressing the philosophy of education, there are some very useful sites from related fields. Websites are rarely quality assured, so the reader needs to be cautious in accessing information from them. Nevertheless, when used carefully, the following sites should help supplement the ideas and debates contained in this book.

Stanford Encyclopedia of Philosophy (http://plato.stanford.edu)

This is an outstanding resource, containing regularly updated entries on a very wide range of topics and philosophers.

Philosophy around the Web (http://users.ox.ac.uk/~worc0337/phil_index.html)

This site offers a guide and links to philosophy web resources.

Philosophy Now Magazine (http://www.philosophynow.org/)

This is the website of the 'popular' magazine, and contains a diverse collection of articles, fiction, news and reports.

Internet for Philosophy (http://www.vts.intute.ac.uk/he/tutorial/philosophy//index.htm)

This very clearly presented site offers a free online tutorial to help students interested in philosophy develop their internet research skills.

The Encyclopaedia of Informal Education (http://www.infed.org/)

As its name suggests, this site focuses on non-traditional approaches to education. It contains entries on a wide range of topics, including brief discussions of philosophers.

Open Directory Project – Philosophy of Education (http://www.dmoz.org/Society/ Philosophy/Philosophy_of_Education/)

The Philosophy of Education section of this comprehensive resource is a useful portal for further sites on philosophers, societies and content.

The Ism Book (http://www.ismbook.com/)

This is 'an intellectual "field guide" that provides brief definitions of theories, doctrines, movements, and approaches in philosophy, religion, politics, science, the arts, and related disciplines.' As such, it is quite a useful reference for students of education.

Philosophy of Liberal Education (http://www.ditext.com/libed/libed.html)

An idiosyncratic, US-orientated resource that is worth exploring nonetheless.

Encyclopaedia of Philosophy of Education

(http://web.archive.org/web/20010210002725/www.educacao.pro.br/entries.htm)
This multi-national, incomplete project provides short articles on a range of topics.

Philosophy of Education Societies

United Kingdom – http://www.philosophy-of-education.org/
United States – http://philosophyofeducation.org/
Canada – http://www.philosophyofeducation.ca/
Australasia – http://www.pesa.org.au

Index